Literacy and Language Diversity in the United States

CΛL

Printed in the United States of America

Editorial/production supervision: Lynn Fischer, Joy Peyton
Editing: Joy Peyton, Donald Ranard
Copyediting: Lynn Fischer
Proofreading: Amy Fitch
Indexing: Kathleen McLane
Interior design/production: SAGARTdesign
Cover: SAGARTdesign

ISBN 1-887744-88-6

This publication was produced with funding from the U.S. Department of Education (ED), Office of Vocational and Adult Education (OVAE), under Contract No. ED-99-CO-0008. The opinions expressed here do not necessarily reflect the positions or policies of ED or OVAE.

Library of Congress Cataloging-in-Publication Data

Wiley, Terrence G.
    Literacy and language diversity in the United States / Terrence G. Wiley.--
2nd ed.
        p. cm.
    Includes bibliographical references (p.) and index.
    ISBN 1-887744-88-6 (pbk.)
    1 Literacy--United States. 2. Sociolinguistics--United States. 3.
Multilingualism--United States. 4. Language policy--United States. 5.
Education, Bilingual--United States. I. Title

LC151.W45 2005
302.2'244--dc22
                                                                        2005041724

Literacy and Language Diversity in the United States

SECOND EDITION

Terrence G. Wiley

CAL

In memory of

Meyer Weinberg (1920–2002)

Contents

List of Figures and Tables

Chapter 5

Chapter 8

Chapter 9

Acknowledgments

I had the privilege of working closely with Meyer Weinberg from 1992 to 1994, while he was revising *A Chance to Learn: A History of Race and Education in the United States* and writing *Asian-American Education: Historical Background and Current Realities*—2 of his 18 books, all of which focus on social justice. Although his 1992–1994 tour of duty at California State University, Long Beach, was his last academic appointment, he never really retired; he finished his final book shortly before his death. Whenever I complained to him that a more scholarly work on a subject should be written, he would say, "Well, get busy." His stern admonition prods me still.

My interest in language diversity began some years ago, when Reynaldo Macías, my doctoral advisor at the University of Southern California, convinced me, an otherwise skeptical student of comparative intellectual history, to assist him in a study on biliteracy. A growing interest in the subject and a dissertation followed. For a time, Reynaldo, Nancy Hornberger, David Spener, and a few others carried this issue. Now, a chorus of scholars has lent a collective voice to biliteracy studies and expanded the field.

In writing the first edition of *Literacy and Language Diversity in the United States* (1996), I benefited from the advice of Reynaldo Macías and from the encouragement and intellectual support of my friends and colleagues at California State University, Long Beach. More recently, I am appreciative of the support of Olga Kagan, University of California, Los Angeles (UCLA); Nariyo Kono, Portland State University and Warm Springs, Oregon; Maria Quezada, California Association for Bilingual Education (CABE); and the late Russ Campbell, Language Resource Program at UCLA, whose infectious enthusiasm is sorely missed.

In preparing the second edition of the book, I am likewise grateful to many people, particularly my wife Eileen and son Aaron. My principal editors, Joy Peyton and Donald Ranard, deserve special thanks for convincing me to revise the book, providing ongoing constructive criticism, and keeping me on task. I am particularly indebted to the reviewers—Donna Christian, Mary McGroarty, and Steve Reder—who provided valuable guidance and content for this edition; I bear responsibility for any recommendations not fully heeded. Thanks also to Lynn Fischer for copyediting and coordinating the production of the book, Elizabeth Peterson for researching statistical data, Amy Fitch for proofreading, Kathleen McLane for indexing, and Vincent Sagart for designing the cover and book for this second edition.

I am also greatly appreciative of the support and encouragement of my colleagues at Arizona State University (ASU), in particular, Carole Edelsky, Jeff MacSwan, and Kellie Rolstad, who continue to probe and critique the constructions of deficiency that persist in the fields of literacy and biliteracy. I am likewise grateful for the ongoing intellectual support of my dean, Eugene Garcia, and ASU colleagues David Berliner, Arnold Danzig, Gene Glass, Josué González, Barbara Guzzetti, Sarah Hudelson, Kay Hartwell Hunnicutt, James Middleton, and Carlos Ovando.

Formative and lasting intellectual debts are owed to many scholars who stimulated my thinking early on, particularly James Paul Gee, Sylvia Scribner and Michael Cole, Brian Street, and James Tollefson. The ongoing work of a number of scholars has given me additional insights and inspiration, especially Elsa Auerbach, Colin Baker, John Baugh, Suresh Canagarajah, JoAnn (Jodi) Crandall, Carole Edelsky, Nancy Hornberger, Stephen May, Teresa McCarty, Mary McGroarty, Sandra McKay, Tom Ricento, John Rickford, Susan Romaine, Richard Ruíz, Otto Santa Ana, and Heide Spruck Wrigley.

Lastly, I would like to thank my current and former students for helping me consider, reconsider, and critique the issues addressed in this book through discussions in my seminars on literacy and social policy, educational language policy, and heritage and community languages. I am particularly indebted to Gerda de Klerk and Wayne Wright for their challenging questions and insights and to Mario Castro for his assistance with tables and data preparation for this text. I am also indebted to those ASU students involved in field projects on heritage and community languages in the United States, especially Karen Johnson, Seok Kang, Ha Lam, Mengying Li, Evelyn Haralson Monat, Chanyoung Park, Elba Ruhl, Rafael Serrano, Kun Yan, Byeon-kuen You, and Jingning Zhang.

Terrence G. Wiley

1

Introduction

The development of a schooled literacy that grew up around the development of Western patterns of schooling gradually privileged one kind of literacy. Literacy was not tied exclusively to just one sense of grammatical correctness, as the term *grammar* school usually suggests to us. Rather the original sense of a common literate discourse was based on a notion of social democracy in the making—a community discourse available to all. . . . We need continually to remind ourselves that other voices need to be heard and not disenfranchised by a single view of a correct language of literacy. (Cook-Gumperz & Keller-Cohen, 1993, p. 286)

In the United States, as in many other countries where the majority of the population is literate and where free public schooling has been available for about a century, illiteracy[1] is often portrayed as a social disease. Concerns about illiteracy and low levels of literacy in the United States are not new; they have long been stressed by the popular media and have captured the attention of generations of policy makers and educators. Historically, when the topic is illiteracy, the spotlight is often aimed at non-English-speaking immigrants and ethnic and linguistic minorities. In the 1990s, after several decades of increased immigration, a number of popular articles raised the specter of mass literacy problems. One article was titled, "Dumber Than We Thought" with the subtitle, "Literacy: A New Study Shows Why We Can't Cope With Everyday Life" (Kaplan, 1993). Taking up half of the first page of the article was a photograph of an early 20th-century classroom populated with adult immigrants from various national origins. The connection between the photograph and the article was clear: The "we" who were "dumber" were more likely to be immigrants and minorities, especially language minorities.

More recent concerns have centered on achieving high standards for all students, including language minorities. Bilingual education, another subject of national concern, has been the target of English-only advocates such as millionaire-activist Ron Unz, who has received national attention for leading successful antibilingual education campaigns in California, Arizona, and Massachusetts; a similar effort in Colorado in 2002 failed. (See Crawford, 2000, and Tse, 2001, for a discussion of current debates on bilingual education.)

Concerns about literacy and language diversity in the United States are not new (Wiley, 2000a). Language issues have been a subject of debate since the earliest days of the republic. Noah Webster (1758–1843) wanted to build a national character by standardizing literacy conventions for a common American English. Webster was a staunch Federalist who contended that the country's language, like its government, should have a common national standard. During his time, a few dubious proposals to make Hebrew or Greek the national language were circulated. For Webster, however, the key to national unity was a linguistic unity based on an orthographic conformity that would eradicate spelling variations within the United States (Lepore, 2002). Interestingly, Webster was more concerned about eradicating regional varieties among English speakers than about the presence of people who spoke other languages. He noted, "the [English] language of the middle States is tinctured with a variety of Irish, Scotch, and German dialects which are justly censured as deviations from propriety and the standard of elegant pronunciation" (Lepore, p. 22). Webster further held that a "uniform national standard of pronunciation for spelling . . . would create a uniform, national standard pronunciation and demolish those odious distinctions of provincial dialects" (Lepore, p. 22).

Because of Webster's commercial influence in selling dictionaries and pedagogical materials, many of his efforts to regularize English spelling were largely successful, but his ambitions to eradicate dialects through spelling reform were never realized. Webster would probably be surprised to see the resilience of regional and social dialects of English in spite of his achievements in regularizing American English spelling.

More recently, in describing literacy problems in the United States, both the media and scholars tend to make cross-group comparisons on the basis of race, immigration status, or language background. The achievements of ethnic and linguistic minority groups[2] seem low when compared with mainstream[3] Whites. Findings from two national adult English literacy surveys conducted in 1985 and 1992 (see Chapter 4) indicate that Whites as a group consistently score higher than other groups, even when adjustments are made for comparable years of schooling. Native speakers of English, those who grew up in an English-language environment, generally outperform nonnative speakers of English. In addition, an analysis of the 1990 U.S. Census data showed that individuals age 16–24 who spoke a language other than English were 3 times more likely than native English speakers to have not completed or to not be enrolled in high school (McArthur, 1993).

Given these and similar findings, one purpose of this book is to examine the issues underlying the differences between the literacy performance and educational achievement of language minorities and native speakers of English. Toward this end, it is necessary to scrutinize the dominant popular and scholarly views governing much of the social and educational policy debates that surround literacy. One must analyze literacy in its traditional context of rhetoric and education as well as consider the major popular and scholarly beliefs on the subject. It is also necessary to consider literacy in terms of other dimensions, particularly race, ethnicity, and social class, and to probe its evolving relationship with the fields of psychology, anthropology, linguistics, sociology, social theory, history, economics, and public policy analysis.

According to Scribner (1988), three basic metaphors underlie most beliefs about literacy: (a) literacy as adaptation, (b) literacy as state of grace, and (c) literacy as power. *Literacy as adaptation* holds that literacy is the key to social and economic access and provides a solution to the functional English problems of individuals. Measuring and defining English functional literacy, however, is complicated: Who defines it? How is it measured? Does literacy in the native language count? Yet, despite the lack of clear answers to these questions, literacy as adaptation tends to be the dominant metaphor in debates about adult literacy policy.

Traditionally, *literacy as state of grace* represents literacy as a kind of salvation in which the literate person or the *literati* are considered to have special virtues. According to Scribner (1988, p. 77), literacy as state of grace is a metaphor that helps perpetuate the belief that there is a "cognitive great divide" between literates and nonliterates. A major focus of this book is a critique of the views derived from this metaphor both as it appears in the general literacy literature (Chapter 3) and as it is reproduced in some of the dominant theoretical constructs in bilingual education theory (Chapter 8).

In recent years, the metaphor of *literacy as power* has become more visible in the literature (Scribner, 1988). In this sense, literacy is seen as a critical tool for transforming existing social relations. Literacy as power differs from literacy as adaptation in that literacy as power becomes an instrument for praxis to promote a more just society (Walsh, 1991). This position has been most notably pursued by Paulo Freire (1970a, 1970b). Drawing on the work of Freire, Valadez argued that literacy generally, and writing specifically, empowers students by breaking the "culture of silence" (1981, p. 173; see also Edelsky, 1996).

Literacy as power recognizes languages other than English as valuable literacy resources (see Ruíz, 1984). Native language literacy is increasingly seen as a means of breaking cultures of silence for those language minorities who are not literate in English. For those who are *biliterate* (literate in more than one language), each language provides an additional channel for voice (see Spener, 1994).

Divided into 10 chapters, this book explores the major issues that scholars and educators face concerning fair and effective educational policies and practices for language minority learners. **Chapter 2** examines some of the common myths and assumptions about literacy and language diversity in the United States. Because literacy is often confused with English literacy, it is necessary to acknowledge the extent of language diversity in the United States in order to recognize the significance of literacy in languages other than English. The chapter also looks at scholarly assumptions about literacy and English literacy that influence the ways in which research questions are framed. The chapter concludes with implications for policy and practice.

Chapter 3 reviews and critiques the major scholarly orientations toward the study of literacy. It also probes the notion of a great divide between literates and nonliterates and between those who have acquired literacy through formal schooling and those who have developed vernacular or restricted literacies without formal schooling. The great divide view of literacy is based on the premise that literates have cognitive advantages over nonliterates and that these cognitive benefits result in social and technological advantages for both literate individuals and literate societies. Because literacy is often associated with schooling, it is also necessary to explore this relationship to determine whether those who are schooled have cognitive advantages over those who are not. After exploring these issues, attention is shifted to the social consequences of literacy, wherein the purported great divide between literates and nonliterates, schooled and nonschooled is seen as largely the result of social and educational practices.

Chapter 4 is divided into four sections: (a) the historical motivations for measuring literacy and intelligence; (b) definitions of literacy and how these definitions can be problematic when measuring literacy, specifically of language minorities; (c) an analysis of the strengths and weaknesses of the three common approaches to national literacy assessment (self-reported measures, surrogate measures, and direct measures); and (d) a review of two literacy surveys, the 1992 National Adult Literacy Survey (NALS) and the 1979 National Chicano Survey (NCS). The chapter concludes with recommendations for national literacy assessments that are more reflective of this nation's language and literacy diversity.

Chapter 5 concerns the purported socioeconomic consequences of illiteracy. The focus on illiteracy as a problem of underskilled individuals lends itself to a blame-the-victim psychology, which perpetuates rather than addresses the problem. Assumptions about the relationship between literacy and economic mobility are probed, and the commonly held view that illiteracy is the cause of individual economic problems is linked to an ideological climate in which a perpetual literacy crisis accompanied by an expectation of failure of particular groups is maintained.

Chapter 6 considers issues related to the ways in which a lower language and literacy status is ascribed to speakers of so-called nonstandard varieties of English. It opens with a discussion of status ascription based on language background, the kinds of labels that are routinely used in education programs, and the attitudes often associated with those labels. The status of nonstandard varieties of language and the promotion of literacy is also discussed. The chapter includes a discussion of African American language and the debate regarding its status and use in schools.

Chapter 7 discusses the importance of ethnographic studies that focus on literacy in the community, in the home, and in school. It notes the usefulness of studies that reflect the social practices orientation to literacy. The chapter also underscores the importance of analyses that include an ideological orientation. Such analyses are needed to demonstrate how the literacy practices and expectations of dominant groups can affect other groups. Lastly, the chapter reviews three education strategies: assimilation, accommodation, and adaptation.

Chapter 8 briefly revisits issues related to the purported cognitive great divide within the context of contemporary bilingual education theory. It reviews some of the efforts over the past several decades to teach language and literacy within social contexts. The chapter closes with a discussion of the contributions that ethnographic studies have made to our understanding of language learning and its use both in and out of school.

Chapter 9 assesses recent developments in the educational standards movement and how they have influenced both language arts generally and English as a second language specifically.

In conclusion, **Chapter 10** reviews the impact of societal attitudes, education policies, and pedagogical practices on language minority adults and children in the United States. It revisits the three major orientations toward literacy education and research (autonomous, social practices, and ideological) and suggests areas in which further research and reflection on policies and practices related to literacy are needed.

Further Reading

Crandall, J. A. (1991). Adult literacy development. *Review of Applied Linguistics, 12,* 86–104.

This article provides a straightforward introduction to many of the issues of adult literacy, including definitions, goals of literacy instruction, choice of language of instruction, and assessment and evaluation.

Guzzetti, B. J. (Ed.). (2002). *Literacy in America: An encyclopedia of history, theory, and practice.* Santa Barbara, CA: ABC-CLIO.

A useful comprehensive encyclopedia on literacy issues in the United States, this work includes hundreds of entries by noted authorities on literacy and literacy education.

2

Common Myths About Literacy and Language Diversity in the United States

It may seem rather indelicate ... to stress ... that biliteracy—the mastery of reading in particular, and at times also writing, in two (or more) languages—is not at all a rare skill among that portion of mankind that has successfully won the battle for literacy. (Fishman, 1980a, p. 49)

A number of popular myths surround discussions of literacy and language diversity in the United States. To adequately discuss literacy, it is necessary to look also at dominant attitudes and beliefs about language diversity. Taken as a whole, these attitudes and beliefs are part of the dominant ideology about language and literacy in the United States, characterized by English monolingualism. *Ideology* refers to beliefs and convictions that dictate, direct, or influence policy and behavior. English monolingualism reflects an ideology that speaking languages other than English is aberrant and socially disuniting (Ovando & Wiley, 2003; Ricento & Wiley, 2002; Skutnabb-Kangas & Phillipson, 1989). This assumption underlies much of the public discussion about literacy and language diversity and sheds light on much of the education research, policy, and practice directed at language and literacy issues.

The first part of this chapter critiques six common myths and misconceptions about literacy and language diversity in the United States by drawing on both historical evidence and contemporary data. The second part of the chapter looks at the impact of the ideology of English monolingualism on the way that scholarly issues and research are framed with respect to language, literacy, and diversity. The chapter concludes with implications for policy and practice.

Common Myths

Myth 1. The United States is most appropriately described as an English-speaking, monolingual nation.

Lamenting the lack of interest by the English-speaking majority in foreign languages in the United States and the country's resulting cultural isolation from the rest of the world, Senator Paul Simon (1988) has said, "We should erect a sign at each point of entry into the United States: Welcome to the United States—we cannot speak your language" (p. 1). Although "we" refers to the majority of monolingual English speakers, U.S. census data indicate that by the year 2000 there were approximately 47 million speakers of languages other than English living in the United States (see Figure 2.1).

Figure 2.1.
People Living in the United States (Age 5+) Who Speak a Language Other Than English

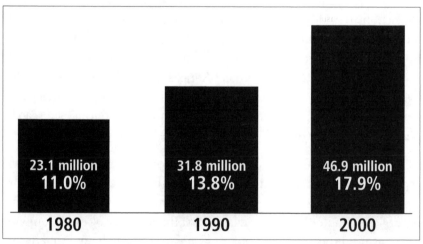

23.1 million	31.8 million	46.9 million
11.0%	13.8%	17.9%
1980	1990	2000

Note. Percentages are of total U.S. population. From U.S. Census 2000, Summary File 3, Table DP-2.

Table 2.1 provides a breakdown of the nearly 47 million speakers by major language groups, and Table 2.2 provides 1990 and 2000 U.S. Census comparison data for selected languages. Based on these data, it is clear that Spanish, Russian, Chinese, and a number of other languages are on the rise, whereas a number of European languages, such as Italian, Greek, and Hungarian, which were on the rise a century ago, are now declining. Most of these changes can be explained by changes in immigration patterns.

Table 2.1.
People Living in the United States (Age 5+) by Language Spoken

Language or language group	Number of speakers
Total	262,375,152
Those who speak only English	215,423,557
Those who speak another language	46,951,595
Spanish or Spanish Creole	28,101,052
Other Indo-European languages	10,017,989
Asian & Pacific Island languages	6,960,065
Native North American languages	381,480
African languages	418,505
Other unspecified languages	1,072,504

Note. From U.S. Census 2000, Summary File 3, Table PCT10. Internet release, February 25, 2003.

Based on both 1990 and 2000 U.S. Census data, it is clear that while English is overwhelmingly the majority language, the presence in this country of nearly 47 million individuals who speak languages other than English indicates that the United States is more appropriately described as a multilingual nation in which English is the dominant language. Census data from 2000 show that nearly 18% of the U.S. population speak a language other than English (Figure 2.1). Table 2.3 further breaks this information down by showing the percentage of individuals in each state who speak a language other than English. The 2000 U.S. Census does not, however, provide information on relative speaking abilities in other languages.

Table 2.2.
Selected Languages Other Than English Spoken in the United States in 1990 and 2000

Language Spoken	1990	2000	Change	% Change
Spanish, Spanish Creole	17,339,200	28,101,052	10,761,852	62%
Chinese (includes Mandarin and others)*	1,319,500	2,022,143	702,643	53%
French (includes Patois and Cajun)	1,702,200	1,643,838	-58,362	-3%
German	1,547,100	1,383,442	-163,658	-11%
Tagalog (Filipino)*	898,700	1,224,241	325,541	36%
Vietnamese	507,100	1,009,627	502,527	99%
Italian	1,308,600	1,008,370	-300,230	-23%
Korean	626,500	894,063	267,563	43%
Asian Indian languages**	644,400	815,450	171,050	27%
Russian	242,700	706,242	463,542	191%
Polish	723,500	667,414	-56,086	-8%
Arabic	355,100	614,582	259,482	73%
Portuguese, Portuguese Creole	429,900	564,630	134,730	31%
Japanese	427,700	477,997	50,297	12%
French Creole (Haitian)*	187,700	453,368	265,668	142%
Greek	388,300	365,436	-22,864	-6%
Persian (Farsi)	201,900	312,085	110,185	55%
Thai, Laotian*	206,300	269,767	63,467	31%
Armenian	149,700	202,708	53,008	35%
Hebrew	144,300	195,374	51,074	35%
Mon-Khmer, Cambodian	127,400	181,889	54,489	43%
Yiddish	213,100	178,945	-34,155	-16%
Navajo	148,500	178,014	29,514	20%
Miao, Hmong*	91,600	168,063	76,463	83%
Hungarian	147,900	117,973	-29,927	-20%

Note. From 1990 Census of Population as reported in *Numbers and Needs*, September 1993, and from U.S. Census 2000, Summary File 3, Table PCT10. Internet release, February 25, 2003.

*1990 and 2000 comparison labels not exactly parallel.

**2000 U.S. Census totals for Gujarathi, Hindi, and Urdu only; 1990 not delineated.

Table 2.3.
Individuals Who Speak Only English and
Individuals Who Speak a Second Language by State

State	Speak only English	Speak a second language	State	Speak only English	Speak a second language
California	60.5%	39.5%	Michigan	91.6%	8.4%
New Mexico	63.5%	37.5%	Pennsylvania	91.6%	8.4%
Texas	68.8%	32.2%	New Hampshire	91.7%	8.3%
New York	72.0%	28.0%	North Carolina	92.0%	8.0%
Hawaii	73.4%	26.6%	Nebraska	92.1%	7.9%
Arizona	74.1%	25.9%	Maine	92.2%	7.8%
New Jersey	74.5%	25.5%	Oklahoma	92.6%	7.4%
Florida	76.9%	23.9%	Wisconsin	92.7%	7.3%
Nevada	76.9%	23.1%	South Dakota	93.5%	6.5%
Rhode Island	80.0%	20.0%	Indiana	93.6%	6.4%
Illinois	80.8%	19.2%	Wyoming	93.6%	6.4%
Massachusetts	81.3%	18.7%	North Dakota	93.7%	6.3%
Connecticut	81.7%	18.3%	Ohio	93.9%	6.1%
District of Columbia	83.2%	16.8%	Vermont	94.1%	5.9%
Colorado	84.9%	15.1%	Iowa	94.2%	5.8%
Alaska	85.7%	14.3%	Montana	94.8%	5.2%
Washington	86.0%	14.0%	South Carolina	94.8%	5.2%
Maryland	87.4%	12.6%	Missouri	94.9%	5.1%
Utah	87.5%	12.5%	Arkansas	95.0%	5.0%
Oregon	87.9%	12.1%	Tennessee	95.2%	4.8%
Virginia	88.9%	11.1%	Alabama	96.1%	3.9%
Georgia	90.1%	9.9%	Kentucky	96.1%	3.9%
Delaware	90.5%	9.5%	Mississippi	96.4%	3.6%
Idaho	90.7%	9.3%	West Virginia	97.3%	2.7%
Louisiana	90.8%	9.2%	Average for the United States	82.1%	17.9%
Kansas	91.3%	8.7%			
Minnesota	91.5%	8.5%			

Note. States are listed by lowest to highest percentage of individuals speaking only English. Percentages are estimations. From Arizona State University, Education Policy Studies Laboratory, Language Policy Research Unit and U.S. Census 2000, Summary File 3.

Myth 2. The predominance of English and English literacy is threatened.

While it is true that the United States is linguistically diverse, it is equally true that English has been the dominant language of the United States since its founding, and there is no reason to assume that the language is in any danger of being eclipsed in the near or foreseeable future.

Estimates of the ethnic origins of the population made during the first U.S. census in 1790 can be taken as implicit indicators of language diversity. According to Pitt (1976), roughly 49% of the population were of English origin, nearly 19% were of African origin, 12% were Scotch or Scotch Irish, and about 3% were Irish; Dutch, French, and Spanish origin peoples represented an aggregate 14%. Lepore (2002) estimates that by 1790, approximately 75% of the U.S. population spoke English as their native tongue—a lower rate than currently—among a population of around 4 million, which included 600,000 Europeans, 150,000 enslaved Africans, and 150,000 Native Americans. Thus, there was a diverse pool of native speakers of other languages.

Through the mid-19th century, a high percentage of immigrants were from predominantly English-speaking areas; however, by the end of the 20th century, the majority of immigrants spoke languages other than English. Native language instruction and bilingual education were not uncommon in areas where language minority groups comprised a major portion of the local population, until legislation was passed mandating English as the official language of instruction in the early 20th century (Kloss, 1998; Leibowitz, 1971). By 1909, the U.S. Immigration Commission reported, among the nation's 37 largest cities, 57.8% of children in school were of foreign-born parentage: In New York, 71.5% of the parents of school children were foreign born; in Chicago, 67.5%; and in San Francisco, 57.8% (Weiss, 1982). In 1910, there were 92 million people in the United States; approximately 13 million (age 10 or older) were foreign born, 23% of whom did not speak English (Luebke, 1980).

A national wave of xenophobia—largely focused on all things German during World War I—and an intense period of Americanization occurred from about 1915–1925. In 1917, as the United States entered the war, restrictions against the use of German and other foreign languages resulted in a rapid decline in both foreign and bilingual education. Although the U.S. Supreme Court struck down the more extreme restrictions on foreign language in 1923 (*Meyer v. Nebraska*), German language instruction never fully recovered (see Wiley, 1998).

Immigration restrictionists note that current immigration has reached historic highs and claim that, as a result, English is threatened. Although in terms of raw numbers there are more immigrants in the United States now than ever before, as a percentage of the total population, the number is moderate in comparison to the past (see Table 2.4). For example,

Table 2.4.
Decennial Immigration Flows to the United States 1830–2000

Decade ending	Total U.S. population (in millions)	Immigrants entering the United States (in millions)	Immigrants as percentage of total population
1830	12.9	0.1	0.8
1840	17.1	0.6	3.5
1850	23.2	1.7	7.3
1860	31.4	2.6	8.3
1870	38.6	2.3	6.0
1880	50.2	2.8	5.6
1890	63.0	5.2	8.3
1900	76.3	3.7	4.8
1910	92.0	8.8	9.6
1920	105.7	5.8	5.4
1930	122.8	4.1	3.3
1940	131.7	0.5	0.4
1950	151.3	1.0	0.7
1960	179.3	2.5	1.4
1970	203.3	3.3	1.6
1980	226.5	4.5	2.0
1990	248.7	7.3	2.9
2000	281.4	9.1	3.2

Note. The data in column 2 are from *Measuring America: The Decennial Censuses From 1790 to 2000* (p. A-1), U.S. Census Bureau, 2002. The data in column 3 are from *Statistical Yearbook of the Immigration and Naturalization Service* (Table 1), U.S. Citizenship and Immigration Services, 2000.

although in 1910 there were fewer immigrants living in the United States than in 2000, the percentage of immigrants of the total U.S. population was significantly greater (9.6%) than today (3.2%).

Contemporary fears that the dominance of English is in danger echo concerns that have been raised periodically for more than 200 years (see Crawford, 1992a, 1992b, 1999, 2000; Macías, 1999; Simpson, 1986). These fears have no basis in reality. Recent statistics on immigration and language diversity in the United States indicate that English is in no danger of being eclipsed by other languages. According to 2000 U.S. Census data, of the nearly 47 million individuals who speak a language other than English at home, only 3.4 million (7.2%) speak English "not at all."

Table 2.5.
Ability to Speak English by Age Group

Age group	Speak only English	Speak another language and			
		speak English "very well"	speak English "well"	speak English "not well"	speak English "not at all"
5–17	80.6	11.8	4.2	2.3	1.2
18–64	80.3	10.0	4.3	3.5	1.9
65+	86.5	6.0	2.9	2.5	2.1
All age groups (5–65+)	81.2	9.8	4.1	3.1	1.8

Note. Figures are percentages of total population for United States and Puerto Rico. From U.S. Census 2000, Summary File 3, Table P19, compiled by Arizona State University, Language Policy Research Unit.

Table 2.5 indicates that the majority of individuals who speak a language other than English also speak English at some level. Among all age groups 5 and older, only 1.8% do not speak any English. Only 1.2% of those age 5–17 do not speak any English compared to 2.1% of those 65 and older.

Myth 3. English literacy is the only literacy worth noting.
Just as there is a failure to acknowledge the extent of language diversity in the United States, there is also a general failure to acknowledge liter-

acy in languages other than English. This omission adds to much of the confusion about literacy. Although millions of people are literate in languages other than English, their abilities are ignored. By ignoring literacy in other languages, *literacy* becomes confused with *English literacy*. This confusion is reflected in most surveys and measures of literacy, which, because they focus only on English literacy, fail to accurately describe literacy characteristics among language minority groups (Macías, 1994; Vargas, 1986; Wiley, 1991a; see also Chapter 4). According to Macías (1990), there are three patterns of literacy among language minority groups in the United States: (a) native language literacy, which is literacy in one's native language; (b) second language literacy (usually in English), which implies no native language literacy; and (c) biliteracy, which is literacy in two languages (typically in one's native language and in English). Nonliteracy (i.e., no literacy in any language) is also an option.

Although English is the dominant language of the United States, and it is important that speakers of other languages learn to speak, read, and write it, it is not the case that English literacy can or should fulfill all the needs of language minority groups (Fishman, 1980a). When all literacy is reduced to English literacy, the myth that the United States is a monolingual nation is promoted (see Bhatia, 1983; Simon, 1988).

Limited English oral proficiency is commonly confused with illiteracy. Some language minority individuals read and write English but may not speak the language well; conversely, some who are fluent speakers of English do not possess English reading and writing skills. The problems of becoming literate in a second language need to be differentiated from the challenges of learning to speak a second language and from initial literacy in a first or second language (Vargas, 1986).

Myth 4. English illiteracy is high because language minorities are not as eager to learn English and assimilate as prior generations were.

A common criticism aimed at recent immigrants and language minority groups is that they are disinclined to learn English or to acquire literacy in English because of loyalty to their native languages and cultures. This myth is based partly on the assumption of the English-speaking majority that languages other than English should be surrendered as a kind of rite of passage (see Kloss, 1971). It is also based on the erroneous assumption that all non-English languages are "immigrant" languages (Macías, 1984). Because approximately 50% of the language minority population were born in the United States (Waggoner, 1993), this assumption is specious. American Indian languages and a language such as Hawaiian are not foreign but indigenous languages. Thus, it is inappropriate to view all language minorities as immigrants—even if one were to accept the assimilationist rite-of-passage viewpoint. Historically, indigenous languages antedate European and English colonization and the formation of the United States as an independent county. English—in addition to being the dominant national language—is also accurately characterized as an "old colonial language," as is Spanish (see Molesky, 1988).

It is also argued that recent non-English-speaking immigrants are different from those of a century ago, who, it is believed, readily surrendered their languages and cultures. However, a study by Wyman (1993) of late 19th- and early 20th-century European immigrants concludes that a high percentage of European immigrants emigrated back to their homelands. As now, millions of immigrants returned to their homelands while millions more remained in the United States (see Table 2.6). Then as now, the image of opportunistic, disloyal immigrants fostered resentment among restrictionists, who, in turn, created a past in which former immigrants were somehow more loyal and willing to be Americanized and Anglicized than those of the present.

What, then, of the current situation? Are individuals who speak languages other than English really reluctant to learn English? Crawford (1992a) notes that in California, on the day that Proposition 63 (a proposal to make English the official language of California) was passed, "more than 40,000 adults were on waiting lists for ESL instruction in Los Angeles alone" (p. 17). According to Veltman (2000), children of immigrants who speak languages other than English are shifting to English at a historically unprecedented rate. This trend is causing concern that the United States is losing a national resource (see discussion in Peyton, Ranard, & McGinnis, 2001).

Table 2.6.
European-U.S. Migration 1908–1923

Nationality/Language	Immigration to United States	Emigration from United States	Remain in United States	Return to homeland (percentage)
Bohemian, Moravian (Czech)	77,737	14,951	62,786	0.19
Bulgarian, Serbian, Montenegrin	104,808	92,886	11,922	0.89
Croat, Slovene	225,914	114,766	111,148	0.51
Dalmatian, Bosnian, Herzegovinian	30,690	8,904	21,786	0.29
Dutch, Flemish	141,064	24,903	116,161	0.18
English	706,681	146,301	560,380	0.21
Finnish	105,342	30,890	74,452	0.29
French	304,240	62,538	241,702	0.21
German	669,546	119,554	550,010	0.18
Greek	366,454	168,847	197,607	0.46
Hebrew	958,642	52,034	906,608	0.05
Hungarian	226,818	149,319	77,499	0.66
Irish	432,668	46,211	386,457	0.11
Italian (Northern)	401,921	147,334	254,587	0.37
Italian (Southern)	1,624,353	969,754	654,599	0.60
Lithuanian	137,716	34,605	103,111	0.25
Polish	788,957	318,210	470,747	0.40
Portuguese	128,527	39,527	89,000	0.31
Romanian	95,689	63,126	32,563	0.66
Russian	210,321	110,282	100,039	0.52
Ruthenian (Russniak)	171,823	23,996	142,827	0.17
Scandinavian (Norwegian, Danish, Swedish)	448,846	97,920	350,926	0.22
Scottish	301,075	38,600	262,475	0.13
Slovak	225,033	127,593	97,440	0.57
Spanish	153,218	61,086	92,132	0.40
Welsh	26,152	3,376	22,776	0.13

Note. From *Eleventh Annual Report, 1923* (p. 133), U.S. Secretary of Labor, 1923.

Myth 5. Many language minority adults favor English-only policies.

Ironically, while language minority populations are sometimes blamed for not wanting to learn English, supporters of English-only and official English initiatives often boast of support by language minority groups. Opinion surveys citing support for learning English often focus only on English and fail to either ask for or report information regarding language minorities' desire to maintain their native languages. To probe this issue, it is useful to consider data on attitudes within multilingual communities toward maintenance of languages other than English. Attitudes toward bilingualism and biliteracy are also of interest. To date, the 1979 National Chicano Survey (NCS) is one of the few national surveys that has provided comprehensive data on such questions. The survey is particularly interesting because it provides data on one of the largest Spanish-speaking subpopulations in the United States. In one survey question, respondents were asked which language individuals of Mexican descent should speak in the United States. The results are reported in Figure 2.2.

Figure 2.2.
"Which language should individuals of Mexican descent speak in the United States?"

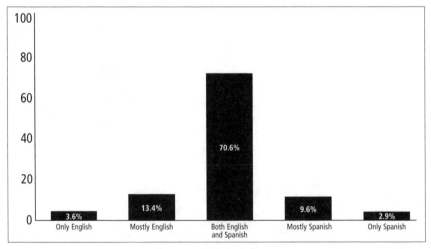

Note. Data from 1979 National Chicano Survey. From *Literacy, Biliteracy, and Educational Achievement Among the Mexican-Origin Population in the United States* (p. 197), by T. G. Wiley, 1988, Los Angeles: University of Southern California. Unpublished doctoral dissertation.

From these data, one could claim that over 87% of the Chicanos surveyed believed that English should be spoken. However, English-only advocates would be little encouraged to learn that less than 4% indicated that exclusively English should be spoken. Over 70% favored dual language use. These data illustrate the importance of framing language-preference questions in such a way that they allow a range of possible responses rather than offering only a simple dichotomy.

In response to the question, "Should children of Mexican descent learn to read and write in both Spanish and English?" the results were solidly affirmative, with nearly 96% of the respondents agreeing that their children should learn both languages. Another question asked if parents should discourage their children from speaking Spanish. Only 1% agreed. When asked if children of Mexican descent should learn to speak Spanish, 99% agreed (Wiley, 1988). These data indicate that nearly all of the Mexican-origin parents surveyed supported the goals of bilingualism and biliteracy for their children. (Subsequent surveys have shown consistent support for bilingualism and bilingual education; see Figure 2.3).

Given the difficulties of acquiring and becoming literate in two languages, it is reasonable to ask why there was such strong support for bilingualism and biliteracy among the Chicano respondents of the NCS. When respondents were asked whether there were advantages to being bilingual in the United States, over 93% answered affirmatively. For a related question, "What are the benefits of being bilingual in the United States?" nine response choices were offered, five relating to "personal benefits" and four relating to "practical benefits." Figure 2.4 shows that the practical benefits of being bilingual in the United States were considered more important to respondents than were the personal benefits: 67.9% chose practical benefits over 31.4% who chose personal benefits. According to survey respondents, the most important benefits of being bilingual were increased employment opportunities (45.1%), improved communication skills (26.4%), and societal and community benefits (10.4%).

Figure 2.3.
Support for Bilingual Education

Question/Statement	Response
Torres (1988) Support for "home language as a teaching tool"	
Parents on Bilingual School Advisory Committee (n=41)	95.1% Agree/Strongly agree
Parents not on committee, but with children in bilingual education (n=106)	99% Agree/Strongly agree
School principals (n=11)	100% Agree/Strongly agree
Youssef & Simpkins (1985) Survey of 44 parents of children in an Arabic bilingual program	
"I am pleased my child is in a bilingual program."	97% Agree/Strongly agree
"Bilingual education should not be part of the school curriculum."	55% Disagree/Strongly disagree
"Do you want your child to attend bilingual classes?"	95% Yes
Attinasi (1985) Survey of 65 Latinos living in northern Indiana	
"Do you want your children in bilingual education?"	89% Yes
Aguire (1985) Survey of 600 parents of children in bilingual programs and 60 teachers in bilingual programs	
"Bilingual education is acceptable in the school because it is the best means for meeting the educational needs of the LEP [limited English proficient] child."	80% Parents agree 90% Teachers agree
Hosch (1984) Survey of 283 subjects from random voter lists, El Paso County, Texas	
"Last year, the state of Texas spent $31.00 per student enrolled in a bilingual education program. Do you think this should be eliminated/decreased or maintained/increased?"	64.3% Support for maintained or increased funding
Shin & Kim (in press) Survey of 56 Korean parents of children in elementary school	
"Would you place your child in a bilingual classroom where both Korean and English are used as a medium of instruction?"	70% Yes
Shin & Lee (1996) Survey of Hmong parents of children in elementary school	
"Would you place your child in a bilingual classroom where both Hmong and English are used as a medium of instruction?"	60% Yes

Note. From *Under Attack: The Case Against Bilingual Education* (pp. 44–45), by S. D. Krashen, 1996, Culver City, CA: Language Education Associates. Copyright 1996 by Language Education Associates. Adapted with permission.

Figure 2.4.
"What are the benefits of being bilingual in the United States?"

Personal benefits	
Improves self-esteem and personal satisfaction	0.6%
Broadens cross-cultural understanding	2.9%
Improves communication skills	26.4%
Improves one's image	1.0%
Provides home/family benefits	0.5%
Total	**31.4%**
Practical benefits	
Provides societal/community benefits	10.4%
Increases employment opportunities	45.1%
Increases education opportunities/success	5.8%
Increases opportunities in general	6.6%
Total	**67.9%**

Note. Data from 1979 National Chicano Survey. From *Literacy, Biliteracy, and Educational Achievement Among the Mexican-Origin Population in the United States* (pp. 199–200), by T. G. Wiley, 1988, Los Angeles: University of Southern California. Unpublished doctoral dissertation.

Other results from this survey support the view that bilingualism confers practical benefits. For example, those who were biliterate were more likely to report being employed (see Chapter 5). In multilingual communities, bilinguals and biliterates have valued skills as translators and as cultural brokers that monolinguals often lack (Valdés, 2001). Thus, it is significant that practical benefits were considered more advantageous than personal benefits by survey respondents, as it is often argued that only English has practical relevance.

Myth 6. The best way to promote English literacy is to immerse language minority children and adults in English-only instruction.

One of the more enduring misconceptions about bilingualism is that raising children bilingually confuses them, inhibits their cognitive development, and interferes with their English language learning. This misconception was bolstered by several generations of biased and flawed research (see Chapter 4; Hakuta, 1986). It continues to underlie much of the opposition to bilingual education. It has led to confusion in schools about language use and languages of instruction and has resulted in generations of language minority parents being advised to not speak to children in their native language at home, even when parents have little facility in English.[1]

It is often argued that the best way to promote English language and literacy development is to push people into English-only immersion programs (for discussion, see Crawford, 1999, and Krashen, 1981). However, neither research nor the historical record support this approach. Current research indicates that bilingual education and two-way immersion programs can be more effective than English-only approaches if students are put into comparable programs with comparable resources (Crawford, 1998/1999). Federally and state-assisted bilingual education programs, however, reach a fraction of the students who meet the eligibility criteria for such programs (Crawford, 1998). Thus, although it is often assumed that lower rates of academic performance can be blamed on bilingual programs, the burden appears to reside more with the English-only programs that do not provide for native language development.

The historical record also raises serious questions about the efficacy of English-only approaches. Although contemporary debates over different approaches to teaching language minorities often frame issues solely in terms of immigrants, the most extreme attempt to implement an English-only education dealt with native peoples. After the Civil War, the U.S. government began to pursue an aggressive American Indian deculturation and domestication program. According to Spring (1994), deculturation involved "replacing the use of native languages with English, destroying Indian customs, and teaching allegiance to the U.S. government" (p. 18).

Education programs were seen as the principal means by which this could be accomplished. Central to this "educational policy was the boarding school, which was designed to remove children from their families at an early age and, thereby, isolate them from the language and customs of their parents and tribes" (p. 18).

Among the strategies used "was an absolute prohibition on Native American children speaking their own languages, and those that did were humiliated, beaten, and had their mouths washed with lye soap" (Norgren & Nanda, 1988, p. 186). In spite of these practices, Weinberg (1995) notes, "Indian children were notoriously slow learners of the English language [not because English was difficult to learn, but because] they had been taught from earliest childhood to despise their conquerors, their language, dress, customs—in fact everything that pertained to them" (p. 206). Sometimes the methods of instruction were punishment enough. Carlisle Indian Industrial School, for example, "taught using a text called *First Lessons for the Deaf and Dumb.* . . . The instructor walked from desk to desk, stopping frequently to guide a student's hand as he or she painstaking formed each letter" (Cooper, 1999, pp. 51–52).

The impact of English-only policies on Cherokee literacy is particularly noteworthy, as illustrated in "The Case of Sequoyah."

Assumptions Underlying Scholarly Work

Scholars are not immune from framing issues related to language and literacy development in terms of an English-only focus. Even in academic discussions about literacy, a number of tenuous assumptions have been made about language diversity. Bhatia (1983) has analyzed these and contends that four dominant assumptions are made about societies that are predominantly monolingual:

1. In comparison to multilingual societies, linguistic diversity is negligible in ML [monolingual] societies.

2. The phenomenon of monolingualism has a feeding relationship with literacy, whereas multilingualism induces a bleeding relationship.

The Case of Sequoyah

By 1822 the Cherokee had developed a syllabary, Sequoyah, named after its inventor, to promote literacy in their own language. Sequoyah was enthusiastically embraced and widely used among the Cherokee (see Lepore, 2002). It provided the basis for a Cherokee financed and governed school system that allowed instruction through high school. The result, estimated by missionaries working with the Cherokee in 1833, was that "three-fifths of the Cherokee were literate in their own language and one-fifth in English" (Weinberg, 1995, p. 184). Cherokee educational progress, based largely on the development of native language literacy, was so dramatic that one observer noted in 1852, "The Cherokee Nation had a better common school system than either Arkansas or Missouri, the two neighboring states" (Weinberg, p. 185).

The overall literacy rate of the Cherokee may have reached more than 90% during the 1850s (Crawford, 1999). By 1906, however, in the aftermath of deculturation policies carried out by the U.S. government, the Cherokee Nation, its reservations, and its school system had been destroyed. "The loss of [Cherokee language] schools spelled the end of the widespread bilingual literacy that had distinguished Cherokees in the nineteenth century" (Weinberg, p. 222).

3. Communication problems are more severe and complex in multilingual than in ML societies.

4. The linguistic situation is too obvious to warrant any serious language planning in ML societies. (pp. 23–24)

These assumptions have important implications for literacy policy. An underlying theme is that language diversity is a problem rather than a resource (see Ruíz, 1984). Most disturbing is the assumption that given the dominance of one language, such as English, the linguistic situation does not require any thoughtful language planning, other than perhaps simply transitioning language minorities into the dominant language. Bhatia (1983) contends that the linguistic situation in so-called monolingual societies is always more complex than is commonly assumed, because no speech community is "either linguistically homogeneous or free from variation" (p. 24; see also Fishman, 1967).

The persistence of the myth of English monolingualism—that the United States is and should be linguistically homogeneous—reflects the dominant relationship of English over other languages in this nation. It is also perpetuated by attitudes toward dialect and register (i.e., the appropriate level of discourse) that view one variety of language, the school-taught standard, as being inherently superior to other varieties. Thus, attitudes toward non-English literacy are often tied to negative predispositions toward nonstandard varieties of English (see Chapter 6).

The emphasis on English in the United States influences the way in which scholars formulate research questions. For example, if researchers assume that an intergenerational shift from other languages to English is desirable and inevitable, they narrow the range of their research findings, and they narrow their research task to one of merely documenting the rate of shift from other languages to English. Veltman (1983, 2000) has made a strong empirical case for the unidirectional shift from other languages to English. He contends that not only is there a general language shift toward English, but also that any movement away from English is so negligible that it is equal to zero. His argument is worth presenting in detail:

> There is almost no in-migration into language groups from the English language group. We are not here referring to the numbers of people from English language backgrounds who learn a minority language. Rather, when we speak of linguistic migration into a language group, we require that a person of English language origin adopt the minority language as his principal language of use. This is a rather stringent test. . . . What is important to understand, however, is that in terms of this definition, there is virtually no linguistic in-migration into minority language groups. *A high degree of bilingualism in a minority language does not constitute linguistic immigration* [italics added]. A linguistic immigrant to the Spanish group is someone who becomes Spanish-

speaking in the full sense of the term. He is an active participant in the daily life of the Spanish language group, not someone who simply speaks Spanish, however well. (1983, pp. 12–13)

Veltman's definition of language shift is so intentionally "stringent" that the *bi* of bilingualism does not count; determining the extent of bilingualism in society is excluded. As a result, language shift is presented as an either/or phenomenon in which one is either an English-speaking person or a speaker of another language. By virtue of facility in English, one becomes a statistic in the world of English speakers, regardless of one's facility in other languages. In other words, the research is designed in such a way that bilinguals are treated as if they were English-speaking monolinguals. In reality, however, some bilinguals, despite their facility in English, drift toward the world of other languages when their spouses, friends, families, and co-workers use these languages more than they use English.

Other scholars who have looked at language maintenance and shift find loyalty to and maintenance of languages other than English, with general shifts toward English over time (Fishman, 1966, 1980b, 1991). Many factors contribute to this, including economic, political, and personal factors, such as a desire to use language as a means of maintaining one's cultural identity. Fishman (1980b) argues that "ethnic newspapers, radio programs, schools, organizations, and churches are not the chief nurturers of language maintenance in the United States; all these institutions may even decrease in number without greatly influencing American non-English-language maintenance" (p. 634). More important are "certain central role relationships within the narrower circles (for example, parent-child, cleric-lay) are preserved in the original . . . language alone. These may be (and usually are) the most intimate or emotional relationships" (p. 634). Additional factors that help explain the maintenance of languages other than English include physiological factors related to advanced age or to aphasia that cause some individuals to lose facility in English or cease identifying with and using the language (Wiley, 1986).

Some writers (e.g., Gardner, 1985; Lambert, 1974; Schumann, 1978; Taylor, 1987; see also Baker, 2001, for a review of major second language acquisition theories) have emphasized attitudes (along with other factors) of the language minority groups toward the dominant language as a major factor in language acquisition. What is frequently ignored, however, is the dynamic interaction between language minorities and members of the receiving or dominant society. It is not unusual, for example, for language minority individuals to encounter the irritation of some members of the English-speaking majority in the United States if they are perceived as imperfect speakers and writers of English. This is especially true for adults, who do not have the same social license as children for deviation from the expected norm. Such encounters with the English-speaking majority have been found to negatively affect the desire of adults to continue attempting to learn a new language (see Perdue, 1984). This indicates that attitudinal studies on second language and literacy acquisition need to concentrate on the interaction between language minorities and the dominant society rather than only on the attitudes of the language minorities.

Beyond the issues related to the motivation to learn a new language or to maintain one's native language is the issue of language rights. To mandate that speakers of languages other than English should not use or maintain their native languages is in violation of what the United Nations has seen as a basic human right, that is, the right to use and maintain one's mother tongue. Thus, more is involved than merely whether an individual *can* change his or her language (see Macías, 1979; Skutnabb-Kangas, 2000; Wiley, 2000a, 2002a, 2002b). Based on the surveys cited in this chapter, most language minority groups in the United States favor both learning English and retaining their ancestral languages. These attitudes tend to promote expanding the language resources of the United States.

Implications for Policy and Practice

To accurately determine literacy, it is necessary to clarify which language or languages are being discussed (e.g., refer to *English literacy* rather than *literacy* if only English literacy is in question). Most national literacy estimates are based solely on English, and this tends to inflate the magnitude of the "literacy crisis." They also stigmatize those who are literate in languages other than English (Wiley, 1991a). Biliteracy, literacy in two languages, likewise has been largely overlooked in most policy discussions despite growing recognition of the importance of the topic (e.g., Greenberg, Macías, Rhodes, & Chan, 2001; Hornberger, 1989, 1990; Hornberger & Hardman, 1994; Kalmar, 1994; Macías, 1988, 1994; Ramírez, 1992; Spener, 1994; Wiley, 1988, 1990, 1990–1991, 1991a, 2002b). Although biliteracy arguably relates to equal abilities in two or more languages, it is unlikely that most biliterates have perfectly balanced abilities, because their language experiences and contexts for learning would have to be parallel across languages (Valdés, 2001).

Again, even though literacy in languages other than English is rarely surveyed in the United States, many individuals are literate in other languages. Thus, claims made regarding the extent of "illiteracy" (meaning English nonliteracy) among language minorities, as well as the assumption that English literacy is the only literacy that counts, must be reevaluated. Whereas English may be the dominant language in the United States, it does not necessarily follow that English literacy can or does fulfill all the literacy needs of language minority groups (see Klassen & Burnaby, 1993). For the elderly, for recent immigrants, and for those who have lacked opportunities to study English, being able to use their native language provides an immediate means for social participation. For indigenous peoples, native language literacy provides a means of preserving languages and cultures and reversing language shift (see Fishman, 1991). In addition, the development of literacy in languages other than English has positive benefits for the English-speaking majority population. Senator Paul Simon (1988) is among those who contend that the United States is at a disadvantage internationally in trade, diplomacy, and national security because it has not further developed its linguistic resources (see Brecht & Rivers, 2000; Peyton, Ranard, & McGinnis, 2001, chap. 1; U.S. Government Accounting Office, 2002).

3

Literacy and the Great Divide: Cognitive or Social?

[If] we believe that literacy is a precondition for abstract thinking, how do we evaluate the intellectual skills of nonliterate people? Do we consider them incapable of participating in modern society because they are limited to the particularistic and concrete? (Scribner & Cole, 1978, p. 449)

Since the early decades of the 20th century, literacy researchers have attempted to determine the cognitive effects of literacy. Some scholars (Goody & Watt, 1963/1988; Havelock, 1963, 1988; Olson, 1977, 1984, 1988; Ong, 1982, 1988) have contended that literacy produces cognitive effects that make literates and literate societies more logical and analytical. In subsequent works, a few of these scholars (Goody, 1986, 1987, 1999; Goody & Watt, 1988; Olson, 1994, 1999) have moderated their earlier positions, which reflected the view that a cognitive great divide exists between literates and nonliterates, resulting from the former having mastered the technology of print.

The assumption of positive cognitive effects associated with literacy would help explain why highly literate societies and highly literate people appear to have economic, political, and social advantages over those who are not literate or not as literate, according to these researchers. In other words, it would help explain the socioeconomic great divide between literate and nonliterate societies. Although a cognitive great divide hypothesis has been the dominant view historically, in recent years a growing body of work has begun to offer alternative views. These alternative views represent a shift in focus from literacy as an autonomous construct to literacies as socially and culturally embedded practices (see Cook-Gumperz,

1986; Cook-Gumperz & Keller-Cohen, 1993; Edelsky, 1996; Gee, 1986, 1991, 1996, 2000, 2001; Langer, 1987; Street, 1984, 1993, 1995; Weinstein-Shr, 1993b).

This chapter examines the cognitive great divide hypothesis from the perspective of three major scholarly orientations toward the study of literacy. Much of the literature discussed here is not specific to language minority literacy issues. Nevertheless, this discussion presents the assumptions that underlie the general field of literacy and are often reflected in the literatures related to second language acquisition, second language literacy, and bilingual education.

Three Scholarly Orientations Toward Literacy

The dispute among literacy experts concerning a cognitive great divide results in part from the different scholarly orientations that researchers have toward literacy. In an effort to analyze and simplify some of these differences, Street (1984, 1993) reduces them to two: the *autonomous* and the *ideological*. Street's schema is roughly parallel to what Tollefson (1991) has called the *neoclassical* and *historical-structural* orientations in the broader domain of language policy. The work of these authors—along with that of Cook-Gumperz (1986); Gee (1986, 1991, 1996, 2001); and others—has been instrumental in identifying a major paradigm shift from the autonomous/neoclassical orientation toward the ideological/historical-structural orientation.

This chapter identifies three orientations toward the study of literacy: the autonomous, the social practices, and the ideological. This schema largely follows Street's; however, the social practices orientation is added to underscore variations within his ideological model. The differences in the three orientations reflect how different scholars view individual versus group factors, intergroup power relations, and the roles of the social scientist in research and the teacher in education (Tollefson, 1991). In fairness to the authors on whose work this framework is based, it should be noted that its heuristic categories are for the purpose of discussion and do not necessarily represent how the authors would structure their own works.

Autonomous Orientation

The autonomous orientation to literacy tends to focus on formal mental properties of decoding and encoding text, excluding analyses of how these processes occur within social contexts. The success or failure of the learner in acquiring literacy is seen as the result of individual psychological processes. The focus on psychosocial factors is limited mainly to studying individual motivation, i.e., the learner's desire to assimilate into the dominant society (Tollefson, 1991; see Wiley, 1999). Researchers and educators operating within the autonomous approach see literacy as having "cognitive consequences" at both the individual and the societal level, giving literates a mental edge over nonliterates. Cognitive consequences are considered to result from the ability to use print rather than from the social practices in which it is used. An autonomous orientation largely ignores the historical and sociopolitical contexts in which individuals live and differences in power and resources among groups. It also neglects the attitudes of dominant groups toward subordinate groups and how the dominant groups treat subordinate groups in school. In other words, it ignores social factors that affect individual motivation to succeed at becoming literate (see Auerbach, 1992).

Social Practices Orientation

According to Scribner and Cole (1981), this orientation differs from the autonomous orientation by approaching literacy as a set of socially organized practices that involve "not simply knowing how to read and write a particular script but applying this knowledge for specific purposes in specific contexts of use" (p. 236). Rather than focusing on the technology of a writing system and its purported consequences, the social practices orientation concentrates on the nature of social practices that determine the kinds of skills associated with literacy. Heath's work (1980, 1983) exemplifies this approach. In particular, her studies of literacy events have helped illuminate literate practices within various ethnic/linguistic communities (for more on Heath's studies, see Chapter 7). Tannen's analyses (1982, 1987) of oral/literate language styles have also confronted the paradox of cognitive differences between orality and literacy, and Cook-Gumperz' emphasis (1986) on the social construction of literacy has been valuable in deepening our understanding of schooling practices.[1]

Ideological Orientation

This orientation subsumes the social practices orientation and adds to it a more overt focus on the differential power relations between groups and social class differences in literacy practices. In the ideological orientation, literacy is viewed as a set of practices that are "inextricably linked to cultural and power structures in society" (Street, 1993, p. 7). The term *ideological* is used "because it signals quite explicitly that literacy practices are aspects not only of 'culture' but also of power structures" (p. 7). For example, Levine (1982) approaches literacy as a social practice within a historical context and against which prevailing political and structural realities are reflected. He sees these literacy practices incorporating activities in which an individual both wishes to engage and may be compelled to engage.

Central to both the ideological and social practices perspectives is the notion of literacy as practice. The distinction between the two views centers largely on the degree of emphasis each places on how literacy relates to ideology and power relations between groups. Freire's work (1970a, 1970b) has helped to inspire both practical and scholarly work involving the ideological perspective and the work of critical pedagogy writers (e.g., Aronowitz & Giroux, 1985; Darder, 1991; Giroux, 1983a, 1983b, 1988; McLaren, 1989). Other recent works are also relevant (see Auerbach, 1989, 1991, 1992; Delgado-Gaitán, 1990; Edelsky & Hudelson, 1991; Freire & Macedo, 1987; Lankshear & Lawler, 1989; Luke, 1998; Shannon, 1989, 1990; Shor, 1987; Stuckey, 1991; Walsh, 1991). While the perspectives of these writers are far from monolithic, they share an ideological orientation whose concerns, according to Grillo (1989, p. 15), include the following:

- The social practices in which literacy products are composed and communicated

- The ways in which these practices are embedded in institutions, settings, or domains and are connected to other, wider social, economic, political, and cultural practices

- The organization and labeling of the literacy practices themselves

---

- The ideologies, which may be linguistic or other, that guide the processes of communication

- The outcomes of utterances and texts produced in these communications

By taking these factors into consideration, the acquisition and use of literacy is viewed as neither a neutral process nor as an end in itself. Rather, literacy practices are seen as being influenced by the dominant social, economic, and political institutions in which they are embedded. Similarly, literacy problems are viewed as being related to social stratification and to the gaps in power and resources between groups. Because schools are the principal institutions responsible for developing literacy, they are perceived as being embedded within larger sociopolitical contexts. Because some groups succeed in school while others fail, the ideological orientation scrutinizes the way schools carry out literacy development. It looks at implicit biases in schools that can privilege some groups to the exclusion of others. Like the social practices orientation, it values literacy programs and policies that are built on the knowledge and resources people already have. In contrast to the autonomous orientation, which sees literacy development as an individual accomplishment, the ideological and social practices orientations locate literacy within various social, cultural, and linguistic networks. Different literacy practices are analyzed within the context of these networks, and individual problems are not separated from them (see Chapter 7).

Building on the social practices orientation, the ideological orientation sees failure as resulting from unequal social and educational resources, inappropriate educational policies, and culturally and linguistically inadequate curriculum models. It views literacy as not only an individual achievement but also as a social achievement acquired by individuals through social participation, as Scribner and Cole (1978, 1981) and Heath (1983, 1988b) have indicated. As markers of social achievement, literacy and educational credentials can be manipulated as gatekeeping devices by those in power (Erickson, 1984; Leibowitz, 1969; McKay, 1993; McKay & Weinstein-Shr, 1993).

The Great Divide Hypothesis

In human evolution, the development of tools and language are often considered the critical achievements that separate the species from the rest of the animal kingdom. Just as technology has had its impact on human societies, it is commonly assumed that writing, as a technology, has had its impact as well. The development and widespread use of writing systems are often seen as qualitatively separating those societies that use writing from those that do not. A number of claims have been advanced about the cognitive divide between literate and nonliterate societies and between literate and nonliterate people, especially by those scholars who subscribe to the autonomous orientation.

Much of the frustration of those interested in proving these claims results from the fact that comparisons of literates and nonliterates have been confounded by schooling; most literates have been to school. Consequently, it is difficult to determine whether alleged cognitive consequences of literacy are actually the result of literacy or of school literacy practices. In other words, do literates have different cognitive abilities because they are literate or because they have been to school? Do the schooled have cognitive advantages, or do they have social advantages? These are some of the questions that we consider in this section, as we review and critique the cognitive great divide hypothesis.

The Autonomous Orientation and the Great Divide Hypothesis

Goody and Watt (1963/1988) argue that the development of an easy-to-use writing system (i.e., an alphabetic system) led to major intellectual changes in ancient Greece, which set the stage for cognitive differences between nonliterate and literate societies. According to Goody and Watt, oral societies were living in mythic time, outside history, which enabled them to maintain an equilibrium where they could transform or forget the events of their past that contradicted their own myths. Literate societies, on the other hand, must confront their pasts because they are maintained in written records. Goody and Watt assert that when a former oral society begins storing its records, a schism develops whereby mythic time gives way to historical time. Then, because these societies are unable to easily readjust the past to fit the needs of the present, historical consciousness gives rise to skepticism regarding the authenticity of the legendary past, which, in turn, gives rise to a general skepticism.

Goody and Watt (1963/1988) contend that, with the rise of skepticism, the desire to test alternative explanations arises. Moreover, the process of writing is more analytic than the process of speaking because of the habitual use of separate, isolated, formal units in writing. Consequently, they reason, formal logic probably could not have arisen without the development of writing. In Goody and Watt's portrayal of the rise of literacy, the Greeks are given singular credit for being the inventors of logic. The ancient achievements in logic by the Egyptians, Indians, Chinese, and others are not acknowledged. Thus, a disturbing characteristic of much of the literature related to the notion of a historical great divide is its Eurocentric focus.

Moreover, Goody and Watt (1963/1988) maintain that oral and literate traditions exist side by side in the modern world in a state of constant tension. According to this view, a residue of the conventions of the oral tradition is seen in certain written texts. Conversely, a literate residue is also posited by Olson (1977, 1984), who contends that literate parents are more "literate" in their speech and thought processes than less literate parents. He maintains that literacy increases the metalinguistic awareness of literate parents and that this metalinguistic awareness is reflected in their speech and oral interactions with their children, which then helps facilitate the acquisition of literacy among the children.

Oral thinking from this perspective, then, represents the antithesis of literate, logical, thinking. Good thinking has often been associated with good writing. At least since the 1890s, educators have viewed nonstandard language as a less logical means for conveying rational thought than standard language. The model for the standard has largely been academic written language (Street, 1984; Stubbs, 1980). As a result, prescriptivists assume that until students have mastered the correct forms of standard academic English, they should not advance their opinions (Wright, 1980). This places speakers of nonstandard varieties of English and speakers of other languages at a considerable disadvantage, because more attention is placed on the form of the language than on its content.

Ong (1982, 1988) has advanced some of the strongest arguments in support of a cognitive divide. Like Goody and Watt, he contends that the origin of various cognitive differences between literate and oral cultures lies in the inherent differences between communication mediated by print and that which is mediated by speech. He argues that speech relies on sound, and sound is transitory. Unlike print, speech cannot be stopped and frozen for observation; it is impermanent. Few would argue that speech and writing are the same, but Ong (1982) deduces that the impermanence of sound in oral systems of communication produces qualitatively different cognitive effects from those produced by written systems. He sees the restriction of words to sounds as determining both the mode of expression and the mode of thought in oral cultures.

Ong (1982) maintains that thought is intertwined with memory systems to such an extent that mnemonic processing even determines syntax. He writes that thought in oral societies must become heavily rhythmic, requiring "balanced patterns, in repetitions or antitheses, in alliterations and assonances, in epithetic and other formulaic expressions, in standard thematic settings . . . in proverbs which are constantly heard by everyone" (p. 34). Ong sees the oral mode of thought as depending heavily on conjunctive or additive devices—such as the word *and*—while the literate mode of thought involves more logical subordination of ideas. Ong argues that the oral "savage" mind (Lévi-Strauss, 1966) *totalizes;* that is, it fails to make distinctions as the literate mind purportedly does.

These purported cognitive differences between oral and literate societies are also believed to have sociopolitical consequences. Extending Goody and Watt's (1963/1988) position, Ong (1982) sees oral societies as having a relatively easy time maintaining social equilibrium, because they can rid themselves of memories that no longer have relevance for the present or readjust genealogies or other historical accounts to match present purposes. In other words, they have the flexibility to invent or alter the rules as they go along. Literate societies, on the other hand, are bound by written records and dictionaries that allow deeds and meanings to become fixed and to be scrutinized critically.

This argument seems particularly weak, because literate societies are not immune from rewriting their pasts, ignoring their histories, or censoring and suppressing information regarding negative or distressful elements of the past (see Street, 1984). Moreover, remembrance of past events tends to vary among cultures. In some oral societies, there is a remarkable emphasis on and skill in recalling past events (see Hall, 1959).

According to Ong (1982), expression in oral cultures carries a heavy load of cumbersome, redundant, formulaic baggage that is generally rejected by so-called high literacy cultures. Gee (1986), however, sees the use of fewer descriptive adjectives in formal (English) writing as an indication of its more analytic nature. Gee argues that Ong's assertion—which claims that communicative devices in oral cultures (such as the overuse of adjectives) are characteristics of the savage mind—is unfounded. Gee sees a similarity between this attitude toward the stylistic devices of oral societies and the attitude of many English teachers toward such stylistic devices in their students' writing. Whether Ong's views are culture-specific notions of style—such as existed among the 17th-century British essayists (Street, 1984)—or whether they are more universally held across literate cultures, is a topic worthy of further investigation.

Ong (1982) maintains that oral cultures are more intellectually conservative than literate cultures and less open to intellectual experimentation. He contends that knowledge in oral societies is difficult to preserve, because much energy must be expended to preserve it; therefore, tradition and preservation outweigh experimentation. Writing is seen as less taxing than speaking, because the context of thought can be stored outside the mind. The technology of writing is seen as freeing the mind's energies for analysis rather than memory.

Ong (1982) and other great divide scholars contend that oral cultures are more concretely grounded in the immediate world of human interaction than are literate cultures, which are better able to deal with abstractions. Ong argues that, unable to store knowledge outside the mind, individuals in oral cultures must ground or contextualize their knowledge in the immediate world of concrete and familiar experience. He maintains that oral cultures are "little concerned with preserving knowledge of skills as an abstract, self-subsistent corpus" (p. 43). Conversely, writing is seen as allowing for more detachment and more abstract thought. (Olson, 1977, also argues that literacy lends itself to more abstract thought than does orality and that oral language is more context embedded or context dependent than written.)

Ong (1982) bases much of his position on Luria's studies (1976) on non-literates' and literates' ability to classify objects. Luria found that the subjects who had attended school for even a short time could perform on a more abstract level than those who had not been to school. The ability for abstract thinking is seen as allowing for a greater degree of objectivity through a disengagement of personal interest. According to Ong, distancing is possible for literates, because writing separates the knower from the known. Conversely, he sees communication in oral cultures as being more participatory and, thereby, more personal and less objective.[2]

The Social Practices Orientation and the Great Divide Hypothesis

Aspects of the great divide hypothesis have been questioned by a number of scholars operating within the social practices perspective (e.g., Edwards & Sienkewicz, 1991; Heath, 1980, 1983, 1988a, 1988b; Labov, 1970, 1973; Leacock, 1972; Scribner & Cole, 1978, 1981; Tannen, 1982, 1987). Scribner and Cole (1978) ask, "If we believe that writing and logical thinking are always mutually dependent, what do we conclude about the reasoning abilities of a college student who writes an incoherent essay? Is this an automatic sign of defective logic?" (p. 449)

Wright (1980) cautioned against the common view that proper form in writing is an indication of logical thinking. Rather, she suggests that this view reflects the "literate" distrust of oral conventions in writing and social class biases concerning propriety rather than clarity of thought. Similarly, the distancing and impersonalization that are manifested in certain types of writing may also be interpreted as stylistic, class-based, or cultural preferences rather than cognitive consequences of writing. From a social practices perspective, Labov (1970) notes that the tendency to distance oneself from a topic through stylistic devices does not necessarily improve the logic of the presentation. Thus, while these authors do not deny that differences between oral and literate discourse exist, they note that differences in style need not necessarily be equated with labels of cognitive superiority and inferiority.

Questions on the relationship between certain writing styles and cognitive development are relevant for practice, because it is apparent that the great divide hypothesis is reflected in the assumptions made by some teachers about their students. Some English and bilingual education teachers tend to categorize students (see Chapter 8) based on their purported concrete or abstract speech and writing, their embedded or disembedded thought, and their field-dependent or field-independent cognitive styles. These dichotomies support the assumption that certain types of communication are less abstract than written communication, a conclusion that has been challenged by Leacock (1972) and Edwards and Sienkewicz (1991). These authors cite a number of examples of logical, abstract practices of communication, including examples in which nonstandard language is used.

The Social Practices Alternative to the Great Divide Hypothesis

The paradigm shift away from the autonomous to the social practices orientation has its roots in studies involving the oral and literate practices of culturally and linguistically diverse groups. Though not overtly ideological in intent, the work of Scribner and Cole (1978, 1981) was significant in pointing to the weakness of the autonomous orientation. Their work focused on a multilingual group, the Vai of Liberia. Scribner and Cole's research (1981) was motivated by a desire to understand "how socially organized activities come to have consequences for human thought" (p. 235). They emphasized that their framework was neither a grand theory nor a formal model but rather "a practice account of literacy" (p. 235). Despite their modest disclaimers, their approach and conclusions have helped lead to the paradigm shift in literacy studies toward the social practices orientation; Gee (1986) and Street (1984) have astutely acknowledged the implications of their work for the ideological orientation.

Scribner and Cole (1981) define practice as "a recurrent, goal-directed sequence of activities using a particular technology and a particular system of knowledge" (p. 236). Skills, as distinct from practice, are "coordinated sets of actions involved in applying this knowledge in particular settings" (p. 236). Practices relate to both whole domains (e.g., law) and to specific endeavors within a domain (e.g., cross-examination), which are "socially developed and patterned ways of using technology, knowledge [and skills] to accomplish tasks" (p. 236). The key point that Scribner and Cole (1981) make is that "cognitive skills, no less than . . . linguistic skills are intimately bound within the nature of the practices that require them" (p. 237). Furthermore, they state,

> In order to identify the consequences of literacy, we need to consider the specific characteristics of specific practices. And . . . we need to understand the larger social system that generates certain kinds of practices (and not others). From this perspective, inquiries into the cognitive consequences of literacy are inquiries into the impact of socially organized practices in other domains (trade and agriculture) on practices involving writing (keeping lists of sales, exchanging goods by letters). (p. 237)

Some of the scholars whose work has been seen as supporting the great divide have not been satisfied with the way in which their positions have been portrayed. In response to the work of Scribner and Cole (1981), several scholars of the autonomous orientation have attempted to clarify, defend, and expand their positions. For example, Goody (1987, chapt. 10), in a critique of Scribner and Cole's (1981) research, suggests that their cognitive tests to determine the effects of literacy on individuals are inadequate indicators of the consequences of literacy, which involve both individual literacy and a society's literate tradition of accumulated knowledge (see also Olson, 1994, chapt. 2.)

Orality Versus Literacy

Scribner and Cole (1978) observed that in several important studies and debates on the differences between oral and literate cultures, schooling was a confounding variable (e.g., Greenfield, 1972; Olson, 1977). According to Scribner and Cole (1978), general claims for cognitive differences between groups are based on research that actually involves the analysis of specific tasks:

> A defining characteristic of the developmental perspective is that it specifies literacy's effects as the emergence of general mental capacities—abstract thinking, for example or logical operations—rather than specific skills. These abilities are presumed to

characterize the individual's abilities across a wide range of tasks. Thus, *based upon a limited sample of performance in experimental contexts* [italics added], the conclusion has been drawn that there is a great-divide between the intellectual competencies of people living in oral cultures and those in literate cultures. (p. 451)

Scribner and Cole (1978) argue that the debate over the great divide parallels an old dispute in education about whether learning is specific or if it strengthens the mind in a general way. They conclude that learning is largely skill specific, embedded within specific contexts. Consequently, literacy (defined as reading and writing) and subject matter in general have been taught as discrete skills that can be identified in behavioral objectives and tested. Most empirical evidence in support of literacy's cognitive effects has been based on specific tasks (as measured by standardized tests). Ironically, claims for global qualitative differences between the literate and nonliterate (regarding competence and proficiency) are based on tests that measure rather limited or specific tasks.

Schooled Versus Nonschooled Literacy

If there were a cognitive great divide, it would be desirable to know whether it is a result of schooling (i.e., specific literacy practices in school) or of literacy in general (i.e., the global effects of using print technology regardless of context). In order to separate the effects of school-based literacy tasks from literacy tasks that occur outside of school, Scribner and Cole (1981) proposed a framework that defines literacy as a practice that is both task and context specific. They looked for a society with individuals who were literate but had not attended school; they found such individuals among the Vai, a multilingual, rural people in Liberia. While the language taught in school in Liberia is English, Arabic is taught to some Vai to facilitate the reading of religious texts. In addition, some Vai men read and write a syllabic Vai vernacular in a script not taught in school.

Scribner and Cole (1981) set up a number of tasks designed to test various cognitive functions associated with literacy. Broadly, these were tests of categorization, memory, logical/syllogistic reasoning, encoding/decoding, semantic integration (processing for meaning as opposed to grammatical form), and verbal explanation. They compared results among those Vai who were literate and had attended English schooling, those who were literate in Qu'ranic Arabic, those who were literate in Arabic, and those who were literate in vernacular Vai but were unschooled.

The expected results were that those who were literate would show more ability in categorization tasks, logical/syllogistic reasoning, and verbal explanations of the tasks performed. However, the actual results found that apart from schooling, literacy did not result in better performances. Neither literacy in syllabic Vai nor in alphabetic Arabic was found to produce the expected cognitive outcomes.

What then of the effects of schooling? Here the results were mixed. Scribner and Cole (1981) found that Vai who had attended school generally had an increased ability to explain the tasks performed. Although these results are consistent with those of previous researchers, this was the first time that *schooling* effects on verbal performance had been separated from other effects. However, schooling did not account for cognitively demonstrated abilities in a number of areas. For example, schooled individuals were not more adept at solving tasks that required abstract reasoning, such as categorizing geometric shapes. Rather, positive cognitive effects appeared to be associated with urbanization, multilingualism, and biliteracy. Attempts to find a correlation between cognitive differences and schooling were only partially successful and prompted Scribner and Cole (1981) to conclude,

> Our results raise a specter . . . even if we were to accept as a working proposition that school produces general changes in certain intellectual operations, we might have to qualify the conclusion to refer only to students, recent ex-students, or those continuing in school-like occupations. (p. 131)

In addition, Scribner and Cole (1981) concluded that schooling does not appear to be a determinant of performance in tasks involving highly specialized skills. As tasks became related less specifically to either Vai or Arabic scripts, the influences of literacy on task performances became more remote. As for the alleged cognitive consequences of literacy, the researchers tentatively concluded that school literacy may be somewhat more important as a factor in producing cognitive effects than nonschooled literacy, but this may be more a result of school bias toward assessing cognitive skills. The message would seem to be that one is usually better at what one has practiced. In a response to this study, Olson (1994) determines,

> My own view is that Western literacy can no more be separated from schooling than Vai literacy can be separated from letter writing. Literacy in Western cultures is not just learning the abc's; it is learning to use the resources of writing for a culturally defined set of tasks and procedures. All writers agree on this point. It is the competence to exploit a particular set of cultural resources. It is the evolution of those resources in conjunction with the knowledge and skill to exploit those resources for particular purpose that makes up literacy. That is why literacy competence can have a history. But it does mean that we cannot grasp the full implications of literacy by means of research which simply compares readers and nonreaders. We require a richer, more diversified notion of literacy. (p. 43)

Seemingly, Olson (1994) endorses a view of literacy that is more encompassing than that of the social practices scholars. Yet for him, Western literacy retains its centrality and autonomy to such a degree that it is indistinguishable from schooling. In the autonomous view, it is literacy, not the social uses to which it is put, that remains the primary concern. By equating literacy with schooling, what are we to make of alternative literacies including those in Western societies that emerge outside of school contexts?

The Ideological Orientation and the Great Divide Hypothesis

The great divide has also been challenged by those scholars whose views more explicitly reflect an ideological orientation (e.g., Gee, 1986, 1996; Street, 1984, 1993, 1995, 1999). These scholars tend to see differences between oral and written styles of communication as cultural and class differences among groups that have unequal social status and authority. Gee (1986) maintains, for example, that more recent versions of the great divide hypothesis represent a new, more subtle version of the savage-versus-civilized dichotomy: Societies labeled primitive were usually small, homogeneous, nonliterate, highly personal, regulated by face-to-face encounters rather than by abstract rules, had a strong sense of group solidarity. They were sometimes said to be "mystical and prelogical" . . . incapable of abstract thought, irrational, child-like . . . and inferior. (pp. 720–721)

Gee (1986) notes the similarity between Ong's contemporary version of this dichotomy and the positions taken by linguists and educators. He charges that Ong should have been aware that many of his claims regarding the cognitive limitations of nonliterates are applicable to individuals of lower socioeconomic status who are less influenced by school-based literacy than are members of the dominant middle-class. Gee (1986) adds,

[It] is striking how similar Ong's features are to characterizations that linguists have offered of the differences between speech and writing, educators of the differences between "good" and "bad" writers, and sociolinguists of the differences between the way black children of lower socioeconomic status and the way white middle-class children tell stories. (p. 726)

Gee (1986) further notes that claims regarding the cognitive effects of literacy tacitly seek to "privilege one social group's ways of doing things as if they were natural and universal" (p. 731). Street (1984) makes a similar point regarding the alleged objective superiority of the essay. In this regard, Street and Street (1991) observe,

We hypothesize that the mechanism through which meanings and uses of literacy take on this role is the "pedagogization" of literacy. By this we mean that literacy has become associated with educational notions of Teaching and Learning and with what teachers and pupils do in schools, at the expense of many other uses and meanings of literacy evident from the comparative ethnographic literature. (p. 143)

Street and Street (1991) make a distinction between the notion of pedagogy "in the narrow sense of specific skills and tricks of the trade used by teachers [and its] broader sense of institutionalized processes of teaching and learning, usually associated with the school but increasingly identified in home practices associated with reading and writing" (p. 144). Recently, however, the notion of alternative literacies (i.e., as alternatives to school-defined literacies) is receiving increased attention (see Cook-Gumperz & Keller-Cohen, 1993).

In summary, from the ideological perspective, the cognitive great divide hypothesis is largely based on implicit assumptions that mask its cultural and class biases. To make this assertion is not to refute the idea that there are differences in the abilities of literates and nonliterates or the schooled and nonschooled. Luria (1976); Scribner and Cole (1978, 1981); Vygotsky (1978); and others have found differences. However, the key, from the ideological perspective, is to underscore the necessity to look at differences within the social, economic, and political contexts in which they emerge. The criteria for evaluating purported cognitive consequences are subject to scrutiny, because they emerge from particular sociopolitical contexts. Attention also needs to be focused on language and literacy practices both within groups and between groups, because the norms, standards, and expectations of dominant groups are often imposed either explicitly or implicitly on less influential or less powerful groups.

Social Consequences of Defective Schooling and Biased Practices

From the perspective of the ideological orientation, a major concern involves looking at the historical and contemporary roles that schools have played in promoting literacy. The more ideologically focused scholars (among them, Carter & Segura, 1979; Leibowitz, 1969, 1971; Spring, 1994; Weinberg, 1995) are concerned with the social, economic, and political effects of schooling. According to these scholars, educational failure is not located solely within the student. The real problem is not that language minority groups come from literacy-deprived oral cultures or that they lack appropriate home environments to do well in school. Rather, in the process of failing to educate these students, schools have become a socially sanctioned mechanism that ascribes a lower status to them (see McDermott, 1987a, 1987b).

Weinberg (1995) maintains that despite persistent efforts to educate themselves, language minority groups have historically been victims of overt segregation and cultural control through a variety of devices, including language suppression, such as that directed at Native Americans (discussed in Chapter 2), and denial of languages other than English for instruction. Language suppression in the United States reached its peak during the World War I era, when English was mandated as the official language of instruction, and bans and restrictions were placed on German and other languages. In many states and U.S. territories, schools prohibited the use of Chinese, Japanese, and Spanish, not only as a means of instruction but even as a means of informal social communication among students during break times (see Crawford, 1992a, 1992b; Leibowitz, 1969, 1971, 1974). Restrictive practices were continued well into the 1960s and still persist in some places. Most importantly, as Leibowitz (1971) contends, the motivation to impose English language and literacy policies on language and other minorities has all too frequently been based on antagonistic attitudes of the majority toward the minority group "usually because of race, color, or religion" (p. 4; see also Crawford, 1992a, chapt. 6).

What have been the consequences of such educational policies and practices? Unfortunately, for a disproportionately large number of language minority groups, the consequences have been oppressive. The impact on many Chicanos has been particularly harsh. Weinberg (1995), citing the findings of a 1970 memorandum of the Commission on Civil Rights, characterizes the educational experience of Chicanos as demonstrating

> (1) a high degree of segregation, (2) an extremely low academic achievement, (3) a predominance of exclusionary practices by schools, and (4) a discriminatory use of public finance. The pattern is similar to that imposed upon black children, who were regarded by the dominant white society as inferior. Denial of an equal education was a powerful instrument of continued oppression. Those who were not permitted to learn were deemed incapable of learning and could, logically, therefore be confined to a lower status in society. (p.177)

Given the historical context of the language minority experience in the United States, underachievement in education by a substantial number of adults is predictable. Consequently, the role of schools in promoting the general rise of literacy cannot be viewed in isolation from sociopolitical ideologies that seek to promote social control (Illich, 1979; Leibowitz, 1971; Street, 1984). Collins (1979) asserts that the widespread use of standardized reading and writing tests has accentuated differences among groups and thereby reinforced social stratification. Thus, schooling does other than promote literacy and cognitive abilities; it reflects differences in social practices and ascribes different values to those practices, because literacy practices associated with schooling and formal education are typically considered to have higher social value than those not associated with schools.

Erickson (1984) maintains that literacy, defined by school achievement, symbolizes the attainment of culture and civilization, wherein the literati, well versed in the classics, knowledgeable of philosophy, the humanities, and fine arts, are held in high status. Being literate in this sense carries the connotation of being well educated, and being illiterate, the stigma of being uneducated. In a critique of this status-ascribing function of the schools, Erickson argues that literacy not only promotes prestige of the literate but also promotes strategic power for them, because it involves mastery of a communication system. Erickson sees the prestige factor as masking power. It masks the distinction between schooling and literacy such that being literate—or lettered—implies that one not only has skills but also that one has been to school. Consequently, this elitist view of literacy may also be characterized as a justification for power. Erickson goes on to raise a number of important questions:

> In current public discourse about literacy, are we talking about knowledge and skill in decoding letters, or are we talking about being "lettered" as a marker of social class status and cultural capital? Do we see the school diploma mainly as evidence of mastery of knowledge and skill in literacy? I don't think so. I think that the high school diploma functions, for low SES [socioeconomic status] students, primarily as a docility certificate. . . . This would especially make good sense if ordinary work in most of the com-

pany's jobs does not really require literacy as schools define it. (p. 527)

Erickson's (1984) analysis has much in common with the social practices perspective. Like Scribner and Cole (1978, 1981), he makes a distinction between literacy and schooling. He also accepts their view that cognitive operations associated with literacy should be seen as "practices" within "task domains." However, unlike Scribner and Cole, Erickson extends his analysis and probes the sociopolitical significance of these differences, which makes his work more representative of the ideological orientation. Literacy tasks at work and in everyday life are seen as being different from literacy tasks at school; each are defined by a different social context. School tasks are often seen as more cognitively demanding than out-of-school tasks, because school tasks are often defined as "context independent," or as in Cummins' terminology, "context reduced" (1981, chapt. 8).

Erickson (1984) argues that the concept of *literacy practices* requires a careful analysis of the relationship between intellectual capabilities and the social situations in which they are put to use. Despite the attempt to make school exercises about the real world authentic, simulations have limitations. Erickson provides an example: Mathematical computations performed in a grocery store are unlike those performed as a classroom activity in a hypothetical grocery store. Although the computation skills appear to be the same in both cases, there is a difference in the social contexts in which the tasks are performed, which affects the attitude and disposition of the learner. In the workbook-oriented and skills-based environment of most schools, the learner is not free to negotiate his or her own choices concerning the computation. This is not only because the classroom computational task is out of context (or in a reduced context) with a real-world situation; it is also because the school exercise occurs "in a context in which the power relations between the student and teacher are such that the student has no influence on problem formulation" (p. 533). Erickson concludes that disproportionate school failure among some groups is related partly to a "schismogenesis" (p. 536), a conflict that results from sociocultural and linguistic differences (see also Giroux, 1983a, 1983b). However, these differences are not the only cause of a learner's failure; rather, failure is "achieved" by a learner's being labeled by the school as an individual of less worth than others.

> [This] view is at once both pessimistic and affirming. It proposes that children failing in school are working at achieving that failure. The view does not wash its hands of the problem at that point. It maintains, however, that intervention to break the cycle of school failure must start by locating the problem jointly in the processes of society at large and in the interactions of specific individuals. (Erickson, 1984, p. 539)

Given the constraints of their socially defined roles, Erickson (1984) portrays both teacher and learner as trapped in an inflexible school culture. More supportive alternative modes of social interaction are possible, but Erickson concludes, "From a sociocultural point of view, literacy, reasoning, and civility as daily school practices cannot be associated and reordered apart from the fabric of society in which those practices take place" (pp. 543–544).[3]

Erickson (1984) calls attention to the work of Scollon and Scollon (1981), who studied the underachievement of Athabaskan Alaskan Natives in written literacy. Scollon and Scollon found that to become literate in the terms of the Western-style school was to lose one's sense of cultural identity (see also Reder & Wikelund, 1993). Thus, the Athabaskan Alaskan Natives resisted school-defined literacy and suffered the consequences of only marginal performance. Most importantly, Erickson's reliance on Scribner and Cole's (1981) definition of literacy as practice helps correct the cognitive great divide notion that school-like literacy tasks inherently involve higher order thinking over nonschool literacy tasks. Debates over language minority groups' disproportionate failure in schools often degenerate either into blaming the victim (i.e., the student and parents) or blaming the schools (see Chapter 5). By locating failure in a complex interrelationship of societal and educational interactions, Erickson concludes that both "cognitive deficits" and "discriminatory school practices"[4] are insufficient to explain the persistence of failure and lower levels of literacy among some minority groups.

Implications for Policy and Practice

Although the literature on literacy is replete with advice on how to improve the literacy skills of individual students, the autonomous orientation offers little practical advice on how to remedy the cognitive great divide. Olson (1984), for example, contends that literate parents privilege their children with literate speech. Because these parents are competent at using language to describe language *(metalanguage)*, their children's awareness of language is heightened, which facilitates the children's literacy development. Stated differently, the progeny of highly literate parents have a cognitive head start over those children with a less cognitively advantaged heritage. Olson (1984) concludes,

> The role of the metalanguage in literacy is not significantly different from the traditional assumption that the antecedents of literacy lie in the knowledge of the language and that children from more literate homes have larger vocabularies than those from less literate ones, both because their parents have larger vocabularies and because they are exposed to books. . . . The link, then, between the structures of society and the structures of the individual are to be found in their sharing a common language which, in this case, is the metalanguage for referring to language. It is in this common language that we may find an identity between what is taught and what is learned. (p. 192)

In recent years, such conclusions have been widely advocated and expanded by Hirsch (1987; Hirsch, Kett, & Trefil, 1988) and advocates of "cultural literacy" (see Walters, 1992, for a critique). Publications promoting cultural literacy and English as the common language have been widely endorsed and marketed. Their popularity is proof of the dominance and persistence of the autonomous orientation.

However, if educators and schools are to be more responsive to the needs of language minority students, more functional analyses are needed of literacy activities as they relate to social practices, especially in education, including analyses of what people actually do with literacy. It is important to note that Scribner and Cole (1978, 1981) do not question that there is a relationship between cognitive abilities and specific literacy practices in specific social contexts. They do, however, question the alleged general, or global, cognitive consequences of literacy apart from a particular context. Following Vygotsky (1978), they caution that the debate over the status of specific skills versus generally transferable, developed abilities "cannot be dealt with by a single formula" (Scribner & Cole, 1978, p. 460).

Along similar lines, Heath (1980) argues that the extent to which all normal people can become literate depends on the functions that literacy plays in their lives, a context or setting in which there is a need to be literate, and the presence of literate helpers in the environment. She contends that becoming literate does not necessarily require formal instruction or a sequential hierarchy of skills to be mastered. Heath (1980) warns that common instructional practices impose a curriculum that slows down opportunities for actual reading experiences by fragmenting the process into skills and activities alien to the parents' and community's experience. Literacy instruction, when construed and implemented as technical pedagogical skills, requires a level of expertise that leaves parents with a sense of inadequacy and results in their seeing little role for themselves in the process of promoting their children's literacy. Heath (1980) concludes that effective instruction needs to be presented in a more natural and functional context than it has been. She contends that if such changes are made in schools, truly functional literacy instruction could "alter not only methods and goals of reading instruction but also assessments of the accountability of schools in meeting society's needs" (p. 131).

According to the ideological orientation, educational practices aimed at promoting literacy always exist within a sociopolitical and sociohistorical context. From this perspective, de Castell and Luke (1983) assert that literacy instruction has been imposed on society rather than derived from it. This distinction is an important one, because the autonomous position assumes that the product of literacy is somehow distinct from the process of acquisition. They ascertain that

> Unless the instructional process itself is educational, the product cannot be an educated individual. The context within which we acquire language significantly mediates meaning and understanding in any subsequent context of use. Our analysis has indi-

cated that the processes and materials of literacy instruction have been based historically on ideological codes. . . . We argue that *the wholesale importation of a literacy model imposed and not locally derived counts as cultural imperialism* [italics added]. (p. 388)

If literacy practices are not to appear alien to language minority learners, education policy formation and curriculum design must be made meaningful and functional for them and their communities. Otherwise, literacy skills will be seen as an imposition on the community by a school system whose values and motives are alien to it. As social practices scholars contend, schools need to become more aware of literacy practices within their communities so that these practices can be incorporated into the school curriculum. Such inclusion does not preclude teaching literacy skills valued by dominant groups; rather, it provides a link between the school and the community that imposed, standardized curriculum models are often unable to make. In the words of Erickson (1984),

> Human learning as well as human teaching needs to be seen as a social transaction, a collective enterprise. Society, culture, teacher, and student interpenetrate in the definition and enactment of learning tasks. . . . The curricular reform attempts of the recent past attempted to change the academic content of instruction without *institutionalizing* the fundamental changes in social relations between teachers and students that would enable the kind of learning environment necessary for teaching higher order cognition. . . . It may be that teachers need more control over their ways of teaching, not less. For classroom teachers to have more authority . . . would be a change in the allocation of power—social change in the schools as institutions and in society that maintains those schools. From a sociocultural point of view, literacy, reasoning and civility as daily school practices cannot be associated and reordered apart from the fabric of society in which those practices take place. (pp. 543–544)

Whether or not there are cognitive differences between literate and nonliterate persons, there are definitely social consequences resulting from the stigma attached to illiteracy. Language minority populations, whose communication abilities (oral or written) in languages other than English may not be recognized, are often unduly stigmatized by a focus on cognitive deficiencies. Although lack of literacy may prevent individuals from achieving their goals, notions of superiority and inferiority can also be manipulated as instruments of social control.

Further Reading

Ernst, G., Statzner, E., & Trueba, H. T. (Eds.). (1994, September). Alternative visions of schooling: Success stories in minority settings. *Anthropology and Education Quarterly, 25*(3), 200–207.

This article attempts to transcend the seemingly endless association between minority status and educational failure through examples of marginal communities that have created successful schools, thereby achieving a balance between what Giroux (1988) has called the language of critique and the language of hope.

Kintgen, E. R., Kroll, B. M., & Rose, M. (Eds.). (1988). *Perspectives on literacy*. Carbondale, IL: Southern Illinois University Press.

This collection provides an excellent complementary set of readings to this chapter and Chapter 7.

Wagner, D. A., Venezky, R. L., & Street, B. V. (Eds.). (1999). *Literacy: An international handbook*. Oxford, United Kingdom: Westview Press.

This comprehensive handbook looks at literacy from historical, philosophical, psychological, sociological, anthropological, pedagogical, and policy perspectives. Some papers are representative of the autonomous, social practices, and ideological perspectives.

4

Defining and Measuring Literacy: Uses and Abuses

Who but the person or group involved can really describe what "effective functioning in one's own cultural group" really means? How is a "life of dignity and pride" measured? The basic question may be: Whose needs are served by generalized statistics about the population? (Hunter & Harman, 1979, p. 19)

There has long been an interest in the United States in assessing the nation's literacy, identifying illiteracy in the population as a whole, and locating deficiencies in certain segments of the population. Literacy surveys have been intended as barometers of national well-being and as indicators of the country's capacity to compete with other nations. Employers have looked at literacy assessment as a means of determining the competency of workers. The military has relied on literacy and intelligence testing to ascertain the preparedness of recruits. Education policy makers have looked to literacy data for feedback on how well schools are teaching skills that students need to participate in the social, economic, and political arenas. There has also been a fascination with measuring intelligence and making cross-group comparisons of IQ based on race, ethnicity, and language background. Unfortunately, results from literacy surveys and intelligence tests have sometimes been used as scorecards of the great divide—the purported cognitive gap between those who are literate and those who are not—rather than as tools to promote an equitable and responsive education system.

Measures of literacy and intelligence are influenced by assumptions about what it means to be literate and intelligent. For example, with few exceptions, national literacy surveys fail to collect data on literacy in languages other than English. Intelligence tests have long been criticized for implicit language and cultural biases (see Mensh & Mensh, 1991). Standards on which both functional literacy and academic achievement are based typically reflect the norms of middle-class, English-speaking populations. These standards are imposed on the overall population with the result that, too often, those who fail to meet these levels are stigmatized.

This chapter examines the uses and abuses of literacy measurements. It begins by looking at some of the early efforts to measure literacy and intelligence; in many instances, the motivations behind these efforts were mired in notions of racial and ethnic superiority. The chapter then deals with the problems of defining and establishing levels of literacy. An analysis of the three major approaches to national literacy assessment—self-reported measures, surrogate measures, and direct measures—is followed by a discussion of two contemporary literacy surveys: the 1992 National Adult Literacy Survey (NALS) and the 1979 National Chicano Survey (NCS). The chapter concludes with recommendations for national literacy assessments that are sensitive to language diversity and biliteracy and that are designed with input from the populations being assessed.

Historical Motivations for Measuring Literacy and Intelligence

Widespread interest in measuring literacy and intelligence increased after the turn of the 20th century, during a time of xenophobia toward non-English-speaking immigrants and racism toward African Americans and other minority groups. Literacy and intelligence test findings were used repeatedly to make cross-group comparisons, usually with race and ethnicity as the determinants. Literacy requirements, for example, were used to discriminate against African Americans at the voting polls (Leibowitz, 1969).

With few exceptions, most national literacy assessments have been conducted only in English. Literacy and prior schooling in languages other than English have been largely ignored as factors in claims made for "innate" differences between groups. With nativists clamoring for immigration restrictions, literacy became a gatekeeping tool to bar immigrants from entering the United States (McKay & Weinstein-Shr, 1993). Immigrant literacy-test bills were passed in Congress in 1896, 1904, and 1916. All received presidential vetoes and failed to become law until 1917, when wartime antiforeigner sentiment bolstered support for restrictionism, and a bill was passed supporting a literacy test over President Wilson's veto. This literacy test required all immigrants 16 years and older to read a short passage from the Bible in their native language (Chermayeff, Wasserman, & Shapiro, 1991), one of the few instances in which native language literacy was assessed (Figure 4.1).

A National Obsession With Testing

During World War I, reports of numerous Army recruits failing entrance exams became well publicized, which raised concern that U.S. census data overestimated the nation's literacy rate (Venezky, Kaestle, & Sum, 1987). As a result, a national testing campaign was initiated.

Figure 4.1.
Cards with Bible passages in various languages used to test immigrants' literacy at Ellis Island, circa 1917

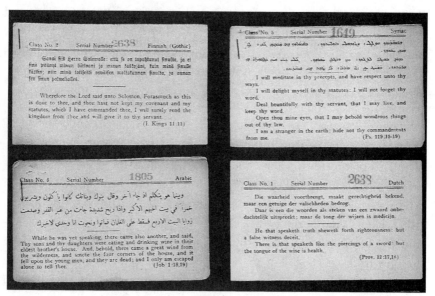

Note. From *Ellis Island: An Illustrated History of the Immigrant Experience* (p. 120), by I. Chermayeff, F. Wasserman, and M. J. Shapiro, 1991, New York: Macmillan. Reprinted with permission of the National Park Service, Statue of Liberty National Monument.

During this period, intelligence testing became a national obsession. Corporate foundations underwrote studies on the inheritance of mental traits, eugenics, and race betterment. A committee on the heredity of feeble-mindedness included prominent researchers such as Edward Thorndike, who, with Lewis Terman of Stanford University, another pioneer in testing and measurement, supported sterilization of the feeble-minded. Thorndike and his student Henry Garret believed that those with lesser intelligence, as measured by standardized tests, were morally inferior. Although English literacy and some formal schooling were requisite for intelligence testing, researchers at the time paid little attention to language, class, and culture bias and presented their findings as "objective," "empirical" evidence that those of Anglo-Saxon origin were of "superior" intellectual and moral stock. In the United States, the so-called scientific testing movement was entangled in racism and linguisism (Karier, 1973; see also Gould, 1981).

In 1916, Terman revised the Binet intelligence test and called it the Stanford-Binet test. According to Weinberg (1983), it was normed on "1,000 white children of average social status born in California" (p. 60). Terman believed that IQ tests would ultimately reveal "enormously significant racial differences in general intelligence, which cannot be wiped out by any scheme of mental culture" (Weinberg, 1983, p. 60). This view was diametrically opposed to that of Binet, who saw intelligence as a practical activity involving "the faculty of adapting oneself, [and he] regarded with 'brutal pessimism' the view of intelligence as an unchangeable quantity" (Weinberg, 1983, p. 59).

Testing and the Growth of Immigration

The rise of the testing movement and the push for restrictive literacy requirements coincided with a record influx of immigrants, a majority of whom spoke languages other than English. Against this background, in 1917, Henry Goddard took the English-language version of the Stanford-Binet test to Ellis Island and administered it to newly arrived immigrants. In one test, he classified 25 out of 30 adult Jews as feeble-minded. "Following Goddard's lead, there was an almost immediate explosion of new tests and research" (Hakuta, 1986, p. 20). More than 1 out of every 10 Ellis Island immigrants during this period were referred for mental testing to determine whether they were mentally impaired. Immigrants were put into inspection lines where they were inspected for behavior that might indicate mental instabilities that would burden the receiving society (see Figure 4.2). Telling symptoms included "facetiousness, nail biting, smiling, or other eccentricities" (Chermayeff et al., 1991, p. 137), such as an Englishman reacting to a question as if he were an Irishman. If observed as acting in such a way,

> They were quickly chalked with an X, removed from the line, and taken to another room for an examination. There, doctors conducted a preliminary interview, asking immigrants about themselves and their families, where they came from, or similar questions. Perhaps they would ask an immigrant to solve a simple arithmetic problem or count backward from 20 to 1 or complete a puzzle. (Chermayeff et al., p. 139)

Figure 4.2.
Immigrants marked with Xs, which indicate suspected mental impairment, await examination at Ellis Island

Note. From *Ellis Island: An Illustrated History of the Immigrant Experience* (p. 138), by I. Chermayeff, F. Wasserman, and M. J. Shapiro, 1991, New York: Macmillan. Reprinted with permission of Culver Pictures.

One Polish woman noted the confusion experienced by immigrants during such interrogation (Chermayeff et al.):

> They asked us questions. "How much is two and one? How much is two and two?" But the next young girl [was asked] "How do you wash stairs, from the top or from the bottom?" She says, "I don't go to America to wash stairs." (p. 138).

Some of the immigration officers expressed skepticism about the mental testing, because many confounding factors such as the "immigrants' diverse backgrounds, languages, cultures, and levels of education . . . affected their behavior [to the extent that one] doctor recalled that the process of identifying mental incompetence . . . was 'always haphazard,' and that often fully competent people were held for examination" (Chermayeff et al., 1991, p. 139).

Meanwhile, on the military front, Lewis Terman sought to extend the use of the Stanford-Binet test even further and, with Goddard, convinced the army to test nearly 2 million draftees. Two English language tests were constructed: one for those who could read and write and another for "illiterates" and "foreigners" (who received instructions in pantomime). Comparisons among ethnic groups were made on the basis of literacy, national origin, and race. Europeans were classified into Nordics, Alpines (those in proximity to the Alps), and Mediterranean races (Hakuta, 1986), with Nordics (Scandinavians) at the top and Mediterraneans (Greeks and Italians) at the bottom; Italians were considered a "superior sort of Chinaman" (Wyman, 1993, p. 100).

In this peculiar scheme of classification, only English literacy counted as literacy. Native language literacy or prior schooling were given little consideration as factors that influenced test results. Length of residency in the United States, however, was considered an influencing factor. The test results, popularized in Carl Brigham's (1923) *A Study in American Intelligence,* found that improved test scores were based on length of residency in the United States, which, as Hakuta (1986) notes, "is obviously related to the knowledge of English and the level of acculturation" (p. 21) to U.S. society. Nevertheless, Brigham discounted this along with the influence of non-English literacy and prior schooling. Imagine how bizarre the pantomimed test must have seemed to those newly arrived immigrants who were unfamiliar with such testing and who could not have suspected the racist assumptions behind the attempt to measure their intelligence.

Because the data indicated that non-English-speaking Nordics had outperformed non-English-speaking Mediterraneans, Brigham concluded that the underlying cause of these differences was race rather than language (Hakuta, 1986; see also Brigham, 1923). Preoccupied with attempting to prove his racial-differences hypotheses, Brigham ignored the possible influence of prior schooling, which would have involved practice in taking tests. Thus, in addition to a language bias, there was a schooling bias. Had Mediterraneans out-performed Nordics, it is hard to imagine that Brigham would not have pursued the salience of other factors than race in his analysis of the data. Brigham's racialization of the Stanford-Binet test data (see Chapter 5) proved beneficial for the political agenda of nativists and eugenicists. According to Weinberg (1983),

> In 1924, Congress passed a general immigration statute that established quotas for each country of origin. Immigration from favored countries—the "Nordiks"—were given higher quotas while those from "inferior" countries in eastern and southern Europe entered under lower quotas. Of the 27 states with sterilization laws by 1930, 20 had been passed since 1918, the end of World War I. Works by eugenicists such as Brigham were an important factor in the passage of this legislation. (p. 61)

A Critique of Army Intelligence Tests

According to Weinberg (1983), Army intelligence tests were critiqued by Herbert B. Alexander in 1922, who concluded that there were more tests of what one had learned in school than tests of aptitude for learning. In 1924, Horace Mann Bond, a young African American student at the University of Chicago, followed up on Alexander's studies and found a high correlation (74%) between schooling and intelligence, which helped confirm Alexander's conclusions. Bond further found that African Americans in Illinois averaged higher scores than Whites from four southern states. Speculating on the implications of these findings, Bond noted, "One wonders how Mr. Brigham squares the facts of southern white deficiency with his theory" (p. 63). Weinberg (1983) adds,

> Would Brigham in other words claim that higher scoring northern whites had migrated selectively? Or, would he concede the overwhelming influence of differential opportunities [because leading testers of the day] such as Terman contended that racial status (as opposed to racial genetics) played only a minor role in the scores? (p. 63)

Despite these critiques, Brigham's work held sway during the 1920s, a period marked by "lynchings and comparatively low educational opportunities for blacks in the South . . . oppressions [that] were ignored by theorists of genetic inferiority" (Weinberg, 1983, p. 63).

In summary, the push to measure literacy and intelligence in the early decades of the 20th century emerged during a period of xenophobia toward foreigners and racial prejudice toward African Americans and other language minorities. Some of the most famous founders of the modern testing and measurement movement used their purportedly scientific tools to affirm their own biases. The results of their studies influenced both public policies and popular stereotypes. Thus, when looking at the results of contemporary cross-group comparisons of literacy or intelligence, it is important to be aware of the abuses to which such information has been put in the past.

Constructive Reasons for Measuring Literacy

Despite the negative legacy associated with efforts to measure literacy, there are also positive reasons to assess it. One of the more important reasons involves the use of literacy data in attempts to redress past discriminatory practices. There are many examples of such practices. During the 19th century, literacy requirements were used as preconditions for suffrage. In the mid-19th century, they were used to disenfranchise English-speaking Irish voters. Following the end of their enslavement and initial enfranchisement, African American males faced literacy requirements designed to bar them from voting (Leibowitz, 1969, 1974). Literacy requirements became one in a growing arsenal of Jim Crow measures that lead to the institutionalization of American apartheid. There was considerable irony in the use of literacy requirements against African Americans, because prior to the Civil War "compulsory ignorance laws" had made it a crime for blacks to receive literacy instruction in most southern states (Weinberg, 1995).

In an effort to redress these practices, Congress passed the Voting Rights Act in 1965 (Leibowitz, 1969). One of the act's provisions called for "the use of ethnicity, voting, and literacy rates to identify possible violations of the act" (Macías, 1994, p. 40). In 1975, the scope of the act was broadened by amendments that included provisions for non-English-language-background Latinos, Asian Americans, American Indians, and Alaska Natives. In 1982, Congress modified its definition of *language minority* by adding "no oral/comprehensive ability in English" and defined *illiteracy* as equivalent to "less than a fifth-grade education" (Macías, 1994, p. 40). Congress required jurisdictions with a sufficient number of language minority groups to be identified. Thus, from the 1960s into the 1980s, the application of language and literacy assessment to the Voting Rights Act coincided with a general expansion of civil rights and a corresponding federal recognition of language minority rights in some legal domains (see Leibowitz, 1982).

Just as language and literacy data are useful aids in redressing past discriminations, so too, are the data essential in determining the need for specialized education services for both children and adults, such as bilingual and English as a second language (ESL) programs. Without such data, it is difficult to convince policy makers and politicians to allocate sufficient resources. (For a discussion of technical issues in data collection, see Macías, 1993; Macías & Spencer, 1984.)

Definitions of Literacy

There is little consensus among scholars or lay people on what it means to be literate. *Literacy* may be defined narrowly in terms of basic skills used in reading and writing, or broadly, as social practices. Defining literacy is often problematic, because the conception of what it involves does not remain static. Resnick and Resnick (1988), as well as other scholars (e.g., Clifford, 1984; Scribner, 1988; Szwed, 1981), have noted a tendency for expectations relating to literacy to inflate over time, which makes intergenerational comparisons difficult. The attempt to define literacy involves many questions, as Kaplan (1983) notes,

> Can one claim that literacy is the ability to write one's name? If so, is there any qualitative difference between being able to write one's name in an alphabetically graphized language versus one which is graphized in ideograms? Or does literacy imply some set of skills, e.g., the ability to complete a form, to address a letter, to compose a letter, to write a list, etc.? If literacy implies broader skills, what skills, in what combination, and to what degree? How does a definition of "basic" literacy correlate with the notion of "technical" literacy or with the notion of "literary" literacy? . . . What does it mean when a government claims that its citizens enjoy a certain percentage of literacy? Under such circumstances is literacy equally distributed among all segments of the population, or is it differentiated by sex, by economic status, by race, by religion, or by any number of other sociological variables? (p. x)

Given these inherent difficulties, researchers often do not proceed far without attempting to constrain or operationalize the notion of literacy for purposes of measurement. Nevertheless, operational definitions rightly remain the subject of heated debate, and lack of consensus results in estimates of illiteracy that vary widely from 15% to 50% (Venezky et al., 1987).

With these concerns in mind, anyone interested in measuring literacy confronts an array of competing definitions. The following list is representative but not exhaustive. Other definitions abound in the literature. In the United States, definitions such as these are usually discussed in reference to English literacy only; however, in the definitions presented here, implications for language diversity are addressed briefly.

Minimal literacy is the ability to read or write something, at some level, in some context(s). At one time, the ability to write one's name or read a simple passage aloud was taken as a sufficient indicator of literacy (Resnick & Resnick, 1988). During World War I, immigrants were required, as a precondition to entering the country, to demonstrate that they had minimal literacy abilities by reading a short passage from the Bible in their native language.

Conventional literacy is the ability to use print in reading, writing, and comprehending texts on familiar subjects and within one's environment (Hunter & Harman, 1979). Although the conventional definition seems straightforward, it is problematic for researchers, because *familiar subjects* and *one's environment* vary widely from community to community. In many language minority communities, texts on familiar subjects would include texts in languages other than English and texts that, for the most part, require fairly high-level reading skills, such as religious texts.

Basic literacy refers to a level of reading and writing that allows for continued, self-sustained literacy development. This definition assumes a threshold that one can build on through one's own efforts (see Macías, 1990; Venezky, Wagner, & Ciliberti, 1990). Essentially, basic literacy is similar to conventional literacy with the added emphasis that one has "enough" literacy to continue learning on one's own. Mikulecky (1990), however, cautions that "there is little evidence that basic literacy in itself wields a magical transforming power for learning" (p. 26). For language minority individuals who have not yet acquired literacy in any language, the native language may provide the most accessible means for developing a level of literacy that allows for self-sustained development.

Functional literacy is the focus of much of the national discussion about literacy. It refers to the ability to use print in order to achieve one's own goals and meet the demands of society by participating effectively within the family, workplace, and community. Functional literacy subsumes conventional literacy, in that it extends the conventional definition to include the ability to use reading and writing to fulfill economic and social purposes at a minimum level of competence. However, competencies for functional literacy education (more recently under the rubric of *life skills*) are usually prescribed by middle-class educators according to their own norms and practices (Hunter & Harman, 1979). Although considered essential for meeting basic needs, functional literacy competencies are rarely grounded in ethnographic research that examines what people themselves wish or need to do with literacy (see Weinstein-Shr, 1990, 1993b). In fact, ethnographic studies (e.g., Klassen & Burnaby, 1993) indicate that many of those lacking literacy in their native languages and in English are often able to function successfully in their daily lives but are blocked from other opportunities for mobility. Other studies (e.g., Taylor & Dorsey-Gaines, 1988) indicate that families in poverty often have more literacy skills than they are usually given credit for and are not necessarily liberated from their poverty by their literacy (see Chapter 5).

Restricted literacy refers to "participation in script activities [that remain] restricted to a minority of self-selected [people]" (Scribner & Cole, 1981, p. 238). It differs from state-supported mass literacy, because it is acquired without formal schooling. There are language communities, such as the Vai in West Africa, where a script has been developed and informally taught outside of school. The Vai script, which is used in commerce and interpersonal communication, is functional but not essential because "those who do not know it can get along quite well" (Scribner & Cole, 1981, p. 238).

> [Significantly, it] does not fulfill the expectations of those social scientists who consider literacy a prime mover in social change, [as it does not necessarily] set off a dramatic modernizing sequence, [nor has it been] accompanied by rapid developments in technology, art, and science. (pp. 238–239)

Generally, restricted literacies do not fulfill the functions of mass literacies (i.e., public school literacies); nevertheless, they offer rich possibilities for enhancing communication within groups and communities.

Vernacular literacy, according to Shuman (1993), is "unofficial [and] defined by its adherence to local rather than academic standards" (p. 267), thereby creating a mismatch between a community's standard of literacy and the standards of the society at large. Shuman contends that the "issue is not only varieties of writing, standard and local, but a privileged channel and genre of communication" (p. 267). The notion of vernacular literacy blurs the distinction between oral and written communication insofar as oral styles may be represented in writing. It also may involve the use of nonstandard as well as nonacademic varieties of language.

Elite literacy pertains to specialized knowledge, skills, and academic credentials, generally acquired in institutions of higher learning; this knowledge in turn becomes sociocultural capital for *strategic power*—that is, the power to advance socially and economically (Erickson, 1984; see Chapter

3). The qualifier *elite* is used because mostly those with social capital have the opportunities and resources to obtain the credentials, which legitimizes their specialized knowledge. Elite literacy is typically given legitimacy by a university degree. Literacy is often represented as a kind of individual possession of knowledge and skills. Typically, however, education credentials and degrees, once attained, tend to be taken as evidence of literacy without the necessity to continue demonstrating mastery; they are markers of one's literate status. Thus, elite literacy is largely synonymous with formal education and with specific types of culturally and socially approved knowledge, especially in the standard language, as certified by recognized institutions of higher learning. Elite education often includes instruction in foreign languages. Ironically, while there has been considerable opposition to bilingual education and the development of literacy in two languages for language minority groups, there has been support for the development of high-status foreign languages as a basic component of elite education.

Analogical literacies refer to knowledge and skills related to particular types of texts, such as cultural literacy (see Field, 1992; Walters, 1992, for a critique of Hirsch's 1987 notion of cultural literacy), computer literacy, mathematical literacy (numeracy), critical literacy, document literacy, and prose literacy. Macías (1990) has cautioned that the "uses of the term very often confuse the issues over literacy itself as well as the analogical uses" (p. 19), for example, *literacy* with *document literacy*.

Literacy as social practices (as discussed in Chapter 3) refers to literacy practices embedded within social and ideological contexts. Scribner and Cole's (1981) and Heath's (1983) works were instrumental in advancing this view, which has allowed for greater understanding of and sensitivity to language diversity (see Cook-Gumperz, 1986; Gee, 1996; Scribner & Cole, 1978, 1981; Street, 1984). Literacies as social practices are ethnographically informed. This perspective sees literacies as always being socially situated, so that "the link between the activities of reading and writing and the social structures in which they are embedded and which they shape [are always understood]" (Barton, Hamilton, & Ivanic, 2000, p. 7).

From this perspective, "there are as many literacies as there are ways in which written language is recruited within specific social practices to allow people to enact and recognize specific social identities . . . and specifically situated social activities. . . . That's why the New Literacy Studies often uses literacy in the plural, literacies" (Gee, 2001, p. iii). The term *multiliteracies* (Cope & Kalantzis, 2000) provides a similar way of referring to situated literacies.

Barton et al. (2000) contend that literacy practices are simply "what people do with literacy" (p. 7). Consistent with Street (1984, 1993, 1995, 1999), they contend that "[literacy] practices are not observable units of behaviour since they also involve values, attitudes, feelings and social relationships" (p. 7).

Three Approaches to Measuring Literacy

Although there have been both uses and abuses in efforts to measure literacy, those efforts have been constrained in part by the methods available. Historically, there have been three common ways of measuring literacy: self-reported measures, surrogate measures, and direct measures.

Self-Reported Measures of Literacy

The U.S. census has been the primary source of national literacy data. Since 1850 the census has collected *self-reported* literacy data (Venezky et al., 1987). From 1850 to 1940, the census determined literacy based on an individual's response to a question asking whether or not he or she had the ability to read and write a simple message in English or another language. Those who answered "yes" were considered literate. Those who answered "no" were considered nonliterate. Gradually, because most people could read and write at some level, *illiteracy* was extended to include people who could read and write but not very well. Although researchers were increasingly concerned with the reliability of self-reported literacy data, the U.S. census remained the primary national measure of literacy. Based on the 1930 U.S. Census, for example, the self-reported literacy rate was 97% for the European American majority, 90% for foreign born, and 84% for Blacks (Venezky et al., 1987).

Researchers and policy makers tend to distrust self-reported literacy information, given the concern that individuals may inflate, or have an inflated view of, their abilities on self-reported survey questionnaires. This may, in part, be related to the structure of the questions, which require respondents to make general claims about their abilities without specifying a context. For example, until 1940, the yes/no format of the census question forced a simplistic dichotomization of literacy. Most of the adult population had at least rudimentary reading and writing abilities, and dichotomizing literacy into literate or illiterate was of little value.

There are other explanations for why self-reported literacy data can be unreliable. Individuals may equate their formal education with their literacy abilities apart from how they actually perform in real-world literacy situations. Much of what is learned in school involves short-term memory. Because knowledge or skills were once learned does not mean they will be retained if there are no practical applications or incentives to maintain them. From this perspective, prior schooling may be confused with current literacy abilities.

On the other hand, those with lesser schooling are sometimes inclined to deflate their actual literacy abilities; that is, they may downplay the skills they use on a daily basis if they associate survey questions about reading and writing with school-like reading and writing practices. Those who speak nonstandard varieties of English or who have learned English as a second language may also indicate on self-reported surveys that they do not use the language very well, regardless of how they perform in English in their everyday lives. For example, a substantial number of Chicanos surveyed in the National Chicano Survey (1979) indicated that they could not speak any language well; this may have been more a reflection of their lack of facility with school-taught languages than of their communication abilities (Wiley, 1988).

There is, however, some evidence indicating that self-assessment can be a valuable tool when proper controls are used (LeBlanc & Painchaud, 1986). In a study sponsored by the U.S. Department of Education in 1982, the U.S. Census Bureau compared self-reported data regarding English proficiency on one survey with direct-measure data from the

English Language Proficiency Survey (ELPS) and found a strong correlation between the two (McArthur, 1993).

Surrogate Measures of Literacy

During World War II, the military again became interested in measuring literacy, as it had during World War I. Trainers contended that draftees' abilities to follow written instructions on military matters were inadequate. In 1940, the army sought to determine the scope of its literacy problem in quantifiable terms by basing literacy on a grade-level surrogate; it equated literacy with completion of the 4th grade. In 1947, the standard was raised to completion of the 5th grade, and in 1952, it was raised to 6th grade (Hunter & Harman, 1979; Venezky et al., 1987).

The grade-level surrogate was largely chosen for the convenience of having a readily accessible measure. Some scholars have argued that an 8th-grade or even 12th-grade equivalency would be more appropriate (Venezky et al., 1987). Still others contend that the number of school years completed is not an accurate measure of literacy skills. Another concern is that there is no guarantee that skills acquired in school will be retained without ongoing practice (Hunter & Harman, 1979; Kirsch & Guthrie, 1977–1978).

The major limitation of the grade-level completion measure is that the number of years of schooling completed is no guarantee of skill mastery, because there is wide variation in individual abilities at any grade level and wide variation in the retention of skills taught. Its strength is that it does provide a measure of exposure to schooling that can be compared across groups; however, such comparisons provide no information about the quality of schooling received.

Direct Measures of Literacy

Given the concerns about grade-level achievement as a surrogate measure of literacy, a number of attempts have been made at more direct measures. However, the problem of how to define literacy remained. Between 1950 and 1975, educational achievement was on the rise for all major ethnic groups (see Chapter 5). Since most of the population was literate at some level, interest shifted to a focus on functional literacy (see "Definitions of Literacy" for a review of *functional literacy*).

Measures of Functional Literacy

In a review of different measures of functional literacy, Kirsch and Guthrie (1977–1978) found a range of 1% to 20% of "functional illiteracy." Among the various literacy tests, one of the best known is the Adult Performance Level (APL). The development of the APL was sponsored by the U.S. Department of Education in 1971. The APL attempted to assess adults between the ages of 18 and 65. It tested 65 competencies held to be necessary in successful adult living, concentrating on the areas of educational, economic, and employment success. The APL sought to determine three literacy levels—individuals who function with great difficulty, those who are functional but not proficient, and those who are highly proficient (Hunter & Harman, 1979). The underlying assumption was that the functional competencies represented and assessed by the test were necessary for a successful adult life. Based on the criteria established, approximately 20% of the APL sample was determined to be "functionally incompetent." An additional 30% was found to be "functioning with difficulty." Thus, the APL found only half of the adult population to be functionally competent (Kirsch & Guthrie).

Since the APL, various attempts have been made to document and measure on a national scale the literacy proficiency of adults in the United States. Educational functioning levels, which form the basic framework and structure of the National Reporting System for Adult Education (NRS), are one attempt to do this, beginning at the program and state levels (U.S. Department of Education, Office of Vocational & Adult Education, Division of Adult Education & Literacy, 2001). Adult education programs collect data on learner literacy levels and report it to states, who then report it to the federal government. The National Adult Literacy Survey (NALS, 1992) is the most recent attempt to measure literacy on a national level. Findings from and limitations of the NALS are discussed later in this chapter.

Drawbacks to Direct Measures

Direct measures of literacy are always preferable to self-reported measures and grade-level surrogate measures. However, despite their assumed objectivity, direct measures have some drawbacks. One concern is their *ecological validity,* the extent to which the tasks tested correspond to what people actually do in the real world. According to Hunter and Harman (1979), any objective criteria used for measurement are only as reliable and accurate as the judgments of the group that defines them. Because direct measures are selected by experts who often are unfamiliar with the life circumstances of those being assessed, they may fail to anticipate the actual literacy needs, realities, and values of the people and communities being assessed. These concerns have been raised in connection with the APL, whose competencies were determined by academicians and adult basic education (ABE) administrators, based on a small sample of students enrolled in ABE programs. Those unable or unmotivated to enroll in programs were excluded from the sample. The APL failed to define success in terms other than economic and educational (Kirsch & Guthrie, 1977–1978).

Another limitation of direct measures relates to the assessment's being a simulation of a real-world event. Test results represent an artificial or contrived approximation of an individual's actual ability (Erickson, 1984). Many of the tasks used in direct measures of literacy and reasoning ability (including the often-cited attempts by Greenfield, 1972; Luria, 1976; Scribner & Cole, 1978, 1981; and Vygotsky, 1978) are actually "tests of the ability to use language in a certain way. In particular they are tests of what we might call explicitness" (Gee, 1986, pp. 731–732). This means that general conclusions about literacy abilities drawn from the results of simulations or from in-school tests must be interpreted with great caution. Because an individual cannot perform a task on a sit-down exam does not mean he or she is unable to perform the real-world task that the test is designed to simulate, nor does it mean that all tasks contrived by test makers represent things that people really have to do in order to function well in society.

Competency-based tests developed in the 1970s were intended to test real-world abilities. Some were particularly open to concerns about ecological validity. However, Hunter and Harman (1979), as cited at the beginning of this chapter, were particularly critical of the tests when they noted, "If we take seriously the dynamic interaction between self-defined needs and the requirements of society, measurement of functional literacy becomes infinitely more elusive. Who but the person or group involved can really describe what 'effective functioning in one's own cultural group' really means?" (p. 19).

Bias in Standardized Tests

Beyond these issues, there has been a long-standing question regarding language and cultural bias in standardized tests, as Wolfram and Christian (1980) contend. First, they note that the testing is analogous to other circumstances, such as employment interviews, "where people are evaluated with standards of behavior from outside their community" (p. 179). Wolfram and Christian further observe,

> Standardized tests have shown disproportionately lower scores for nonmainstream groups in our society. We should ask why this is so. High socioeconomic groups achieve the highest test scores, an achievement that could be due to some kind of inherent superiority. An alternative explanation is that proportionately higher scores for mainstream groups result from an environment that provides them with certain cultural advantages, and, in some cases, perhaps even physical ones such as proper nutrition or health care. A third possibility may reflect a bias built into the testing instruments themselves. It suggests that certain groups may be using language diversity to their advantage at the expense of others. (p. 179)

The standardized test creates a social event in which the test administrator and the test taker have different expectations and agendas; the test, in fact, is an attempt to manipulate and evaluate the test taker's behavior. "While procedures for taking standardized tests are presumably the same everywhere, test takers may respond quite differently to those procedures" (Wolfram & Christian, 1980, p. 180). Wolfram and Christian further note that the performance of a test taker may be positively or negatively affected by the language of the test, as well as by other social factors, such as outsiders asking them a lot of questions. In a testing situation, no aspect of culture is more likely to raise the issue of cultural bias than language itself. This is especially the case for speakers of nondominant varieties of language, as Wolfram and Christian observe:

People who speak nonmainstream dialects are made aware at an early age that the way in which they express themselves, including the very form of the words and sentences they use, conflicts with the norms of the wider society. They are used to being corrected by teachers; they notice that when people in their community are speaking carefully at the most formal occasions, they tend to shift their language in the direction of the mainstream norms; they sometimes see or hear the typical speech of their community stereotyped and mocked. They can perceive a test on language abilities as an instrument designed to measure them according to someone else's standards, not their own. (p. 181)

This puts speakers of nondominant varieties of English at a disadvantage, because rather than follow their "first intuitions about what is correct, [they must try to consider how] someone else would speak. [Even] the most articulate person, the one best able to express complex thoughts clearly, may not be the one who receives the highest score" (Wolfram & Christian, 1980, p. 182), because the test lacks real-world validity for them.

Strengths and Weaknesses of the Three Approaches to Measuring Literacy

The positive role of measurement as an assessment tool should be to determine the kinds of literacy necessary for society as a whole and desired by individuals within their own communities. Unfortunately, all too often, the testing itself has negative social results by labeling groups and certifying their incompetence.

All three of the basic approaches to measurement—direct measures, surrogate measures, and self-reported measures—have strengths and weaknesses. Given their attempts at objectivity, direct measures such as competency tests and simulations of real-life skills are generally preferable to self-reported measures, but they lack adequate controls for ecological validity. Because amount of schooling (i.e., surrogate measures) represents a kind of status attainment, it is worth measuring in its own right. However, self-reported measures are generally preferable to surrogate measures, since surrogate measures provide no guarantee of competency. Thresholds of functional literacy should not be taken as absolute cutoff points. Conclusively, no single approach can be taken as a foolproof means of assessing literacy.

What has been and still is missing in nearly all national surveys is a focus on literacy in languages other than English. This omission reinforces the common notion that in the United States, English literacy is the only literacy worth measuring.

Conceptual Issues in Reporting Literacy Findings: Dichotomies, Thresholds, and Domains

In reporting literacy data, there has long been a tendency to dichotomize findings into *literacy* or *illiteracy*. Some authors have suggested that literacy should be conceptualized as a single set of skills measured along a continuum, while others argue that it is better portrayed as the ability to perform specific print-related practices in specific social contexts, thereby implying many literacies rather than one type of literacy (Heath, 1980; Scribner & Cole, 1981; Street, 1984; see also Crandall & Imel, 1991, for a discussion of definition issues). Unfortunately, national assessments using the latter definition are not very feasible.

One way to resolve the problem of dichotomizing literacy and illiteracy is to make more distinctions among various kinds of literacy and to see literacy as a continuum within various domains (Kirsch & Guthrie, 1977–1978). In an attempt to implement this approach, Kirsch and Jungeblut (1986, p. 64) developed three broad domains of literacy assessment:

- *Prose literacy* is the skills and strategies needed to understand and use information from texts that are frequently found in the home and community;

- *Document literacy* is the skills and strategies required to locate and use information contained in contextual materials, which include travel maps, graphs, charts, indexes, forms, and schedules; and

- *Quantitative literacy* is the knowledge and skills needed to apply arithmetic operations.

This approach was used by the National Adult Literacy Survey (NALS, 1992), and although it better aligns literacy skills with task types, a number of questions remain: Are all skills that are identified as being specific to one domain (e.g., prose skills) confined to that domain? Are all tasks involving documents distinct from those involving quantitative tasks? (For example, tax forms would seem to involve both document-related skills and quantitative skills.) How do simulated tasks represent real-world tasks? How many of the skills assessed have been learned but forgotten due to lack of need or practice?

There is evidence that literacy tasks assessed in one context do not necessarily transfer to another. For example, school-based literacy tasks do not necessarily carry over to work-related literacy tasks (Harste & Mikulecky, 1984; Mikulecky, 1990). Therefore, to what extent can we expect a test to realistically reflect individual capabilities? Moreover, in interpreting findings, threshold levels of competency (i.e., cutoff points based on scores) are established for each domain. Do these thresholds become functionally equivalent to the former dichotomization of literacy/illiteracy? In other words, have we merely exchanged the long-term concern about illiteracy with one over low levels of literacy?

Furthermore, does the notion of a continuum of literacy skills hold up across languages or only within a language? If literacy is embedded within social practices, is there a continuum that reflects these various social practices? It is possible that the very notion of a continuum of literacy skills is more a reflection of curriculum planners' attempts to provide a rational sequence of instruction than a reflection of what individuals know how to do in actual nonschool contexts.

We also need to know what happens when these literacy domains are applied to multilingual populations. If the focus of an assessment is specifically English literacy, the relationship between literacy in English and in other languages in various social domains is lost. *Domain* refers here to multilingual communities where languages are used for different purposes in different social contexts.

For example, in the Vai's use of Qur'anic for religious practices, the Vai language for interpersonal and business relations, and English for academic instruction, each language and literacy ability within that language is tied to specific social, economic, and religious domains (Scribner & Cole, 1978, 1981).

In their comparisons of Vai who were English-school literate with those who were only Vai and Qur'anic literate, Scribner and Cole (1981) found that those who had been educated in English schools could perform more tasks in specific areas of categorizing, understanding syllogisms, encoding and decoding texts, and giving verbal explanations than could those who were only Vai or Qur'anic literate. Significantly, however, although the English-educated Vai were able to perform more tasks, they were unable to perform some tasks as well as those who were Vai or Qur'anic literate. For example, in tests of memory ability, Qur'anic literates outperformed English-educated and Vai literates. This finding is not surprising, because Qur'anic literates receive more training in rote memorization and incremental recall. Similarly, Vai literates outperformed the others in tests involving semantic integration of syllables. Again, because the Vai script is syllabary, this high performance level should not be surprising (see Scribner & Cole, 1981, for a detailed summary of their comparisons).

The majority of skills tested were associated with the English literacy skills practiced in school. Therefore, if English alone had been used to determine the distribution of literacy abilities, the literacy resources of this population would have been underestimated, because there were many Vai who had not attended English schools. For those who had attended English schools and were biliterate, it was important to know what skills they had in languages other than English. As they learned more and more about the Vai community through their ethnographic work, Scribner and Cole (1981) were forced to refine their literacy assessment instruments.

Given the linguistic diversity in the United States, as in this West African community of the Vai, a focus only on English literacy underestimates the literacy resources of this country and stigmatizes those literate in other languages but not in English. It also fails to inform us about how literacy in languages other than English operates in various social domains.

Limitations of National Measures of Literacy

National measures of literacy are limited in their effectiveness by their focus on English and the scholarly biases discussed in Chapter 2. Four types of limitations are particularly noteworthy: ignoring literacy in languages other than English; overemphasizing English oral language proficiency; sampling biases; and ambiguity in linguistic, ethnic, and racial identification.

Ignoring Literacy in Languages Other Than English

Regardless of the approach used to measure literacy, a major limitation of most national assessments has been the lack of attention to literacy in languages other than English. Measures of literacy in the United States are limited when they "implicitly or explicitly assume English literacy as the focus of the survey. [Even when surveys collect background information on bilingualism and biliteracy] this information is frequently ignored by researchers and policy makers" (Macías, 1994, p. 20). For the past 2 decades, the United States has undergone its second greatest period of immigration. By the 1980s, the country was home to one of the largest Spanish-speaking populations in the world (Simon, 1988); today, with 28 million Spanish speakers, the United States has more than many Spanish-majority countries (U.S. Census Bureau, 2000). By failing to distinguish between insufficient literacy in the native language and insufficient English literacy, literacy is equated with English literacy, and the literacy picture of the United States remains both incomplete and distorted. By concentrating only on English literacy, surveys inflate the perception of the extent of the "literacy crisis" in the United States and stigmatize many individuals who are literate in other languages.

Overemphasizing English Oral Language Proficiency

National demographic surveys often include questions regarding oral fluency in English at the same time that they neglect to seek information about literacy in languages other than English. Similarly, adult education programs for language minority populations seem to emphasize the acquisition of oral English and fail to survey either English or native language literacy. Because native language literacy provides a foundation for the acquisition of second language literacy (Baker, 2001), there is a need for better data on native language literacy in both national surveys and in adult English as a second language programs.

Sampling Biases

Noting "significant problems with undercount of specific groups for the 1990 [U.S.] Census," Macías (1994, p. 30) contends that there may be bias related to the sampling of language minorities. Similar issues were noted prior to the 2000 U.S. Census. Sampling characteristics tend to be based more on the characteristics of the general population than those of language, ethnicity, and social class. Unless oversampling is incorporated into surveys, generalizations based on those language minority persons sampled are unreliable. Moreover,

> [Because most] surveys were designed to assess English literacy, samples may have excluded individuals with little or no proficiency in English from being respondents. [In the absence of bilingual surveyors and assessment instruments] even if there is a substantial representation of language diversity in the sample, some subjects may be excluded from selection or from analysis because of their limited English proficiency. (Macías, 1994, p. 22)

Such was the case for the limited-English-proficient (LEP) individuals excluded from the 1984 and 1986 National Assessment of Educational Progress (NAEP).

Ambiguity in Linguistic, Ethnic, and Racial Identification

Macías (1994) notes a considerable ambiguity in how labels related to language background and ethnic identification are used in studies of literacy: "It has become an easy surrogate [for language background] to use ethnic identifiers for language minorities. [This] confuses the two categories" (p. 35). For example, the terms *Hispanic, Latino,* and *Spanish-speaking* are often used interchangeably in popular usage, even though Spanish-speaking is the only linguistic label. Moreover, if language minority groups are defined by "non-English household languages, then

English monolinguals who are members of ethnic minority groups are excluded. [Conversely, if] we define language minority groups as the same ethnic groups within which there are large numbers of non-English language background (NELB) speakers, this should be made clear" (Macías, 1994, p. 35).

Findings From National Literacy Surveys

Findings from two contemporary national surveys, the 1992 National Adult Literacy Survey and the 1979 National Chicano Survey, illustrate the limitations and the benefits of literacy measurements.

The National Adult Literacy Survey

The most current, comprehensive data on English literacy in the United States comes from the National Adult Literacy Survey (NALS). The NALS grew out of a 1988 congressional initiative in which the U.S. Department of Education was requested to gather information on the nation's literacy. In response, the Department's National Center for Education Statistics (NCES) and Division of Adult Education and Literacy undertook a national household survey to assess the literacy skills of adults in the United States. The Educational Testing Service (ETS) was the prime contractor and Westat Incorporated, its subcontractor.

The NALS builds on the model developed for the Young Adult Literacy Survey (YALS) that conceptualizes literacy along a continuum within three domains (prose, document, and quantitative literacy). Each of these domains is assessed through simulated real-world literacy tasks and seeks to determine five levels of literacy. For example, in the domain of document literacy, one might be asked information about an employment application or to determine the gist of a section of prose. The documents and prose are scaled, based on their purported levels of difficulty.

To the credit of its designers, the NALS was more sensitive to issues of ethnic diversity than most previous studies and included demographic questions related to language diversity. The NALS oversampled for Latinos and African Americans, and it provided both English and Spanish versions of the background questionnaire (Macías, 1994). It also attempted to diversify the subgroups that it identified as Hispanic/ Mexican origin, Hispanic/Puerto Rican origin, Hispanic/Cuban origin, Hispanic/Central or South American origin, and Hispanic/Other. Given the diversity within other generically labeled groups (e.g., Asian and Pacific Islander), it is regrettable that further subgroup analysis was not attempted. Nevertheless, the attempt to identify some Latino subgroups represents an advance over most previous surveys. (See Macías, 1988, which also takes this approach in an analysis of U.S. census data.)

In *Adult Literacy in America: A First Look at the Results of the National Adult Literacy Survey* (Kirsch, Jungeblut, Jenkins, & Kolstad, 1993), the authors note demographic changes in the population between 1980 and 1990: an increase of nearly 100% in the Asian and Pacific Islander origin population (from 3.7 to 7.2 million individuals) and an increase of 6–9% (more than 22 million individuals) in the Hispanic origin population, with some 32 million people speaking languages other than English. The authors observe, "Given these patterns and changes, this is an opportune time to explore the literacy skills of adults in this nation" (p. ix). However, despite the significant number of people in the United States who speak languages other than English, the NALS only assessed English literacy. Hence, although the NALS is more sensitive to language diversity than most prior surveys,[1] its focus is still on only English literacy.

Like most literacy surveys, the NALS was motivated by concerns about the preparedness of individuals and the nation to compete in a global economy. The report quotes the 1990 National Governors Association's goals (endorsed by Presidents Bush and Clinton): "Every adult American will be literate and will possess the knowledge and skills necessary to compete in a global economy and exercise the rights and responsibilities of citizenship" (Kirsch et al., 1993, p. xi).

However, what the NALS did not consider was what kinds of literacy skills, in which languages, are necessary to compete in a global economy and whether one can exercise the rights and responsibilities of citizenship in languages other than English.

Responding to the National Governors Association's goals, "Congress passed the National Literacy Act of 1991 'to enhance the literacy and basic skills of adults . . . and to strengthen and coordinate adult literacy programs'" (Kirsch et al., 1993, p. xi). The report (Kirsch et al.) continues,

> "Any national program for improving literacy skills would have to be based on the best possible information as to where the deficits are and how serious they are" (Carroll & Chall, 1975, p. 11). Surprisingly, though, we do lack accurate and detailed information about literacy in our nation—including how many individuals have limited skills, who they are, and the severity of their problems. (p. xi)

Again, because the focus of the NALS was on English literacy, deficits implicitly become English literacy deficiencies, and recent ethnic and linguistic shifts become important only as they help to explain deficits in English literacy.

Initial Findings and Analyses

The NALS findings attracted national attention, making their way into the headlines of many leading newspapers and magazines. Among some of the more sensationalized findings were that 40 to 44 million adults (21–23% of the nation's 191 million adults) could perform only at the lowest levels of tasks involving prose literacy. A whopping 90 million could not perform tasks above Level 2. A careful reading of the initial report, however, lends itself to a more prudent interpretation. For example, Kirsch et al. (1993) note,

> The approximately 90 million adults who performed in Levels 1 and 2 did not necessarily perceive themselves as being "at risk." Across the literacy scales, 66 to 75 percent of adults in the lowest level and 93 to 97 percent in the second lowest level described themselves as being able to read or write English "well" or "very well." Moreover, only 14 to 25 percent of the adults in Level 1 and 4 to 12 percent in Level 2 said they get a lot of help from family members or friends with everyday prose, document, and quantitative literacy tasks. *It is therefore possible that their skills, while limited, allow them to meet some or most of their personal and occupational literacy needs* [italics added]. (p. xv)

These findings present a dilemma for interpretation. First, self-perceptions are not particularly reliable. Nevertheless, as noted in Chapter 3, performance on school-based or simulated tasks may not be representative of how individuals perform in the real world. Thus, the NALS data should not be interpreted as 90 million people were nonfunctional. To do so is to fall into the trap of inventing a literacy crisis (see Welch & Freebody, 1993, pp. 14–16).

In attempting to account for the large number of individuals who functioned at the lowest level, Kirsch et al. (1993) explain,

> Many factors help explain why so many adults demonstrated English literacy skills in the lowest proficiency level defined (Level 1). Twenty-one percent of the respondents who performed in this level were immigrants who may have been just learning to speak English. (p. xiv)

Note that the emphasis here is on learning to speak English and that there is no discussion of prior literacy. Wrigley, Chisman, and Ewen (1993) maintain that "the NALS does not tell us how well nonnative speakers of English can deal with the language and literacy challenges in their daily lives. It only tells us they can read the kinds of items contained in the test" (p. 19). They also observe that because the NALS assumes familiarity with U.S. society, it may be especially biased against newer arrivals (see also Chisman, Wrigley, & Ewen, 1993).

Although they make for smaller headlines—and probably sell fewer newspapers—recent reports have attempted to correct the original claims. According to Mathews (2001), only 5% of those surveyed should be considered not literate because they failed to answer any questions. There were also problems related to the 5-level scale for each of the three domains. The scale was supposed to increase in difficulty, so that Level 1 tasks should be easier than Level 2 tasks. However, some items did not scale as predicted; that is, some test takers did better on items predicted to be difficult and failed items predicted to be easy, thus raising concerns about the validity of the scale (see Mathews, 2001; cf. Berliner, 1996).

Race, Ethnicity, and Language Background

As with so many standardized assessments of literacy, intelligence, or aptitude, the salient categories for comparison in the NALS were race, ethnicity, and language background. Results showed that Black, Asian and Pacific Islander, American Indian, and Hispanic adults were more likely than White adults to perform in the two lowest literacy levels. Performance differences were affected by many factors. For example, with the exception of Asian and Pacific Islander, most of the adults had completed fewer years of schooling in this country than had White adults. Further, many adults of Asian and Pacific Islander and Hispanic origins were born in other countries and were likely to have learned English as a second language (Kirsch et al., 1993). Given this emphasis,

> This report describes the literacy proficiencies of various subpopulations defined by characteristics such as age, sex, race, ethnicity, and educational background. While certain groups demonstrated lower literacy than others on the average, within each group there were some individuals who performed well and some who performed poorly. . . . Such statements are only intended to highlight general patterns of differences among various groups and therefore do not capture the variability within each group. (p. 13)

This disclaimer addresses an important consideration not always acknowledged in cross-group comparisons: variations within groups may exceed variations between them. Although further analysis is needed to identify the factors that would explain intergroup differences, the report deals with one, prior schooling: "Nearly two-thirds of those in Level 1 (62 percent) had terminated their education before completing high school" (Kirsch et al., 1993, p. xiv). Additionally,

> It is impossible to identify the extent to which literacy shapes particular aspects of our lives or is, in turn, shaped by them. For example, there is a strong relationship between educational attainment and literacy proficiencies. On the one hand, it is likely that staying in school longer does strengthen an individ-

ual's skills. On the other hand, it is also true that those with more advanced skills tend to remain in school longer. (p. 13)

Similar to many prior surveys, NALS data indicates that Whites outperformed other groups, averaging 26–80 points higher than the other groups assessed (see Figure 4.3). In attempting to explain these differences, Kirsch et al. (1993) note that the amount of schooling respondents had received accounted for about 50% of the variance. Factors that may account for the other 50% of the variance are considered: "In making the comparisons between White adults and those of either Hispanic or Asian/Pacific Islander origin, it is important to remember that first language spoken and country of birth may contribute substantially to the proficiency differences that are observed" (Kirsch et al., p. 38).

What is not clear from this statement is how language and country of origin contribute. Could it be that the test instrument and the situation are contributing factors, as some have long contended (see Wolfram and Christian, 1980)? Further exploration of this seems warranted. It is worth noting that African Americans were not considered as a language minority, because many are native speakers of a different variety of English (see Chapter 7). It is also noteworthy that social class does not figure more overtly into the analysis, because it might help account for some of the remaining variance among groups. It might also prove to be illuminating if class differences were explored both within and across groups.

A positive feature of the NALS was the conscious attempt to oversample groups from language backgrounds other than English. An attempt was also made to collect more demographic data related to language diversity than in previous national assessments. Because of the possibility of constructing a biliteracy variable from the self-reported information collected in the survey, Macías (1994, p. 39) observed, "NALS bears close watching and deserves secondary analysis."

Such a secondary data analysis was undertaken in 2001 by Greenberg, Macías, Rhodes, and Chan. Based on data from the states surveyed in the 1992 NALS, it allows for finer demographic analyses (see Figures 4.4 and 4.5). The secondary analysis shows that among language minorities, bilingualism was highest among individuals from Asia. As shown in Figure 4.5,

Figure 4.3.
Average Literacy Proficiencies of Young Adults by Race/Ethnicity and Age

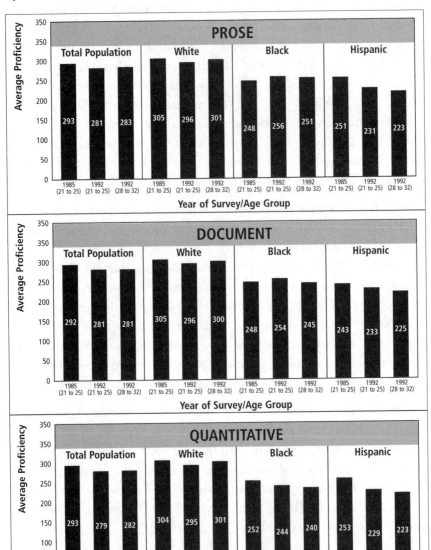

Note. From *Adult Literacy in America: A First Look at the Findings of the National Adult Literacy Survey* (p. 24), by I. S. Kirsch, A. Jungeblut, L. Jenkins, and A. Kolstad, 1993, Washington, DC: National Center for Education Statistics, U.S. Department of Education.

biliteracy rates for Hispanics were highest among Puerto Ricans and Cubans. Additional findings are reported in Chapter 5.

After the NALS

The National Assessment of Adult Literacy (NAAL) survey was conducted in 2003; the results, to be published in 2004, will provide the first indication of the nation's status in adult literacy since the 1992 NALS. Like the NALS, this is a household survey of functional literacy. New components of the NAAL include the following:

Fluency Addition to NAAL (FAN). FAN assesses the ability of adults to decode and recognize words and to read (English) with fluency. Tasks include reading lists of words and numbers and reading text passages. Oral directions and questions are provided in English or Spanish. Words-per-minute and reading accuracy are recorded for analysis.

Adult Literacy Supplemental Assessment (ALSA). ALSA assesses low-literate English-speaking adults and Spanish-speaking adults whose literacy levels in English are not high enough for them to take the FAN. Participants are assessed on their ability to identify letters and numbers and to comprehend simple prose and printed information from actual products and documents. Oral directions and questions are provided in English and Spanish, and respondents may answer questions in either English or Spanish.

NAAL health literacy score. The health literacy score is derived from 26 health-related questions embedded in the participant's primary literacy assessment (either the main NAAL or ALSA), plus 10 health-related questions included in the enhanced background questionnaire. The health questions assess the ability of adults to apply literacy skills to understand health-related materials and forms.

The NAAL should give us more information than we have had about the Spanish and English literacy skills of the Spanish-speaking adult population.

Figure 4.4.
Average Literacy Proficiencies by Hispanic Subgroup

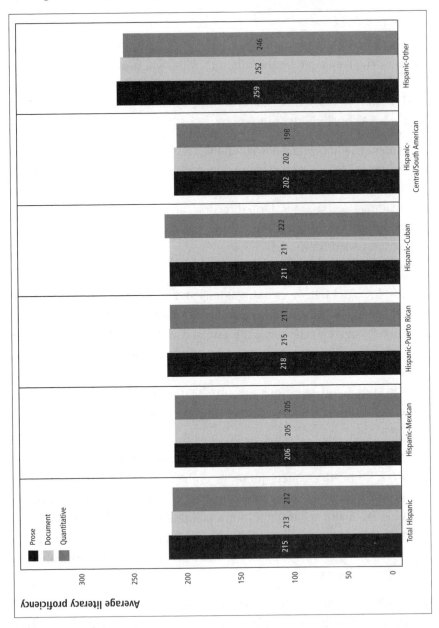

Note. From *English Literacy and Language Minorities in the United States: Results From the National Adult Literacy Survey* (p. 58), by E. Greenberg, R. F. Macías, D. Rhodes, and T. Chan, 2001, Washington, DC: National Center for Education Statistics, U.S. Department of Education.

Figure 4.5.
Literacy Levels by Hispanic Subgroup

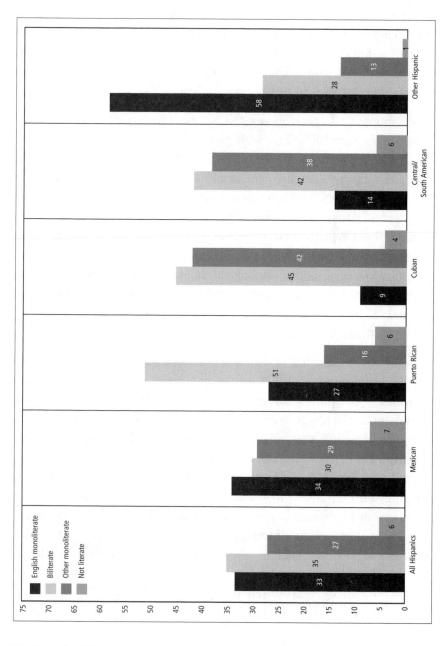

Note. From *English Literacy and Language Minorities in the United States: Results From the National Adult Literacy Survey* (p. 32), by E. Greenberg, R. F. Macías, D. Rhodes, and T. Chan, 2001, Washington, DC: National Center for Education Statistics, U.S. Department of Education.

Research on Biliteracy:
The National Chicano Survey

A high percentage of those who are illiterate in English are literate in other languages. Consequently, there is a need to design national surveys that allow for an analysis of literacy across languages whenever possible. The National Chicano Survey is the only nationally representative survey to date that has allowed for such an analysis.

The National Chicano Survey (NCS) was conducted in 1979 by the Institute for Social Research, with grants from the Ford Foundation and the National Institutes of Health. It was a bilingual survey of a nationally selected and representative sample of the Mexican-origin population in the United States. The NCS was not explicitly designed to measure language and literacy characteristics. Rather, its purpose was to gather information about many different aspects of Chicano life, including social, demographic, political, and mental health characteristics "to compile a statistically representative and comprehensive body of empirical information about the social, economic and psychological status of Chicanos" (Arce, 1985, p. ii). Nevertheless, it is unique in that it allows for a focus on biliteracy through secondary analysis.

The NCS was designed as a national sample (or, more accurately, as a sample representative of 90% of the national Chicano population) and provides opportunities for generalization regarding the U.S. Chicano population. The NCS collected self-reported language, literacy, and schooling data and involved no direct assessment. Though limited to self-reported information, its data tend to be far richer in terms of biliteracy than those of the U.S. census or other surveys such as the 1976 Survey of Income and Education (SIE). The NCS includes parallel literacy-related questions in English and Spanish, which allows for assessment of biliteracy. The majority of the Chicano population in the United States is bilingual, so a biliteracy analysis allows for the determination of literacy characteristics of the population. The NCS also allows for the construction of a surrogate, years-of-schooling measure of literacy.[2]

Limitations

Despite the strength of the NCS in allowing for biliteracy analysis, it has several limitations. For example, the literacy variables tend to dichotomize literacy and illiteracy and do not allow assessment based upon text types or within specific social settings.

Major Findings

Secondary data analyses of the NCS show an overall U.S. Chicano literacy rate of 74%, with 52% English literate, 42% Spanish literate, and 22% biliterate in English and Spanish. If English literacy alone had been measured, illiteracy would have been recorded as 48% rather than 26% (Macías, 1988; Wiley, 1988, 1990). Tables 4.1, 4.2, and 4.3 provide further detail on biliteracy and grade-level achievement. Unfortunately, the NCS and the secondary data analysis of the NCS (Greenberg et al., 2001) are among the few sources from which this issue can be addressed. Despite some of the design limitations of the NCS, Macías (1994) concluded,

> The design options for national surveys have to be widened to include the language and ethnic backgrounds for understanding English literacy as well as biliteracies; [thus] it is not only possible, but very desirable to pursue another National Chicano Survey. (p. 38)

Beyond a new NCS, similar studies of other groups are also desirable. Where cost prohibits direct assessments of native language literacy, surveys (using bilingual surveyors) that collect self-reported data could be undertaken.

Conclusion

In addition to the need to collect data that better reflect literacy and language diversity in the United States, there is a need to be aware of the historical efforts to measure literacy and intelligence and how some of these data have been used. There is also a need to negotiate the kinds of information collected to better reflect the literacy needs and interests of the populations being surveyed. Quantitative data are needed to monitor the effectiveness of schools and adult education programs. However, there are limits to what can be assessed by direct measures or through self-reports. Thus, there is also a need for more ethnographic studies of literacy practices within various linguistic communities and between them and the dominant linguistic community. Beyond this, there is a limit to the utility of language and literacy data when they are linked solely to race, ethnicity, and culture. Greater attention needs to be placed on social class as a factor both within and between groups.

Table 4.1.
Frequencies for Biliteracy in Four Values

Value label	Frequency	Percent	Valid percent	Cumulative percent
English-literate dominant	305	30.8	31.7	31.7
English-Spanish biliterate	194	19.6	20.1	51.8
Spanish-literate dominant	214	21.6	22.2	74.0
Limited or nonliterate	250	25.2	26.0	100.0
Missing cases	28	2.8	Missing	—
Total	991	100.0	100.0	—

Note. Valid cases = 979. From "Literacy, Biliteracy, and Educational Achievement Among the Mexican-Origin Population in the United States," by T. G. Wiley, 1990, *Bilingual Research Journal, 14,* p. 116. Copyright by *Bilingual Research Journal.* Reprinted with permission.

Table 4.2.
Frequencies for Grade Level Achievement

Value label	Frequency	Percent	Valid percent	Cumulative percent
< 6 years	264	26.6	27.0	27.0
6–11 years	392	39.6	40.0	67.0
> 11 years	323	32.6	33.0	100.0
Missing cases	12	1.2	Missing	—
Total	991	100.0	100.0	—

Note. Valid cases = 979. From "Literacy, Biliteracy, and Educational Achievement Among the Mexican-Origin Population in the United States," by T. G. Wiley, 1990, *Bilingual Research Journal, 14,* p. 117. Copyright by *Bilingual Research Journal.* Reprinted with permission.

Table 4.3.
Literacy by Nativity, Sex, Age, and Age at Immigration

	English literate		Biliterate		Spanish literate		Limited or nonliterate	
	Number	Percent	Number	Percent	Number	Percent	Number	Percent
Nativity								
United States	290	30.1	148	15.4	26	2.7	131	13.6
Mexico	15	1.6	46	4.8	188	19.5	119	12.4
Sex								
Male	109	11.3	74	7.7	103	10.7	98	10.2
Female	196	20.4	120	12.5	111	11.5	152	15.8
Age								
18–25	51	5.3	31	3.2	38	4.0	29	3.0
26–35	124	13.0	54	5.6	73	7.6	64	6.7
36–45	74	7.7	43	4.5	51	5.3	33	3.5
46–55	34	3.6	30	3.1	22	2.3	55	5.8
56–65	11	1.2	21	2.2	13	1.4	35	3.7
Over 65	9	0.9	12	1.3	17	1.8	32	3.3
Age at immigration								
5 and under	5	1.4	5	1.4	4	1.1	9	2.5
6–8	3	0.8	3	0.8	—	—	4	1.1
9–11	3	0.8	5	1.4	1	0.3	3	0.8
12–15	1	0.3	11	3.0	10	2.8	8	2.2
16–18	—	—	7	1.9	30	8.3	23	6.4
19 and over	3	0.8	15	4.1	140	38.7	69	19.1

Note. Valid cases = 979. From "Literacy, Biliteracy, and Educational Achievement Among the Mexican-Origin Population in the United States," by T. G. Wiley, 1990, *Bilingual Research Journal, 14,* p. 117. Copyright by *Bilingual Research Journal.* Reprinted with permission.

5

Literacy, Schooling, and the Socioeconomic Divide

(with Mario Castro)

The idea of mobility hinges on the belief that there is equal opportunity in education and through education, opportunity for social mobility and a more equitable society. . . . The germane point is that the idea of mobility through literacy and education remains persuasive, despite . . . the historical experience of most people. (Collins, 1991, pp. 234–235)

In the 1980s, the release of the highly touted *A Nation at Risk* (National Commission on Excellence in Education, 1983) rekindled debate over the nation's "literacy crisis," a predicament purportedly brought on by a lack of fundamental literacy skills in the United States. The report brought national polemics about literacy and education to a level not seen since the Sputnik era. According to Freebody and Welch (1993), the literacy debate in the United States had paralleled that in other nations such as Canada, where there had been "the ready ascription of the causes of the 'crisis' to areas of societal and political practice . . . notably about workers, immigrants, and the 'Back to Basics' school curriculum" (p. 15).

The concern of these authors is that inappropriate education programs, mustered to solve the crisis, can be used "to further marginalize certain segments of society" (Freebody & Welch, 1993, p. 15). Calls for higher national standards dominate the literacy debate in such a way that language minorities appear to be the cause of the crisis. Moreover, the "Back to Basics" and "Teach 'em English" remedies offered are rooted in "a technicist definition of literacy [that has] underpinned the principal models of literacy in North America this century" (Freebody & Welch, p. 15; see also de Castell & Luke, 1983, 1986; Wagner, 1999). Although it is pointless to argue that a strong association between literacy and economic position does not exist, the concern is how language minority populations are positioned in discussions about the crisis and whether the policy and program goals focused on them are appropriate.

This chapter reviews and critiques some of the common assumptions about the relationship between literacy and economic position and discusses their implications for language minority groups. It also presents data on the relationship among literacy, biliteracy, schooling, and employability. Data related to young adults and adolescent immigrants' schooling are presented with implications for policy and practice.

Naming the Disease While Blaming the Patient

Historically, social reformers have pointed to illiteracy and underachievement in education as causes of crime, juvenile delinquency, and unemployment. In the 19th century, the common school movement emerged, in part, as an educational remedy for problems associated with illiteracy. In the early decades of the 20th century, adult Americanization programs were initiated as a means for promoting linguistic assimilation, English literacy, and patriotism (see McClymer, 1982). Since then, illiteracy has continued to be depicted as a personal misery "whose public consequences—unemployment, crime, and so on—cannot be abated without [the assistance of educators]" (Brodkey, 1991, p. 44). If educators are to avoid offering educational placebos for problems that are fundamental, they must understand the nature of the "disease."

Today, in the popular media and in policy debates, illiteracy and educational underachievement are seen as indicators also of a lack of national well-being and competitiveness. Illiteracy is associated with problems of the poor, immigrants, refugees, racial and ethnic minorities, and non-English and limited-English speakers. These labels are treated as if they were similar. Their continued use in popular media gives reason for concern, since, as Brodkey (1991) contends, "all definitions of literacy project both a *literate self* and an *illiterate other.* [They stipulate] "the political as well as cultural terms on which the 'literate' wish to live with the 'illiterate'" (p. 161).

A quarter century ago, Michael Lewis (1978) observed that explanations for success and failure in this society take the form of a popular ideology or belief system that justifies a "culture of inequality [and] mandates the existence of visible failure [and] the persistence of major social problems" (p. 192) such as illiteracy. In the culture of inequality, the illiterate and poor are caught in a cycle of failure and victimization that Lewis calls the "calculus of estrangement" (p. 192). Lewis warned that the need for such victimization would intensify as the disparity between rich and poor widened. He observed that educational failure plays a unique role in the calculus of estrangement: "If the problem is educational failure, we do little except . . . to blame such failure on the backgrounds of those who fail; we certainly do not attempt extensive reform of those school systems which often appear inadequate" (p. 193). Being successful in society is thus attributed to an individual's ability to take advantage of educational opportunities and to become literate. As Collins (1991) concludes, "By defining the relevant measures of social position narrowly enough, social mobility seems to work: We succeed through our 'own' efforts, as represented by the match of education and job" (p. 235; see also Lankshear & Lawler, 1989; Ryan, 1972).

Immigrant and native-born language minority groups have been particularly vulnerable to stigmatization, because they fail to meet the expectations of the majority (see Portes & Rumbaut, 2001), who often assume that the educational system and the job market provide sufficient opportunities for everyone. Rarely are the expectations of the majority, the equity of the educational system, or the opportunities within the job market questioned. Often, the existence of educational programs is taken as sufficient proof that equal opportunity and appropriate instruction have been provided. In a system of English-only instruction, the student is the target, and illiteracy in English is seen as the result of a personal, rather than systemic, failure. When specific education programs, such as bilingual education, are provided for language minority populations, critics attack the programs as inappropriate, because they are not English-only practices.

Over the years, the impact of blaming the victim has influenced the way in which literacy issues are framed. Literacy problems persist generation after generation regardless of advances made in literacy and education.

Thus, the persistence of a *perpetual literacy crisis* raises questions concerning how education reform efforts that offer only English literacy and basic skills education, but no access to satisfactory jobs, can address the more fundamental problems that result from economic inequity among individuals or solve structural problems within the economy.

Literacy and Socioeconomic Problems

At the national economic level, the connections between literacy development and economic improvement are also not as causally linked as they appear in the popular media. As Coulmas (1992) has observed,

> The reduction of illiteracy from 50 percent to 40 percent which was accomplished in Nicaragua by a literacy campaign during the 1980s will likely have no immediate or medium-term consequences for the development of social wealth in that country. Thus the socioeconomic value of literacy cannot be measured on a scale with linear progress. (p. 211)

It is also commonly argued that low literacy levels among a substantial portion of the total labor force must have a negative effect on the national economy because, "in a technological society, the need for the nation's workforce to be continuously replenished by adequately trained and functionally literate workers becomes increasingly important" (Vargas, 1986, p. 9)—so much so that "concerns about the human costs of limited literacy have, in a sense, been overshadowed by concerns about the economic and social costs" (Kirsch, Jungeblut, Jenkins, & Kolstad, 1993, p. x). Despite such concerns, the causality between literacy and national economic well-being may be overestimated.

> What, maybe, the American example illustrates more clearly than any other is that a high level of economic and technological development is not incompatible with relatively high rates of illiteracy. As a matter of fact, in virtually all advanced countries that have taken the trouble to investigate the matter, it was found that functional illiteracy is much more pervasive a problem than had previously been thought. (Coulmas, 1992, p. 214)

What then of the impact of the mass literacy campaigns of the 19th century? Even when mass literacy campaigns were carried out, social problems persisted. Graff (1979, 1987), who studied the impact of such campaigns in Canadian history, locates the cause of economic and social problems not in illiteracy but in social and economic inequality. He concludes that

> Criminal prosecution, and probably apprehension as well, derived from the facts of inequality. Punishment, stratification, and illiteracy too were rooted in the social structure; pervasive structures of inequality which emanated from the ethnic and sexual ascription [that] ordered groups and individuals. . . . Achievement of literacy or education had little impact upon these structures, and in many cases only reinforced them. (p. 210)

Graff (1987) contends that while English literacy was touted as a panacea, gains in literacy actually increased social stratification. So, historically, basic literacy education has been used as a normative agent. Both Street (1984) and Graff (1979) argue that mass literacy campaigns hide a deeper motive, which is to pacify and manage those who do not match middle-class expectations.

The connection then between socioeconomic problems and illiteracy needs to be reversed: Illiteracy may be more a *result* of socioeconomic problems than a *cause*. Literacy is obviously related to social and economic mobility, but the essential question is, does literacy precede or follow gains in mobility?

To answer this question, it is necessary to separate individual cases from general trends. There are instances where individuals have come from unprivileged backgrounds and became literate and ultimately successful. Nevertheless, the historical trend has been that literacy and upward mobility tend to follow rather than precede improvements in a family's economic position, and intergenerationally, children have tended to fare slightly better than their parents, at least until recently (Weinberg, 1983, 1995). Improved economic, political, and social positions have more often been the result of long-term organized efforts to advance better working conditions and benefits than of merely increasing literacy. For example, the gains in economic positions that occurred during the 1930s were more the result of the great expansion of unionism than gains in literacy. Many of those who joined the ranks of unions were from immigrant, language-minority backgrounds. Despite having been stigmatized for their lack of English literacy, they were able to improve their economic positions through organized activity. From their improved economic positions, their children benefited and increased their literacy levels. In other words, the second generation's rise in literacy reflected the economic gains of the previous generation (see Wagner, 1999).

However, there are also constraints on the impact that literacy can have on one's position. Historically, according to Coulmas (1992), "Those who can barely write their name do not have significantly better economic changes than those unable to write at all" (p. 211). Those who are literate but who lack formal schooling and education credentials usually cannot fully benefit in the job market from the literacy skills they do have. As taxpayers, they are shortchanged, because they contribute to services (such as higher education) in which they do not participate. Thus, they are unable to reap the full benefits of citizenship (Vargas, 1986). Often they are recruited into adult literacy and English as a second language (ESL) programs with only a vague sense that improving their literacy and oral English skills will in some way benefit them. In the absence of formal education credentials, these individuals are often blocked from achieving social and economic gains, even though they acquire some degree of English literacy.

The Link Between Literacy and Economic Position

When contemporary data on literacy and educational achievement are analyzed, the data indicate that there is a correlation between the lack of literacy and lower educational achievement in any language (especially in English) and one's economic situation. However, these data are often mistakenly interpreted as indicating a causal relationship between literacy and economic position.

The National Adult Literacy Survey (NALS), for example, indicates that only about 25% of the respondents living in poverty were able to perform at Level 3 or higher on the prose, document, and quantitative literacy tasks (see Chapter 4 regarding NALS literacy levels and task domains). Among those receiving food stamps, only 1% were able to perform Level 5 tasks; of those who received interest from savings or other bank accounts, 83–85% could perform Level 5 tasks.

As indicated in Chapter 4, one of the limitations of the NALS is that it only directly assessed literacy in English. Some comparison with the National Chicano Survey (NCS), which does allow for an analysis of Spanish literacy and biliteracy in English and Spanish, is useful (as long as one remembers, as noted in Chapter 4, that the NCS data were based on self-reported information). Figure 5.1 compares language(s) of literacy among Chicanos by level of family income. The data indicate a strong association between English literacy and family income but show that Spanish literacy is also important. Biliterates and those literate in only Spanish had higher levels of income than those who were not literate in either language, which would seem to confirm the importance of assessing literacy in languages other than English. Family income among biliterates was only slightly lower than among those literate in only English. Interestingly, biliterates were somewhat more likely to be employed than those literate in only English (68% to 62%). As one would expect, the amount of schooling attained also appeared to be significant. Over 73% of those with 12 or more years of schooling were employed, compared with only 50% of those with 6 to 11 years, and only 42% of those with less than 6 years (Wiley, 1988).

For the most part, secondary data from the NALS confirmed these findings (see Figure 5.2). Immigrant biliterates reported slightly higher incomes than English monoliterates and considerably higher incomes than those monoliterate in languages other than English. Biliterate Hispanics reported only slightly lower incomes than English-monoliterate Hispanics. As in the NCS, nonliterates reported substantially lower incomes than those who were monoliterate or biliterate.

These data confirm that low levels of literacy and educational attainment do diminish employment prospects for language minorities. This points to the need to increase educational resources to promote English literacy for those who are already literate in their native language, and to pro-

Figure 5.1.
Chicano Literacy by Family Income

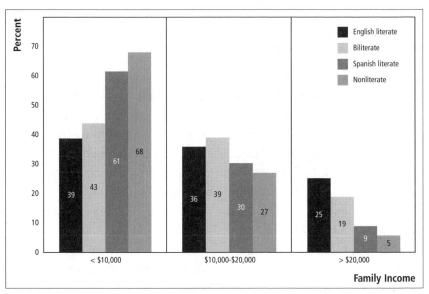

Note. Data from 1979 National Chicano Survey.

mote literacy in native languages for those who are not. However, literacy programs must be explicitly linked to improving both academic and economic opportunities. It is here that the agendas of policy makers, employers, and adult students are often at odds.

Playing Catch-Up:
The Dilemma of Rising Expectations
and Rising Standards

As historical background to the perpetual literacy crisis, Resnick and Resnick (1988) note the impact of ever-rising standards for literacy. They provide a useful analysis of continually changing perceptions of being literate. Having analyzed several historical patterns of literacy education in Europe and the United States, they conclude that current expectations regarding mass literacy have been held for, at most, three generations. In the past, literacy expectations were aimed at achieving a high level of literacy for the children of the upper and middle classes but minimal levels for those at the lower end of the socioeconomic scale. Thus, recent calls

Figure 5.2.
Mean Annual Earnings by Self-Reported Literacy Proficiencies (for 1992)

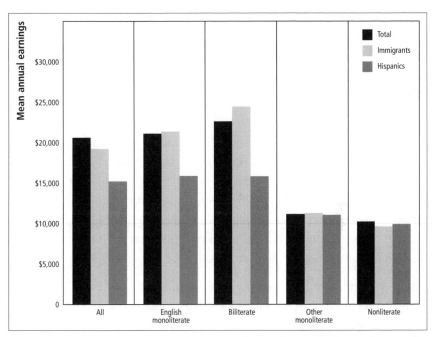

Note. From *English Literacy and Language Minorities in the United States: Results From the National Adult Literacy Survey* (p. 120), by E. Greenberg, R. F. Macías, D. Rhodes, and T. Chan, 2001, Washington, DC: National Center for Education Statistics, U.S. Department of Education.

for high levels of mass literacy can be seen as replacing the standard that once applied for only the more privileged members of society and now applying it universally.

This rapid rise of a standard for literacy raises the issue of the appropriateness of instructional goals, because the clamor for higher standards does not always originate from the populations to which they will be applied. Whereas the emphasis for mass education was formerly on basic literacy skills, now criteria applied to literacy in the United States emphasize the ability to read new material and glean new information from it.

As expectations have risen and literacy competencies have increased throughout society, some authorities have argued that competencies and skills once specialized have become generalized and, ultimately, have come to be devalued. Levine (1982), for example, observed that workers in the unskilled sector must increasingly demonstrate a higher level of competence than they would have been expected to demonstrate in an earlier generation. Similarly, Collins (1979) has noted the tendency to devalue educational credentials as they become widespread. He held that there is often little relationship between educational credentials and job skills; similar conclusions have been reached by others (e.g., Harste & Mikulecky, 1984; Hull, 1997; Mikulecky, 1990; O'Connor, 1993).

Extending this argument, Levine (1982) sees a parallel inflation and corresponding devaluation of literacy skills outside of work. Individuals must attain minimal mastery to just pass as literate in public. As literacy programs and schools more effectively equip their students with literacy skills, the acceptability threshold continues to inflate. As a result of this inflation in literacy criteria, there appears to be no threshold where those with below-norm educational achievement can compete on an equal basis for jobs or command the same status as those above the norm.

The implications of this for language minority groups in low socioeconomic strata are that marginal gains in educational achievement are minimized by gains made across all groups. For example, although it is generally acknowledged that open access to higher education in the late 1960s and early 1970s led to dramatic gains in education among language minority groups, it is rarely pointed out that Whites who spoke only English also entered universities and colleges in record numbers (see Freebody & Welch, 1993).

Thus, while literacy and educational gains are apparent within groups, from one generation to the next, these gains must be seen as relative within the larger sociohistorical setting. Universal adult literacy and high school completion have become common expectations. Because groups are not usually compared only to themselves (e.g., African Americans in 1950 to African Americans in 1990), but to other groups as well, within-group gains have less significance when educational gains are being made in society generally.

The job market worth of these gains may be negated by what Collins (1979) calls "credential inflation": Even as ethnic, racial, and language minorities (of lower socioeconomic status) improve their literacy skills and educational performance, members of dominant groups are making gains, too. For example, between 1950 and 1975, major gains in educational achievement were made across all groups. Given an end to legal segregation and an expansion in educational opportunities generally, African Americans and Latinos showed dramatic gains in years of schooling completed. However, Whites also benefited from the expansion in educational opportunities, and they continue to maintain educational advantages.

These data indicate that despite gains in the amount of education received by African Americans and Latinos, those gains were somewhat negated by the educational gains among the White population. Thus, between 1950 and 1975, underrepresented groups were able to take advantage of additional educational opportunities, but they were not the sole beneficiaries of them.

Trends in Educational Progress Across Ethnic and Linguistic Groups

As Table 5.1 indicates, there was a substantial increase of school-age language minority children from 1979 to 1989. What is the relationship between these increases and national trends in educational progress? There is no simple answer to this question, because the data on educational progress can be interpreted based on which groups have the highest and lowest percentages of below-modal grade-level progress or the sharpest increases and decreases in below-modal grade-level performance (see Table 5.2).

Based on the former criterion, Whites from homes where only English was spoken had the lowest below modal grade percentage (22.3%; i.e., the highest educational progress) in 1979 and the second lowest (32.6%) in 1989. However, data concerning educational progress across ethnic and linguistic groups indicate several surprising trends when increases and decreases are compared within and between groups. Aggregated data for students from ages 8–15 indicate that performance in school generally declined. Table 5.1 indicates that nearly 10% more students were below modal grade level in 1989 than in 1979. The sharpest increases in percentages of students below modal grade level were among White and Latino students (10.3% and 11.6% respectively) who came from homes where only English was spoken.[1] Comparatively, there was only a 1.1% increase among White students who came from homes where a language other than English was spoken and only a 1.8% increase for Latino students from homes with similar language backgrounds. However, there was a net gain in modal grade achievement among students in the "other" category. The majority of these students were probably of Asian ancestry.

Table 5.1.
Educational Progress of Students Age 8–15 by Race/Ethnicity and Language Spoken at Home (for 1979 and 1989)

	Total	White	Black	Hispanic	Other
1979					
Enrolled in school	26,741	20,611	3,857	1,783	490
% below modal grade	24.9	22.4	32.4	35.5	30.0
Speak only English at home	3,965	19,540	3,677	474	274
% below modal grade	24.0	22.3	32.8	27.0	22.8
Speak other language at home	2,098	619	53	1,238	188
% below modal grade	35.0	25.0	B	39.4	43.1
1980					
Enrolled in school	25,572	18,028	3,884	2,668	992
% below modal grade	34.7	32.6	41.0	41.4	29.9
Speak only English at home	20,890	16,191	3,503	762	434
% below modal grade	34.2	32.6	41.2	38.6	27.7
Speak other language at home	2,961	615	88	1,768	489
% below modal grade	36.3	23.9	36.6	42.1	31.0

Note. Figures are in thousands. Students for whom no language characteristics were reported are included in the total but are not designated by race/ethnicity or by language spoken at home. B = base less than 75,000. From *Language Characteristics and Schooling in the United States, a Changing Picture: 1979 and 1989* (NCES Publication No. 93699, p. 26), by E. K. McArthur, 1993, Washington, DC: National Center for Education Statistics, U.S. Department of Education.

Table 5.2.
Educational Progress of Hispanic and Non-Hispanic Students by Birthplace and Language Spoken at Home (for 1979 and 1989)

Ethnicity, birthplace, and percent below modal grade	Total	Language spoken at home	
		Only English	Other
1979			
Hispanic	1,783	474	1,238
% below modal grade	35.5	27.0	39.4
Born in 50 states and DC	1,365	455	910
% below modal grade	31.8	25.5	34.9
Born elsewhere	347	19	328
% below modal grade	52.4	B	51.8
Non-Hispanic	24,958	23,491	860
% below modal grade	24.1	23.9	28.6
Born in 50 states and DC	23,753	23,184	569
% below modal grade	24.0	24.0	22.3
Born elsewhere	597	306	290
% below modal grade	31.1	21.5	41.3
1980			
Hispanic	2,668	762	1,768
% below modal grade	41.4	38.6	42.1
Born in 50 states and DC	2,075	744	1,331
% below modal grade	40.1	39.1	40.7
Born elsewhere	396	14	381
% below modal grade	·44.4	B	45.3
Non-Hispanic	22,904	20,128	1,192
% below modal grade	33.9	34.0	27.8
Born in 50 states and DC	20,598	19,784	813
% below modal grade	33.6	33.9	26.4
Born elsewhere	554	195	359
% below modal grade	36.1	43.9	31.8

Note. Figures are in thousands. Totals for Hispanic and Non-Hispanic include students whose birthplace and/or language spoken at home may not have been reported. *Elsewhere* includes Puerto Rico and other outlying U.S. areas, as well as all other countries. B = base less than 75,000. From *Language Characteristics and Schooling in the United States, a Changing Picture: 1979 and 1989* (NCES Publication No. 93699, p. 27), by E. K. McArthur, 1993, Washington, DC: National Center for Education Statistics, U.S. Department of Education.

Table 5.2 makes even finer distinctions between Latinos and non-Latinos by disaggregating data based on national origin. When this is done, the data indicate that the largest declines (i.e., increases in percentage of students below modal grade level) were at 9.9% for U.S.-born non-Latinos (from homes where only English was spoken) and 22.4% for those born outside the United States. However, even finer distinctions than language background and national origin need to be made to understand the educational and literacy needs of many students.

The significance of social advantages and disadvantages based on national origin for some immigrants is illustrated by the National Adult Literacy Survey (NALS) secondary data analysis (Greenberg, Macías, Rhodes, & Chan, 2001). Hispanic adults born in the United States, for example, attained higher levels of education than those who had immigrated here (see Figure 5.3). Spanish-speaking immigrants generally had lower levels of education compared with immigrants who spoke other languages (Figure 5.4). These data suggest social class differences among immigrants of various language backgrounds. Figure 5.5 shows that immigrants were far more likely to drop out of high school for financial reasons than were U.S.-born individuals (34% compared to 12%) and less likely to state personal reasons or pregnancy (7% to 18%) or lost interest, behavior, or academic problems (18% to 27%) as causes for discontinuing school.

Table 5.3 profiles a number of demographic characteristics of Hispanic students (Grades K–12) that suggest correlations between language background and immigration. Students' parents who spoke mostly English were also more likely to have graduated from high school or attended some college. Those who were bilingual were more likely to have had some college education. Similarly, those who knew mostly English were more likely to have incomes above $30,000 than those who were bilingual or spoke only Spanish. Generally, bilinguals had advantages over Spanish monolinguals.

Populations With Special Needs: Late-Entrants

Frequently, policy discussions about students and adults who do not speak English concentrate only on that fact. From the standpoint of educational equity, this exclusive focus on English proficiency overlooks a major policy concern: students' and immigrant workers' educational histories and cultures (Hull, 1997; McDonnell & Hill, 1993; Stewart, 1993). In addition to knowing students' level of English literacy and what country they are from, it is also necessary to know about their native language literacy and prior schooling (Reder, 1999). Older students entering school present the greatest challenge and the largest proportion of likely candidates for adult ESL programs. As McDonnell and Hill (1993) observe,

Figure 5.3.
Levels of Educational Attainment by Hispanic Adults
Who Immigrated to the United States and
Hispanic Adults Born in the United States

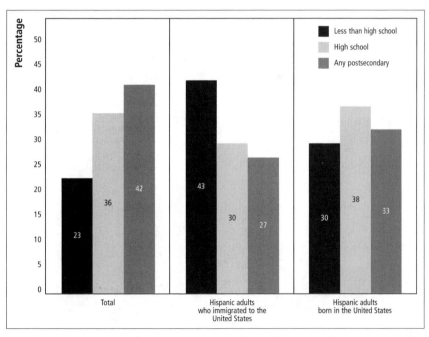

Note. From *English Literacy and Language Minorities in the United States: Results From the National Adult Literacy Survey* (p. 75), by E. Greenberg, R. F. Macías, D. Rhodes, and T. Chan, 2001, Washington, DC: National Center for Education Statistics, U.S. Department of Education.

Figure 5.4.
Levels of Educational Attainment by Native Language

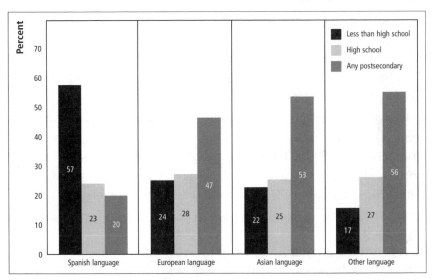

Note. From *English Literacy and Language Minorities in the United States: Results From the National Adult Literacy Survey* (p. 74), by E. Greenberg, R. F. Macías, D. Rhodes, and T. Chan, 2001, Washington, DC: National Center for Education Statistics, U.S. Department of Education.

Figure 5.5.
Reasons for High School Noncompletion by U.S.-Born and Immigrant Adults

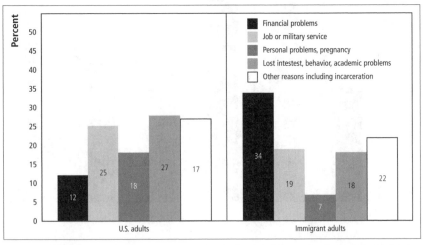

Note. From *English Literacy and Language Minorities in the United States: Results From the National Adult Literacy Survey* (p. 91), by E. Greenberg, R. F. Macías, D. Rhodes, and T. Chan, 2001, Washington, DC: National Center for Education Statistics, U.S. Department of Education.

Table 5.3.
Distribution of Hispanic Students (Grades K–12) by Demographic Characteristics and Language Spoken at Home

| | | Language spoken at home by student | | |
Demographic characteristic	Total	Mostly English	English and Spanish equally	Mostly Spanish
Total	100.0	100.0	100.0	100.0
Language spoken at home by mother				
English	48.3	82.0	6.0	2.0
Spanish	51.0	17.2	93.7	98.0
English + other language or other language only	0.7	0.7	0.3	0
Mother's place of birth				
United States or U.S. territory	46.8	73.8	15.8	8.3
Other country	53.2	26.2	84.2	91.7
Mother's first language				
English	32.8	56.1	3.1	1.5
Spanish	65.2	41.3	96.6	98.3
English + other language or other language only	2.0	2.6	0.3	0.2
Parents' highest level of education				
Less than high school diploma or GED	30.4	17.2	45.8	50.7
High school diploma or GED	27.9	28.4	25.2	28.5
Some college, vocational, technical	25.2	32.5	18.8	12.9
Bachelor's degree	9.0	11.5	5.5	5.3
Graduate/professional school	7.5	10.4	4.7	2.6
Household income				
< $10,000	21.0	17.5	21.5	28.6
$10,000–$20,000	24.6	19.1	33.6	31.6
$20,000–$30,000	26.7	23.7	31.4	30.4
$30,000–$50,000	11.5	15.5	6.8	4.9
> $50,000	16.2	24.2	6.7	4.5

Note. Percentages may not equal 100.0 due to rounding. From National Household Education Survey (Parent Interview Component, Table 6.4), by National Center for Education Statistics, 1999, Washington, DC: U.S. Department of Education.

The instruction given older immigrant students depends profoundly on their academic preparation. *Immigrants who enter elementary school at grade three or above can have serious problems catching up with regular instruction* [italics added]. Whether this happens in a particular case depends primarily on the student's social class and country of origin. . . . However, students whose schooling was delayed or disrupted due to poverty and war are often far behind. (pp. 69–70)

It is difficult to estimate the size of this population, as McDonnell and Hill (1993) point out: "The limited visibility of immigrant students is evidenced in the lack of precise estimates of their numbers" (p. 2). Most of the available data on the immigrant population come from the U.S. census rather than from schools. Based on 1990 U.S. Census data, McDonnell and Hill report that five states (California, New York, Texas, Florida, and Illinois) account for 70% of the school-age immigrant population. California has 41% of the U.S. immigrant youth population, followed by New York with 12%. Among those cities with the largest percentages of immigrant youth are Los Angeles (21%), San Francisco (19%), and Miami/Dade County (18%).

According to government sources in 1988, more than 76% of Mexican-born 20-year-olds in the United States had not completed high school, compared with 21% of the entire U.S.-born population (Stewart, 1993). Secondary data analysis of the National Chicano Survey (NCS; 1979) indicates that 80% of the Mexican-born population entered the United States at age 15 or older. If these patterns have persisted, then the majority of Mexican immigrants enter the United States after the age of compulsory school attendance (age 16).

Students who immigrate at younger ages, especially those who enter the United States without grade-level equivalency, may still not be able to complete their education. This group has been called the *1.5 generation* (Harklau, 2003; Harklau, Losey, & Siegal, 1999), which differs both from the first generation immigrants, who were already beyond the age of compulsory schooling when they arrived in the United States, and the second generation immigrants, who were born in the United States or arrived here as young children and will have the opportunity to attend all or almost all of their schooling in this country.

Late-entrant adolescents are in a double bind, because their lack of English interferes with their taking the required classes for graduation, if those courses are available only in English. Most of their high-school years are spent learning English. Where available, bilingual programs can help students develop literacy in their native language as they learn English. Unfortunately, the availability of bilingual programs at the high-school and middle-school levels is extremely inadequate.

For late-entrant students, adult ESL and adult basic education (ABE) programs may be the only avenues that further their development of literacy (unless they are qualified to study for and take the GED high school equivalency exam). Yet, because ESL courses generally emphasize oral English, late-entrant students are not well served by these programs in the development of their literacy skills. Even when English literacy is offered, there is little articulation between ESL programs and programs that might lead to the kinds of academic and vocational credentials needed for job mobility (see Chisman, Wrigley, & Ewen, 1993; Wrigley, Chisman, & Ewen, 1993), a circumstance that may help explain the high dropout rate among students in adult ESL programs (see Figure 5.6). Clearly, there is a need for content instruction in native languages at the adult level, because students who must learn academic and vocational skills are involved in a race against time.

As the educational ante continues to rise, this may provide a disincentive for language minority students to stay in school. A large number of English-speaking White students may likewise fail to see advantages to staying in school given the recent corporate trend toward downsizing, which has led to a reduction of well-paying jobs in some industries even for native English speakers with higher levels of literacy and educational credentials. This has also led to increased job competition for groups that have historically been discriminated against or disadvantaged by lacking access to the traditional informal social networks that have been used by Whites to gain employment.[2]

Figure 5.6.
Participation in ESL Classes by Country of Birth

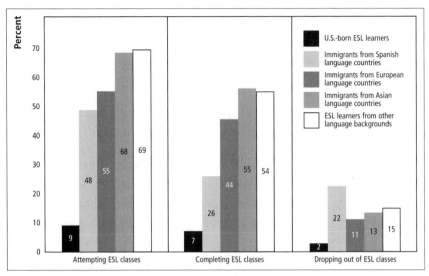

Note. From *English Literacy and Language Minorities in the United States: Results From the National Adult Literacy Survey* (p. 96), by E. Greenberg, R. F. Macías, D. Rhodes, and T. Chan, 2001, Washington, DC: National Center for Education Statistics, U.S. Department of Education.

In spite of these trends, Kirsch, Jungeblut, Jenkins, and Kolstad (1993) conclude that, "although Americans today are, on the whole, better educated and more literate than any who preceded them, many employers say they are unable to find enough workers with the reading, writing, mathematical, and other competencies required in the workplace" (p. x). This commonly held view must be reconciled with the reality that many among the "educated" middle class are losing social position and mobility (see Phillips, 1993). As the highly English literate, college educated lose their jobs in aerospace and computer industries, an underclass, disproportionately populated by immigrants and other language minorities, appears to be growing. During the 1990s, in a job market in which unemployment lines were increasingly populated by both the well educated and the undereducated, intergenerational mobility—once the hope of poor parents for their children—appeared to be waning (Galbraith, 1992). No wonder that some became disenchanted by the lure of educational solutions to employment problems and fail to believe that education will give them a real advantage (see Gibson & Ogbu, 1991, for a related analysis; Portes & Rumbaut, 2001, for an extensive analysis of second generation immigrants). Similar concerns emerged following the 2001 economic downturn.

Conflicting Agendas of Students, Programs, and Policy Makers

National policy discourse and adult education program goals typically depict ESL instruction as instrumental in promoting cultural assimilation, economic mobility, and political participation. Programs usually describe their content in terms of survival skills, life skills, academic English skills, and employment skills. The connection between curriculum and goals, however, often becomes amorphous. The missing factor is a delivery plan that offers a coherent transition from ESL programs to academic programs for which students can receive credit (Chisman, Wrigley, & Ewen, 1993). In vocational ESL programs, job skills are often geared to a specific job, which may or may not be tied to a career track. From the perspective of job mobility, all too often, students, teachers, and policy makers know that English language skills are necessary but not sufficient to lead students to better jobs that usually require both English language skills and academic credentials.

Students, employers, and policy makers often have conflicting goals. Students may be enticed to participate in educational programs by the lure that learning English will do them some good, but they may not find sufficient reason to continue participating (see Comings, Parrella, & Soricone, 1999, for a discussion of persistence patterns in adult learners). Employers are not necessarily interested in promoting ESL and literacy as goals in themselves but see them as a means to improving communication, safety, and efficiency in the workplace. In fact,

> Improved mobility for the student is commonly touted as one of the major goals of literacy policy. Ironically, while the success of the learner in acquiring literacy skills may promote his or her mobility, it can pose a threat to individual employers in the following ways: The employer may grasp the benefits of workplace literacy in improving communication and efficiency, but how

much internal mobility can the enterprise absorb? Some employers may feel they are supporting costly educational programs only to lose their investment when successful learners demand promotions, more pay, or move out of the enterprise to seek better opportunities elsewhere. Employees may feel frustrated when they successfully complete noncredit programs but still lack access to further training that "really counts," training that bestows diplomas, degrees, and credentials required for mobility. These issues are not easily resolved. They demonstrate that there are more fundamental structural issues that relate to whether programs will be successful in meeting the lofty goal of preparing students for full participation. (Wiley, 1993, pp. 19–20)

Conclusion

If the national debate over the perpetual literacy crisis is to be productive, more attention must be shifted to issues of educational equity and economic justice. From the standpoint of education for language minority populations, there must be a recognition that while English language education is needed, it is not sufficient to overcome the barriers facing those who have not had access to an equal education, either here in the United States or—if they are immigrants—in their countries of origin. Raising standards without looking at the special educational needs of specific groups does little except ensure that many will fail to meet the standards and as a result will remain underskilled and underqualified.

6

Language, Diversity, and the Ascription of Status

If we are to invite children into the language of the school, we must make school inviting to them. . . . We must reconnect them to their own brilliance and gain their trust so that they will learn from us. We must respect them, so that they feel connected to us. Then, and only then, might they be willing to adopt our language as one form to be added to their own. (Delpit & Dowdy, 2002, pp. 45, 48).

Prevailing educational terminology about language use and abilities reflects deeper social beliefs about literacy. Terminology can be both descriptive and ascriptive. When used ascriptively, it assigns a social status or social worth to those it labels. This is especially true in the case of *illiteracy,* which refers to the absence of *literacy,* the ability to read and write something at some level. A sense of social stigma, however, is implied by the term *illiterate.* To be illiterate is to be "ignorant" and lacking in formal education. Moreover, illiteracy is a mark of *"inferiority* [italics added] to an expected standard of familiarity with language and literature" (*American Heritage Dictionary of the English Language,* 3rd ed., s.v. "illiteracy"). At one time, an individual who "could read in a vernacular language or handle accounts and correspondence" (Bailey & McArthur, 1992, p. 498) was still considered illiterate if he or she lacked a liberal education and therefore did not know Latin and Greek.

To avoid the stigma associated with the term illiterate, the labels *preliterate* and *nonliterate* are preferred in academic discussions; yet illiterate persists in common usage. A term such as preliterate carries a sense of expectation that individuals and even whole societies will become literate;

the term nonliterate carries no such expectation. The label semiliterate acknowledges some ability to read and write at some level but implies the absence of a formal education.

From the perspective of language diversity, these labels take on special relevance. Speakers of nondominant varieties of English are sometimes looked down on as being illiterate and, therefore, unintelligent because of how they speak the language. Similarly, non-English-speaking people who are literate in languages other than English are treated as if they were illiterate simply because they do not speak English.

The racial, ethnic, and linguistic labeling that occurs in the popular media is also a problem.[1] Consider, for example, the terminology used in reporting census data: White (non-Hispanic), Hispanic, Black, Asian/Pacific Islander, and American Indian represent a kind of grab bag of human typecastings based on rather vague notions of race, culture, and geographical origin, while other dimensions of possible group identification, such as social class, are rarely represented. Individuals of Asian and Pacific geographical origin are melded into a Pan-Asian/Pacific group that seems to function as a quasi-racial category when, in fact, academic performance data among Asian and Pacific students vary widely. In California, for example, Cambodian American students have one of the lowest rates of admission to the University of California and other institutions of higher education (Weinberg, 1997). Nevertheless, there has been considerable debate about whether they should be eligible for special educational assistance, because Asians as an undifferentiated group tend to be overrepresented, and Cambodians are Asian.

The term *Hispanic* tends to be more of a cultural and linguistic designation; despite the disclaimer on census forms that Hispanics can be members of any race, the term now functions like a racial classification because Whites are considered a racial group. As a blanket term, Hispanic ignores distinctions among significant subgroups such as Chicanos, Cuban Americans, and Puerto Rican Americans, as well as distinctions between Hispanics born in the United States and Hispanic immigrants.

Attempts to label and group people into these few categories may be called *racialization*. Miles (1989) defines racialization as "a process of delineation of group boundaries and an allocation of persons within those boundaries by primary reference to (supposedly) inherent biological (usually phenotypical) characteristics. It is therefore an ideological process" (p. 74). A parallel process to racialization involves labeling people according to their language characteristics. Language labeling can be purely descriptive, such as "so and so is a Spanish speaker," but classifications such as non-English speaker ascribe status based on what one does not speak rather than on what one does speak (see Wink, 1993).

This chapter begins by discussing status ascription based on language background and the types of labels routinely used in educational programs and the attitudes often associated with them. The status of nonstandard—or nondominant—varieties of language and the promotion of literacy in schools are also considered, specifically, Ebonics and debates about its status and use in schools. The chapter concludes with implications for practice.

Status Ascription Based on Language

Bilingualism in the United States tends to be seen as either an asset or a problem. This ambivalence is reflected in educational policies that attempt to provide a rapid transition for language minority students from their native languages to English and to teach monolingual English-speaking students foreign languages. In the first case, the United States fails to develop languages other than English, and in the second case, it spends millions to teach them.

These policies, however, are not as contradictory as they appear, because they apply to two different populations. Transitional bilingual education was developed as a remedial program for students who had historically been discriminated against (see Lyons, 1990), whereas foreign language instruction is associated with a tradition of education for college-bound students. Many of the opponents of bilingual education claim that they support foreign language instruction, in effect, denying dual language development for those who already speak a language other than English, while supporting second language instruction for English speakers.

Language is a marker of status. Like race and ethnicity, language provides one of the important means by which individuals and groups identify and distinguish themselves from others. Prejudice on the basis of language is not unlike other forms of prejudice and may work in conjunction with them or serve as a surrogate for them. Weinberg (1990) defines *racism* as a systematic, institutional procedure for excluding some and privileging others. It is premised not on the moral foundation of equal human worth, but on the belief that some are inherently superior to others.

As a related or surrogate form of racism, discrimination on the basis of language may be called *linguicism*. Linguicism has been defined as "the ideologies and structures which are used to legitimate, effectuate and reproduce an unequal division of power and resources (both material and nonmaterial) between groups which are in turn defined on the basis of language (i.e., the mother tongue)" (Phillipson, 1988, p. 339). Phillipson continues:

> Linguistic ideology has affinities with the way racism is affirmed [because] it essentially involves the dominant group/language presenting an idealized image of itself, stigmatizing the dominated group/language, and rationalizing the relationship between the two, always to the advantage of the dominant group/language.

> It is of the essence of hegemony that injustices are internalized by both the dominant group and the dominated groups as being natural and legitimate. However, neither the structures nor the ideologies are static. Hegemony is lived experience which is in a constant process of negotiation, recreation and adjustment. It is therefore open to contestation. (pp. 341–343)

Historically in the United States, language and literacy requirements, like racial policies, have served to bar individuals from immigrating, voting, and seeking employment in some occupations (see Baugh, 1997; Leibowitz, 1969, 1974; Lippi-Green, 1997; McKay, 1993; McKay & Weinstein-Shr, 1993; Wiley & Lukes, 1996). Thus, through linguistic status ascription, language minority groups in various historical contexts have experienced exclusion on the basis of language and literacy that has been functionally parallel to racial exclusion. As with other forms of discrimination, language discrimination can be taken as the denial of equal human worth (Weinberg, 1995).[2]

From LEPs to Lepers

Metaphors and labels used to portray immigrants and language minorities in the media have tremendous power to shape both national discourse and popular perceptions of minorities. The labels used by English language and literacy programs in the assessment and placement of students often ascribe a lower, language/literacy status to students who need English instruction (see Wink, 1993). At the high school, community college, and university levels, it is not uncommon to find some international and language minority students who wish to avoid taking ESL classes, because they feel stigmatized as "ESL students." They are embarrassed to be in courses that are often seen as remedial rather than as developmental. The fact that ESL course credits often are not accepted as a part of the total credits needed for graduation does little to discourage this view.

Consider also the label *limited English proficient* (LEP). This term originated in the bilingual education legislation of 1968 and, initially, referred only to oral abilities in English. In 1978, its definition was extended to include reading and writing. It was "determined that English proficiency would be the exclusive criterion for the LEP population, irrespective of the person's proficiency in the non-English language" (Macías, 1994, p. 35). As an educational classification, the label is based solely on the English language skills a student lacks rather than on those skills the student may have in another language. Abilities in other languages are thereby rendered invisible by this educational labeling. How such labels are tossed about in daily use—for example, in lunchroom conversation when language minority students are jokingly referred to as *lepers*—provides insight into the status ascribed to language minority students.

Labeling students on the basis of their English language proficiencies is problematic in other ways. For example, Macías (1993) contends that educational assessments tend to ignore relationships between languages and focus only on the notion of limited English proficiency. From an educational standpoint, this is significant since "programs and policies that were developed to address a student's limited English proficiency often ignore or de-emphasize race and ethnicity in general" (Macías, 1993, p. 231). Yet, he argues, "debates over bilingual education and cultural literacy are as much about race" (p. 231) and ethnicity as they are about language (see Crawford, 1992a, Chapter 6 on "Hispanophobia").

Furthermore, educational assessments frequently ignore the social class of students (or their prior social class in the case of immigrants and refugees). Social class is usually a major determinant of educational opportunities. Students' prior educational histories need to be considered together with their English language proficiency. For children and adults, LEP and non-English language background (NELB) designations can inappropriately lead to an emphasis on English oral language development while excluding English literacy or literacy in the students' native language (see Skutnabb-Kangas & Phillipson, 1989).

Currently, in an effort to reduce the stigma applied to language minority students, the phrase *English language learner* (ELL) is being used by many. Although less stigmatizing than the previous labels, its focus is still on what language minority students are trying to develop, i.e., English, without acknowledging the additional language(s) they already know. For this reason, the term *heritage language learner* has been catching on in the United States to call attention to this dimension of linguistic identity (see Peyton, Ranard, & McGinnis, 2001).

For some, the fuss over nomenclature is easily dismissed as mere political correctness. Yet these terms are not without social consequences. As Skutnabb-Kangas (2000) contends, it is necessary to see the importance of even the minority label, because it provides a basis for human rights claims (see Wiley, 2000a, 2000b). Underscoring the significance of the language minority label, Skutnabb-Kangas (2000) points out that "many groups strive toward being granted the status of minorities [because that status in international law guarantees rights to education, which] immigrants, migrants, guest workers and refugees do not have" (p. 489).

Not all heritage language learners should be characterized as language minority students. Nevertheless, those who do qualify for language minority status should reflect on the potential benefits of that status. For those who do not qualify, or who choose not to, it remains useful for them to consider the importance of the struggle of language minorities for linguistic human rights and how that struggle benefits their own efforts to learn heritage languages (cf. Mayo, 1999).

Literacy and Nondominant Varieties of Language

From a historical perspective, Illich (1979) explores the promotion of standardized forms of academic language and literacy and the role of schools in promoting those forms of language as a means of social control. In his provocative critique of the rise of modern schooling practices as they relate to vernacular language and literacy, Illich argues that instructional language policies impose a prescribed language in school, and by so doing, vernacular values associated with local common languages are diminished. He explains, as an example, that the imposition of literacy (using standardized language) actually restricted vernacular functions of literacy in late 15th- and early 16th-century Spain (cf. Boone & Mignolo, 1994; Mignolo, 1995, 2000). Rather than developing a tongue naturally in common with others, people had to receive it inauthentically through schools as socially sanctioned institutions. Thus, students would be formally taught the rules of grammar of their mother tongue as if it were Latin or a foreign language. Illich sees this change from the use of vernaculars to standardized mother tongues, by official sanction and imposition, as fostering the idea that the school is the only legitimate vehicle for promoting literacy:

> Now there would be no reading, no writing—if possible, no speaking—outside the educational sphere. . . . We first allow standard language to degrade ethnic, black, or hillbilly language, and then spend money to teach their counterfeits as academic subjects. Administrators and entertainers, admen and newsmen, ethnic politicians and "radical" professionals form powerful interest groups, each fighting for a larger slice of the language pie. (p. 55)

Illich's (1979) radical goal called for *de-schooling* society. Although educational anarchism (see O'Neill, 1983) has never had a wide following in this country, Illich's observation underscores how the school's choice of language and standard forms are instruments of social control. For language minority populations, whose languages or regional and social varieties are not reflected in the schools, the relevance of these observations should not be lost, because those whose language and literacy practices are considered normative have a strategic social advantage over those whose language is considered nonstandard. In this regard, Bhatia (1983) concludes,

> Linguistic factors specific to ML [monolingual] societies govern the pattern of literacy. Some recent research indicates that the patterns within ML societies are neither randomly nor uniformly distributed. There is a systematic correlation between the rate of literacy and the distance between local dialects and the standard language. . . . The relative difference in the distance between the high and low varieties of Tamil, Telugu, and Sinhala plays an important role in the indices of literacy in . . . South Asia. A similar phenomenon has been observed in the United States, where the literacy rate among speakers of Black English is considerably lower than that for speakers of Standard English. (p. 28)

Again, the issue of whose language variety is taken as normative relates directly to who has advantages in the acquisition of literacy at school and who does not. Some students are advantaged, because their language variety and their language practices become the norms for the rest of society. As the speakers of the standard language become advantaged, the speakers of other varieties become disadvantaged. This is especially true when assessment and placement decisions about language levels and language proficiencies of students are based on standardized tests of academic English. Norms for standard language are based on written rather than oral varieties of language (Milroy & Milroy, 1985). Judgments made on the basis of these tests are determined and constrained by the instruments used. Moreover, when those tested speak, read, or write more than one language, judgments about language proficiency are constrained by the language of the test (see Cook-Gumperz, 1993; Hewitt & Inghilleri, 1993). Thus, our notions of language proficiency are influenced by "standard" and "literate" forms of the specific language of the assessment, which is the variety of language taught in schools.

The Case of Ebonics

In a discussion of literacy and language diversity in the United States, it is important to address the issue of *Ebonics*, the variety of English that many African Americans speak. Ebonics is often seen, by those who are unfamiliar with its history and grammar system, as substandard and a barrier to the acquisition of standard English literacy. As a home and community language, Ebonics has also been referred to as *African American English, African American Language, African American Vernacular English (AAVE), Black English,* and *Black Vernacular English (BVE)*.

Although most African Americans are native speakers of English, their linguistic history, related to their sociopolitical and economic history, is substantially different from that of many European-origin Americans. To understand the persistence of purportedly high rates of illiteracy and low rates of educational achievement among African Americans, it is important to take these factors into consideration by first confronting the legacy of stigmatization that many African Americans face.

Africans were first brought to the British colonies in 1619, a year before the arrival of the Mayflower. Initially, some were indentured servants, but by the early decades of the 18th century, a brutal system of slavery was enforced by the legal systems of first the colonies and then, until the end of the Civil War in 1865, the southern states. Thus, unlike most European-origin peoples who came to the United States either voluntarily or as political, religious, or economic refugees, the migration of most African-origin peoples was forced (see Ogbu, 1991; Ogbu & Matute-Bianchi, 1986). Enslaved Africans were not allowed to use their native languages, and in many southern states, "compulsory ignorance" laws were passed, which made it illegal to teach enslaved Africans to read and write.

Of the 12 million souls wrenched from their homelands and brought to the Americas during the 4 centuries in which the Atlantic slave trade ravaged Africa, it is estimated that between 2 and 3 million were Muslims who were literate in Arabic (Lepore, 2002). A minority within that group were sent to the English colonies and, subsequently, to the southern states.

> [The] enslaved Muslims' literacy could be dangerous. Marked as educated, Muslim slaves may have been subject to special persecution and punishment, designed to crush any possibility of

rebellion in much the same way that the antebellum slave codes forbade teaching slaves to write in English. Yet enslaved Muslims labored to preserve their Arabic literacy, bartering for pen, ink, and paper, trading for copies of the Koran. Such efforts were not always successful. However much such men and women employed their literacy, it was often not enough to sustain it. (Lepore, p. 121)

Mainstream U.S. history textbooks have often ignored the fact that some among the enslaved were literate upon arrival. Mixing enslaved peoples of various language backgrounds attained a forced language shift to English. After the abolition of slavery, African Americans continued to be barred from equal participation in education, and English literacy requirements were often used to restrict their political participation (see Leibowitz, 1969).

The Development of African American Speech

Coming from a variety of largely West African language backgrounds and faced with English-speaking enslavers, African Americans developed an English creole.[3] African American speech was ascribed a lower status and developed a diglossic[4] relationship with higher status varieties of English. Roy (1987) explains:

Over time, generations [of African Americans] had more and more contact with English through location, employment, and education and more of the stigmatized features were dropped and more of the forms hypothesized as English were added. Successive generations transmitted to their children a less marked[5] creole system except in those areas where there was only minimal contact with English. This process of language change, a process of differential linguistic acculturation termed decreolization, is responsible for the movement of Plantation English Creole toward English and for the range of social, regional and individual dialects that have been described as Black English (BE) and Black English Vernacular that can be heard in the urban and rural Black communities today. (p. 232)

In contrast, European-origin immigrant groups and their offspring "with rare exceptions have not passed through the pidginization, creolization, and decreolization processes that are responsible for the wide range of language forms that are present in communities using Black English [Ebonics]" (Roy, 1987, p. 237). Today, according to Roy, the high degree of correspondence between African American speech and standard English obscures some of its systematic differences from the school-based variety of English. These linguistic differences have sparked considerable debate over education policy among African Americans. While some argue that Ebonics is an inappropriate vehicle for literacy development in standard English, many who have worked with African American children contend that beginning with the linguistic knowledge of the child provides the best basis on which to build. Building from the child's knowledge of Ebonics, while noting systematic differences between Ebonics and standard English, enables children to better understand both their own language and standard English.

Although Ebonics has been ridiculed as being nonstandard, linguists have long identified and documented its rule-governed nature, and African American scholars have long regretted that Ebonics has not been appreciated. For example, in the 1930s, Woodson (1933/1990) lamented that in "the study of language and schools" (p. 19), African American students had been taught to scorn their own language rather than to study it, which he argued would certainly be "more important to them than the study of French or historical Spanish grammar" (p. 19).

Ebonics and the Law

A major legal challenge, *Martin Luther King Junior Elementary School Children v. Ann Arbor School District* (1979), asserted that the differences between the language of African Americans and the language of school were great enough to warrant "accommodation"—that is, special educational treatment—by the schools. The suit was filed because, despite a district integration plan, African American children performed at a significantly lower level than their White peers. The plaintiffs argued that the school's failure to take into account the language differences of their students was discriminatory. To prove the plaintiffs' position, it first had to be established that the children actually spoke a distinctly different variety of language. According to the presiding judge,

> This case is not an effort on the part of the plaintiffs to require that they be taught "black English," or that a dual language program be provided. . . . It is a straightforward effort to require the court to intervene on the children's behalf to require the defendant School District Board to take appropriate action to teach them to read in the standard English of the school, the commercial world, the arts, the sciences, and the professions. This action is a cry for help in opening the doors to the establishment . . . to keep another generation from becoming functionally illiterate. (as cited in Norgren & Nanda, 1988, p. 190)

Note that the judge's chief concern was "to keep another generation from becoming functionally illiterate" in standard English. Following extensive testimony by linguists who demonstrated that African American English was systematically distinct from standard English, the federal judge sided with the plaintiffs, granting that linguistic differences between the two were significant enough to warrant special educational treatment (Labov, 1982). The decision was one of *linguistic accommodation,* in which teachers were to be sensitized to systematic language differences, foster a receptive attitude toward African American English by making more explicit the differences between it and the dominant school-based variety, and avoid biased assessment and testing practices. This was all toward the goal of helping African American students master standard, school-based English.

Since the time of that decision, there has been no indication that the attitudes of most teachers toward Ebonics have changed. Neither is there evidence that language differences have been accommodated in any systematic way in public schools in the United States. Indeed, an ongoing concern continues to be the lack of knowledge of many teachers and the public regarding differences in grammar and pronunciation between standard English and Ebonics.

Significantly, the court's decision ignored the issue of whether students should receive instruction in Ebonics, an issue that has subsequently become the subject of considerable controversy (see Dillard, 1972). For example, there have been occasional calls for the development of "dialect readers" to promote literacy among those whose speech is markedly different from speakers of the dominant variety of English. According to Wolfram (1994), in the 1970s, a series was developed for middle and high school students called *Bridge: A Cross-Cultural Reading Program* (Simpkins, Simpkins, & Holt, 1977). The rationale for such materials is similar to the one for bilingual education: Language and literacy are better promoted when a student learns his or her own language before attempting to learn a second language (see Lemoine, 1999, for a more contemporary approach to accommodating the needs of Ebonics speakers).

The use of dialect readers, however, has been met with great opposition from teachers and parents who feel that using them would deprive students from learning the dominant language that is needed for full participation in U.S. society. Complicating the debate is the fact that many of the issues regarding the education of African American children have been put forth by White social scientists such as Baratz (1973), Stewart (1964), and Wolfram and Fasold (1973). Occasionally, their intentions and prescriptions have been severely criticized by some commentators (e.g., Sledd, 1969, 1973; see also O'Neil's, 1973, criticism of bidialectical instruction and Shuy's, 1980, thoughts on the debate during the 1960s and 1970s). Wolfram (1994) observes,

> It is quite clear that vernacular dialects have been defined in our own society as inappropriate vehicles for literacy, and it is apparent that children are socialized regarding this functional differentiation from the onset of their socialization regarding literacy. In this respect, the U.S. situation is akin to some third-world situations, in which unwritten minority languages are considered inappropriate for literacy vis-à-vis official state languages even when knowledge of the official language is minimal or nonexistent. (p. 74)

Advocates for Instruction in Ebonics

In spite of such opposition, a small number of advocates have continued to support literacy instruction in Ebonics. Williams (1990), for example, advocates what essentially is a language maintenance policy. Maintenance bilingual policies attempt to cultivate the minority language of students while "strengthening their sense of cultural identity and affirming the rights of an ethnic minority group in a nation" (Baker, 2001, p. 152). Among the issues that such proposals encounter are practical difficulties such as lack of materials, the cost of producing them, and the need for staff development—the same issues that have plagued bilingual education reform efforts.

While Williams (1990) agrees that there are significant phonological and grammatical differences in the language of African Americans that are based on historical West African influences, he rejects the notion that the purported language problems reside in the speech of the African American student. If there is a language problem at all, according to Williams, it resides in the differential power between groups, English-speaking European Americans and Ebonics-speaking African Americans, and the ability of the former to impose its language norms on the latter (see also Smith, 1993).

Williams (1990) also rejects commonly used labels such as *Black Dialect, Black English,* and *Black Vernacular English,* contending that they ascribe a lower status to the language spoken by many African Americans and obscure its West African influences. He prefers instead the terms *Ebonics* and *African American Language,* which, he believes, confer the legitimacy enjoyed by English and other languages.

Providing a linguistic rationale for literacy instruction in Ebonics, Wolfram (1994) argues that there are enough differences between Ebonics and standard English to justify using Ebonics instruction to facilitate the transition to standard English. Wolfram notes that although there are international examples in which the differences between language varieties used in and out of school are sufficient to cause developmental reading problems, in the United States the differences between Ebonics and the written standard are too insufficient to interfere with reading development. Even speakers of the dominant variety do not find an identical match between what they read and how they speak, Wolfram points out.

In a related discussion, Ferreiro and Teberosky (1982) consider the implications of diverging from standard Spanish for some Indian children in South America, and they reach a similar conclusion. They believe that when the divergence is not too great and learners are allowed to read texts in the same way as they speak, reading in the dominant language is not a problem. The divergence between written and spoken language becomes a problem when teachers confuse reading with pronunciation (i.e., when processing print for meaning is confused with speaking correctly). This is one reason why approaches to reading that are based solely on phonics are inappropriate for speakers of nondominant language varieties. Because phonics approaches assume that one must move from sound to meaning, students are presumed to be unable to read until they have mastered the sounds of the dominant variety. Given the prevalence of this approach, it is not difficult to see why speakers of nondominant varieties lose interest in school early and as adults, are reluctant to go back.

Ebonics Today

Today, the term Ebonics has generally been embraced by both the lay and scholarly community. In some alternative schools that emphasize an Afrocentric curriculum, Ebonics is being systematically taught much as other languages are taught in public schools. This promotes its status and positively reinforces students' cultural identity.

However, many researchers, teachers, and parents remain vehemently opposed to teaching Ebonics and developing Ebonics readers, because they assume it deprives students from learning the language variety that is needed for full membership and participation in U.S. society. The debate became front-page news in 1996, when the Oakland Board of Education (California) endorsed instruction in Ebonics. Experts in applied linguistics defended the board's decision, even as it was widely denounced on the Internet and in the popular media (see Baugh, 1999, 2000, 2001; Perry & Delpit, 1998; Ramírez, Wiley, de Klerk, & Lee, 1999; Rickford & Rickford, 2000; Wiley, 2000b; Wolfram, Adger, & Christian 1999).

Commenting on the hotly debated issue from a 20-year perspective, Wolfram (1994) observes,

It is now two decades since the dialect reader controversy erupted and yet we still reap the effects of the phobia that it engendered in many educational and popular circles. Applied social dialectologists are still often reminded by an unforgetting and unforgiving educational establishment and general public that a few of us once attempted to convince educators that it was at least worthwhile to experiment with dialect readers to see if they helped incipient readers gain access to the literate world. (p. 72)

Conclusion and Recommendations

Whether to teach Ebonics to facilitate the acquisition of standard English or to teach standard English only does not have to be an either-or choice. Students need to be aware of the characteristics of the varieties of language they speak, read, and write. For example, learning how to describe the systematic characteristic features of their own language variety can help native speakers of Ebonics see where it is similar to standard academic English and where the two varieties differ. Students who speak Appalachian English could likewise benefit from systematically learning about their language.

Language minorities are not the only ones who can benefit from learning about language differences. In a society as racially, ethnically, and linguistically diverse as ours, speakers of standard English can benefit from learning about the differences between the spoken and written forms of language and about the richness of other varieties, such as Ebonics and Appalachian English. Such knowledge should help children and adults appreciate language differences and develop more tolerant attitudes toward language variations.

The question of whether Ebonics instruction should be part of a full-scale bilingual education program is more complex. The uses of Ebonics are not parallel to those of Spanish, for example, which has its own dominant and nondominant varieties and its spoken and written forms. Given its diglossic relationship with English, Ebonics has been confined mostly to oral language and vernacular literacy practices. Allowing students to learn more about Ebonics and its use in vernacular writing will expose them to the richness of the language. Many works of African American writers, such as Langston Hughes, Paul Dunbar, and Maya Angelou, provide excellent examples (Wolfram, 1994).

To develop a complete Ebonics bilingual education program, much more would be required of the language, including extending its use to a wider range of social practices. Such a full-scale Ebonics-English bilingual program seems utopian.

With the range of language varieties represented in schools in the United States, it is essential that teachers have some knowledge of and training in *sociolinguistics,* the study of language in its various social contexts (see Adger, Snow, & Christian, 2002). Teachers need this knowledge to adequately assess their students' abilities and learning and to provide appropriate instruction. Both teachers and students need to better understand and appreciate language diversity. Without an understanding of language differences, language prejudice and status ascription based on language are perpetuated. Given the pervasiveness of bias toward nondominant varieties of language, language prejudices all too easily become surrogates for ethnic, racial, and class biases.

Further Reading

Adger, C. T., Christian, D., & Taylor, O. (Eds.). (1999). *Making the connection: Language and academic achievement among African American students.* Washington, DC, and McHenry, IL: Center for Applied Linguistics and Delta Systems.

This collection, which appeared in the wake of the Oakland Ebonics controversy, includes a broad range of topics written by a number of recognized authorities. It offers scholarly and practical perspectives for educators, teacher trainers, and policy makers.

Santa Ana, O. (2002). *Brown tide rising: Metaphors of Latinos in contemporary public discourse.* Austin: University of Texas.

This important theoretical and empirical study provides an extensive analysis of prevalent metaphors related to Latino immigration and their influence on the media and public discourse.

7

Literacy and Language Diversity in Sociocultural Contexts

Anthropologists who study literacy and social process have much to offer educational policy and practice. By helping to make explicit what social as well as educational resources adults bring with them, anthropologists can help educators to build on resources adults already have. By discovering the meanings and uses of literacy for members of diverse cultural communities, anthropologists can help educational planners take into account what adults want literacy to do for them. (Weinstein-Shr, 1993b, p. 291)

The more that literacy practices of schools are seen as the sole models for the ways people become literate, the more difficult it becomes to see other possibilities for acquiring literacy. As indicated in Chapter 1, the popular media often perpetuate stereotypes about illiteracy, paying scant attention to the actual ways that people use literacy in their daily lives. Concerning this point, Heath (1988a) observes,

> The public media today give much attention to the decline of literacy skills as measured in school settings and to the failure of students to acquire certain levels of literacy. However, the media pay little attention to occasions for literacy retention—to the actual uses of literacy in work settings, daily interactions in religious, economic, and legal institutions, and family habits of socializing the young into uses of literacy. (p. 349)

This chapter addresses literacy in the broader context of how it relates to social practices. It attempts to demonstrate the value of the social practices orientation (see Chapter 3) by looking at literacy in both school and community contexts and the relationships between them. The social practices orientation greatly adds to an understanding of literacy, yet there is still a need to view literacy practices not only *within* groups, but also *between* them. It is likewise necessary to look at ways that school literacy practices and expectations privilege some students and disadvantage others. It is one thing to talk about standards that all students should achieve by the end of the educational process; it is another to see how implicit expectations favoring one group affect others. Social practices viewed from an ideological orientation are likely to illuminate structural and institutional inequities that produce educational success and failure, often in spite of lofty goals and good intentions.

Ethnographic Studies of Literacy in Sociocultural Contexts

Ethnographic studies of literacy describe what children and adults do with literacy in actual social and cultural contexts (see, for example, Barton & Ivanic, 1991; Camitta, 1993; Cook-Gumperz & Keller-Cohen, 1993; Cushman, 1998; Delgado-Gaitán & Trueba, 1991; Fishman, 1988; Heath, 1980, 1983, 1986, 1988a, 1988b; Hull & Schultz, 2002; Kalmar, 2001; Schieffelin & Cochran-Smith, 1984; Schieffelin & Gilmore, 1986; Scollon & Scollon, 1981; Street, 1984, 1993; Taylor, 1983; Taylor & Dorsey-Gaines, 1988; Trueba, Jacobs, & Kirton, 1990). They demonstrate the importance of studying literacy in a variety of linguistic, ethnocultural, and socioeconomic contexts by providing a more complete picture of the functions of literacy in daily activities. Ethnographic studies have identified a wide range of community literacy practices, many of which are neither taught nor used as a basis for further learning in the schools. These studies are concerned with the literacy activities that people find both practical and meaningful, such as those related to interpersonal communication, entertainment, and leisure.

Rather than dichotomizing literacy and orality, ethnographic studies often focus on literacy events and analyze the interaction between *those events*. The literacy event is a useful conceptual tool for examining specific communities to determine "the actual forms and functions of oral and literate traditions and co-existing relationships between spoken and written language . . . in which a piece of writing is integral to the nature of participants' interactions and their interpretive processes" (Heath, 1988a, p. 350). For example, the following list is a summary of the functions of literacy in one community studied by Heath (1980, pp. 128–129):

- Literacy has an instrumental function. It provides practical information used in transportation and daily business transactions.

- Literacy has social-interactional functions. It provides information useful in daily social communication, as illustrated by letter writing and sending greeting cards or reading and writing recipes.

- Literacy has a major news-related function.

- Literacy has a memory-supportive function, which is illustrated by the use of calendars, telephone books, and appointments books.

- Literacy substitutes for direct oral communication, as in the case of parents and teachers conveying messages by means of notes.

- Literacy provides a basis for keeping permanent records of an official nature.

- Literacy provides a basis to confirm beliefs that are already held, as in the case of appealing to authoritative texts such as dictionaries, code books, or religious texts.

By expanding the range of social contexts in which reading and writing are studied, it is possible to "de-school" the notion of literacy and open it up to possibilities beyond the classroom. By so doing, we may find ways to move beyond stereotypical school-based notions of literacy and perhaps enrich literacy practices in the classroom (see Barton & Ivanic, 1991; Camitta, 1993; Cook-Gumperz & Keller-Cohen, 1993; Reder, 1999; Street, 1993; Weinstein-Shr, 1993b).

Ethnographic research explores literacy practices as they function within different communities. By focusing on literacy events, it is possible to see the interaction between oral and written modes of language use. Understanding literacy events within different communities helps us understand what children already know about language and literacy at the time they enter school. Such knowledge is useful to the schools because, as discussed in Chapter 3, one cannot equate literacy practices generally with school literacy practices specifically.

Literacy is often seen only in terms of what individuals can do with print. Can they read and write, and if so, at what skill levels? Ethnographic studies, in contrast, see literacy embedded in group-specific sociocultural practices. As Schieffelin and Cochran-Smith (1984) note,

> To understand the observed behaviors of any social group, we have to know what literacy means to the group. We have to understand which genres are seen as appropriate to master at different points in time. . . . Without serious consideration of what literacy means and does not mean for those people who are introduced to it, it will be impossible to make sense of the ways literacy organizes and is organized by different social groups. (pp. 20–22)

Literacy Practices in Context: Two Studies

Schieffelin and Cochran-Smith (1984) arrived at their conclusion following several studies they undertook, two of which are briefly reviewed here. One study focuses on the introduction of English literacy into a nonliterate community in New Guinea. Literacy was introduced by missionaries as a tool for changing the local religious beliefs and cultural practices. (Conditions in New Guinea have changed markedly since this study was undertaken.) According to Schieffelin and Cochran-Smith, literacy was introduced through its association with the practices of a foreign religion into a culture where an oral tradition predominated. Reading practices involved Bible reading; instruction concentrated on syllabication with an emphasis on correct pronunciation. English-based words were used for new concepts. The literacy practices introduced were passive, because they were limited to reading and reciting texts rather than writing or interpreting them.

Under these circumstances, there appeared to be no incorporation of literacy into the traditional culture. Therefore, interactions between children and adults were not conducive to an intergenerational transmission of literacy. Children were discouraged from using or handling the books, which were seen as valuable artifacts. Apart from its religious function, book reading had little relevance to the broader social practices of the community. In Scribner and Cole's (1981) terms, this is *restricted literacy*, because it is limited to specific religious practices and taught outside the domain of school. Further, it is literacy that is not tied to economic development, although there may have been individual economic incentives for associating with foreigners. From the social practices approach, literacy in this context can be seen in terms of its limited functions, associated with a rather narrow range of religious practices. From an ideological perspective, the literacy practices of one culture are being used to facilitate a change in the belief system of another. They are tools for the conversion of one people to the beliefs of another. In this instance, the conversion appears not to be forced, although history is full of examples of one society forcibly imposing its literacy practices on another.

Another study reported by Schieffelin and Cochran-Smith (1984) involves a Chinese Vietnamese family living in Philadelphia. This study challenges several commonly held beliefs and raises several questions about literacy in immigrant families who speak languages other than English. The first belief challenged by the study is that children whose parents do not speak English will have difficulty acquiring English literacy, because parents are assumed to be the principal literacy tutors of their children. It is also assumed (largely from an English-speaking, middle-class point of view) that a home must have plenty of (English) books and magazines to provide a literate environment (see Clark, 1976; Morrow, 1983).

According to Schieffelin and Cochran-Smith (1984), in this family, as in many immigrant and refugee families, the parents were not literate in English, but they were literate in Chinese. There were not many books and magazines in the home, and the ones that were there were in Chinese. Nevertheless, Schieffelin and Cochran-Smith note that the children lived in a literate environment, because "reading and writing are very important in their lives" (p. 19). The children's father regularly read letters from relatives aloud to the family, and family members frequently wrote letters. Similarly, in many language-minority households, newspapers, magazines, and books in languages other than English allow adults to utilize their native language literacy and maintain currency within both their communities and the larger society.

A second common belief challenged by the study is that interaction with responsive adults is essential to the literacy development of children (e.g., Clark, 1976, 1984). In the case of the Chinese Vietnamese family, the pattern for English literacy was reversed, with the child having to negotiate literacy events in English for his parents—a reminder that in immigrant and language-minority families, there is no reason to assume that the literacy practices of parents and children should parallel those of monolingual English-speaking, middle-class families. If the children are bilingual or have acquired some English literacy, they may have to assist their parents with English literacy tasks. They become brokers for their parents by acting as translators and scribes. This frequently involves them in complex bilingual and biliterate events not required of their monolingual peers.

Another issue was the inability of the child's non-English-speaking parents to help him with school-related activities:

> Because he cannot receive assistance in school-related activities from his non-English-speaking parents, his requests for assistance are directed primarily to English-speaking adults who are outside his family network. . . . Thus, the non-English-speaking child must develop a range of social relationships that are very different from those of the English-speaking child, who may expect to receive assistance from family members. (Schieffelin & Cochran-Smith, 1984, p. 15)

Several issues emerge from this conclusion. First, if the child's literacy development was tied to his access to English speakers, he was fortunate to have these contacts, because many language minority children do not have these opportunities. Second, his search for help outside the home is what one might expect in situations where no bilingual education is available. If there had been a bilingual program or a family literacy program, the child's parents could have assisted him with his academic schoolwork while he was further developing English. The entire family would have been able to develop English literacy and utilize their Chinese literacy. In the absence of a bilingual program, or a program to give him access to adults who could help him with the English-only curriculum, this child apparently had to fend for himself, and he had been fortunate thus far.

Another question is whether or not the school recognized and built upon the considerable knowledge and skills the child developed, more or less on his own. In a passive learning environment, this child's negotiation skills—which were probably more developed than those of his monolingual peers—might not be recognized. If language and literacy skills are defined solely in terms of school practices, such children may never be allowed to shine in school.

In this regard, Wells (1986) offers several relevant observations and suggestions. He contends that too much emphasis is placed on age-grade comparisons of student performance and too little on mapping the individual progress of children. It is often assumed that children from lower socioeconomic backgrounds are deficient in their oral language abilities (a deficit view). In his own studies on the relationship between language use in the home and in school, Wells found little support for a deficit view, especially when a variety of measures were used to evaluate language. He observed that teachers gave students far fewer opportunities for exploratory and collaborative talk than parents did, regardless of their social class. Thus, teachers can unwittingly reduce children to a passive role and underassess their language abilities (see also Barnes, 1976). Wells concludes that because schools value literacy at the expense of orality, schools may inadvertently be accentuating the literacy disadvantage of some children while ignoring a strength (particularly at the lower grades)—oral language.

Schieffelin and Cochran-Smith's (1984) work helps illustrate how literacy is tied to sociocultural practices and how social practices orientation is valuable. It also demonstrates the value of microethnographic approaches to investigating language use. However, in order to formulate literacy policies that are culturally sensitive, a macroanalysis of how they differentially impact groups is also needed. For such analyses, an ideological orientation is more powerful.

Hidden Strengths: A Study of
Hmong Adults in Philadelphia

Much can also be learned from ethnographic studies of adults acquiring literacy. For example, in a study of Hmong adults living in Philadelphia, Weinstein-Shr (1993b) details the limitations of assessing students' abilities based solely on their performance in English as a second language classrooms. She compares two Hmong students—Pao Youa, an active leader in the Philadelphia Hmong community, and Chou Chang, a good student of English who does not wield any influence in his community. Her comparison of the capabilities of the two students *in* and *out* of class is particularly insightful:

> When I first met Pao Youa in the classroom, I could only see him as a dismally failing student with no hope for making it. Chou Chang, on the other hand, plodded through, allocated the time and resources necessary to complete enigmatic grammar exercises, learned the rules of classroom behavior, and came out with his high-school equivalency degree. A teacher who met these two men in the classroom would have missed much—she could not have imagined the kinds of resources at the command of the older student, nor could she have imagined the kinds of resources at the command of the star pupil, who would eventually leave Philadelphia in despair of his social isolation. (p.291)

Thus, if one were to rely solely on classroom assessments of functional English literacy, one could easily underestimate the abilities of a student who was failing. In this regard, Taylor and Dorsey-Gaines (1988; see also Cushman, 1998) have cogently admonished,

> If we are to teach, we must first examine our own assumptions about families and children, and we must be alert to the negative images in the literature ("dropouts come from stressful homes"). Instead of responding to "pathologies," we must recognize that what we see may actually be healthy adaptations to an uncertain and stressful world. As teachers, researchers, and policy makers, we need to think about the children themselves and to try to imagine the contextual worlds of their day-to-day lives. (p. 203)

Ethnographic studies such as these underscore the fact that speaking a language other than English in itself is not a liability, and they illustrate that students, whether children or adults, may have skills and abilities that are not noted, valued, or built upon in the schools. These studies also underscore the importance of having a *literacy network* that spans two languages, through which children can receive the school-related help they need and through which adults can accomplish what they need in order to function. The studies also suggest that if literacy is viewed as a group resource rather than as an individual's asset, there can be a better appreciation of both the resources and needs of the group.

How Home and School Interact: Heath's Piedmont Studies

Among some of the better known and highly acclaimed ethnographic studies of literacy are those of Heath (1983, 1988a, 1988b), who sought to look at how home and school literacy events interact across different communities. Based on the literacy-orientations framework (discussed in Chapter 3), Heath's Piedmont studies are largely within the social practices orientation. In her studies, Heath did extensive research on three individual communities in the Carolinas to which she gives the pseudonyms Maintown, Roadville, and Trackton. Maintown is described as a middle-class community; Roadville as a working-class White community; and Trackton, a working-class Black community. Heath portrays the three communities as literate. Nevertheless, children from literate, working-class parents did not perform as well in the schools as their middle-class, mostly White, peers.

As Heath (1988b) detailed the relationship between the literacy practices from each community, she documented the extent to which the literacy practices of each group matched the practices and expectations of the schools. Not surprisingly, she found that the literacy practices of the middle-class group corresponded closely to the literacy practices and expectations of the schools. "Children growing up in mainstream communities are expected to develop habits and values which attest to their membership in a 'literate society'" (1988b, p. 163).

Heath (1983, 1988a, 1988b) demonstrates that children from the two working-class communities often knew much more about language and literacy than they were credited for by the schools (see Wells, 1986). Many of these children were perceived as lacking school readiness skills and were labeled *deficient* at the point of entry into school. Similarly, the parents and caretakers were often stereotyped as deficient in their ability to provide home support for their children. As the reasoning goes, if they are not deficient, why do such children continue to fail in the schools?

Heath's (1983, 1988a, 1988b) work helps dispel some of the common stereotypes surrounding literacy levels based on economic and racial divisions. Heath demonstrates how nonmainstream adults and children regularly participate in literacy events, although their communicative styles—their "ways with words," as Heath (1983) puts it—differ from those of the mostly White, middle-class community. But if illiteracy is not the problem, what is? On one level, it is the mismatch between the literacy practices of the schools and those of the nonmainstream communities. But on a deeper level, it is the schools' lack of understanding about and respect for the knowledge and skills that some students bring with them. Terms such as "mainstream" and "Maintown" underscore the differential value attributed to the practices of the schools.

Given the close cultural fit between middle-class homes and school, the mostly White middle-class children were the most advantaged among the three groups. They were the most likely to make the initial adjustment to school and continue to do well. They had a head start that benefited them throughout their lives. Because schools historically have largely been the creations of middle-class Whites whose literacy practices are normative, success for this group comes as no surprise. All this suggests is that the schools reflect implicit class, linguistic, and cultural biases. Heath (1983) underscores the importance of these issues:

> Unless the boundaries between classrooms and communities can be broken, and the flow of cultural patterns between them encouraged, the schools will continue to legitimate and reproduce communities of townspeople who control and limit the potential progress of other communities and who themselves remain untouched by other values and ways of life. (p. 369)

Although these conclusions reflect an ideological orientation (see Chapter 3), Heath (1983) chooses to concentrate on those "skills needed for teachers and students as individuals to make changes which were radical for them" (p. 369). She emphasizes a social practices orientation by focusing on literacy events within each of the three communities. This approach goes a long way toward deposing stereotypical notions of cultural deficiency that working-class Whites and African Americans often must endure. It also provides a basis for schools to recognize and incorporate some of the nonmainstream literacy practices that Heath recommends.

A Critique of the Social Practices Studies From the Ideological Perspective

From an ideological perspective, additional analysis is needed. Specifically, there is a need to probe the way in which literacy practices function to perpetuate differences in power and privilege between the middle class and groups that have suffered racial and class discrimination. There is a need to go beyond description, valuable though it is, precisely because the norms of the White middle class dominate both the schools and the workplace, creating implicit standards against which the practices of working-class communities are assessed. Consider, for example, this description of how adults in Roadville (the White working-class community) tell stories and talk about things they have read:

> Roadville adults do not carry on or sustain in continually over-lapping and interdependent fashion the linking of ways of taking meaning from books to ways of relating that knowledge to other aspects of the environment. They do not encourage decontextualization; in fact, they proscribe it in their own stories. They do not themselves make analytic statements or assert universal truths, except those related to their religious faith. . . . Things do not have to follow logically so long as they fit the past experience of the individuals in the community. Thus, children learn to look for a specific moral in stories and to expect that story to fit their facts of reality explicitly. (Heath, 1988b, p. 180)

Similarly, characterizations of Trackton's African American working-class residents imply a standard against which these practices are measured:

There are no bedtime stories. . . . Instead, during the time these activities would take place in Maintown and Roadville homes, Trackton children are enveloped in different kinds of social interactions. They are held, fed, talked about, and rewarded for nonverbal, and later verbal, renderings of events they witness. . . . Children do not have labels or names of attributes of items and events pointed out for them, and they are asked for reason-explanations not what-explanations. . . . Children come to recognize similarities of pattern, though they do not name lines, points, or items which are similar between two items or situations. (Heath, 1988b, p. 180)

Although these characterizations are presented as descriptions, they could easily be construed as evaluations that imply deficits based on departures from, or the lack of, middle-class practices that are seen as normative. In this regard, Auerbach (1989) has observed, "Since authority is vested in those belonging to the mainstream culture, the literacy practices of the mainstream become the norm and have higher status in school contexts" (p. 173; see also Stuckey, 1991). Given that low levels of literacy and educational achievement tend to persist for some groups across generations, more is needed to explain their lack of educational progress than differences in literacy practices. In a review that reflects an ideological perspective, Rosen (1985) finds much to praise about Heath's (1983) book, *Ways With Words: Language, Life, and Work in Communities and Classrooms*, but also observed,

Heath sets out . . . to satisfy a "need for a full description of the primary-face-to-face interactions of children from community cultures other than [the] mainstream one" (Heath, 1983, p. 3) . . . and in the end "help working-class black and white children learn more effectively" (p. 4). . . . Here "working class" is being contrasted with "mainstream." What then does "mainstream" imply? Middle class? . . . It raises more questions than it answers: What are the *fundamental* determinants of class? How do the practices of everyday life relate to them? (p. 449)

Some clues to the answers of these questions are provided in Heath's (1988a) work. Everyday literacy practices such as applying for employment, working on the job, and seeking a loan are described. In these situations, Heath found that Trackton's African American residents were usually not required—or allowed—to use the literacy skills they had. In one instance, she reports that African Americans applying for millworker jobs had their applications filled out for them by White employment officers. When asked about this practice, the employment officers offered the explanation, "It is easier if we do it. This way, we get to talk to the client, ask questions not on the form, clarify immediately any questions they have, and, for our purposes, the whole thing is just cleaner" (Heath, 1988a, p. 362). What conclusions can be drawn from an ideological perspective? Working-class African Americans were able to acquire and secure jobs (which paid better than other types of employment that demanded greater literacy skills), but they were not empowered, because they were not in control of the literacy events affecting their lives.

In these communities, working-class individuals with little formal education were neither empowered nor disempowered by literacy. To understand the sociopolitical significance of their position, an analysis of their relationship with the dominant middle-class White community is needed. In this regard, Rosen (1985) further contends that racism and the unequal power between African Americans and Whites needs to be emphasized:

> Yes, indeed, communities have different social legacies. A major component of this legacy must be the experience of racism and its continued existence. Why has Heath chosen to warn us off? Black English is the expression and negotiation of Black experience. Racism does no more than lurk in the shadows of this text, raising questions which are not posed by Heath. (pp. 451–452)

Without explicitly focusing on racism, Heath's work (1988a) provides clues to deeper social realities. She describes situations outside the mills where African Americans lacked control over information and documents about themselves when interacting with bank, credit union, and loan office personnel. Heath notes that, typically, they were asked questions about information in their folders without being able to look at the information. As in the employment interviews, these literacy events involved interactions between individuals with unequal social power, with only one person having control over the direction of communication.

This dynamic is significant in several respects: First, the so-called functional literacy skills of the interviewees were not important, because they were not allowed to be important. Second, by being placed in a passive oral response mode, the interviewees were judged only on the basis of oral language and may well have been socially evaluated based on the extent to which their speech sounded "literate." In communities dominated by members of a specific group (i.e., ethnic, racial, or speech), the members of that group often control literacy events by virtue of their social position. Whether teachers in schools, supervisors in offices, or loan officers in banks, they are the gatekeepers, and their norms become the criteria for evaluating and ascribing social status to those with whom they interact.

Implications for Practice

Schools can play a powerful role in helping to maintain social stratification on the basis of their language policies and practices. A better understanding of the role that language, literacy, and cultural differences play in homes, the community, and the schools helps us to understand how social stratification is maintained and reproduced. However, the recognition that students (children and adults) come from communities with literacy practices that differ from those of the school does little to ensure success for all if we merely make aspects of the so-called hidden curriculum explicit. Knowledge of such biases can be acted upon. Several courses of action are possible: *adaptation, accommodation,* and *incorporation.*

Adaptation

Adaptation places most of the burden of change on those whose knowledge and practices are considered subordinate and, thereby, substandard. In schools and other social institutions, adaptation involves the expectation that children and adults who are held to have substandard knowledge and skills will acculturate to the norms of those who control the schools, institutions, and workplace. In schools, this approach is often defended as maintaining standards (i.e., middle-class norms and practices). Applying this expectation to adults, Heath (1988a) contends,

> In work settings, when others control access to and restrict types of written information . . . especially those in financial and legal settings, Trackton residents recognize their deficiency of skills . . . not literacy skills, but knowledge of oral language uses which would enable them to obtain information about oral language uses. . . . Learning how to do this *appropriately, so as not to seem to challenge a person in power* [italics added], is often critical to obtaining a desired outcome and maintaining a job or reputation as a "satisfactory" applicant, or worker. (p. 365)

Accommodation

Accommodation applies more to the action of those who exercise social control by virtue of their role or position. It seeks to meet learners halfway, working with them in an effort to change their language and literacy practices, to make them more compatible with schooled, middle-class norms. While this approach is sensitive to learners' background experiences and needs, it nonetheless implies deficiencies on their part.

Accommodation requires teachers, supervisors, personnel officers, and gatekeepers to develop a better understanding of the communicative styles and literacy practices among their students. Historically, in schools, as Wright (1980) indicates, working-class children had little opportunity to adapt to teacher-controlled question-and-answer dyads, because teachers typically did not model answers to their own questions. Teachers used a formal question register and expected students to answer in an equally formal recitation register. Student discourse was often limited to short-answer responses, which were scrutinized more for being in the correct form than for their content. Without making the expected form explicit, children (and previously unschooled adults; see Klassen & Burnaby, 1993; Miller, 1991) quickly learned that their oral performance was inadequate even if they did not know why. With accommodation, teachers help students understand the differences between the language they use in their homes and communities and the language variety that the school expects them to use. To implement this approach, teachers need to understand both the language and literacy practices of their students and the culture- and class-based literacy practices valued and expected by the schools. Accommodation can be an appropriate response if there is no intention to alter standards.

Incorporation

Because school practices tend to correspond to middle-class literacy expectations regarding language use, one way to neutralize the advantages that White middle-class students have is to incorporate some of the practices of other groups into school practices. This alternative requires an understanding of those community practices that have not been valued previously by the schools and incorporating them into the curriculum. Heath (1988b) suggests as much:

> It must be admitted that a range of alternative ways of learning and displaying knowledge characterizes all highly schooled, successful adults in the advanced stages of their careers. Knowing more about how these alternatives are learned at early ages in different sociocultural conditions can help the school to provide opportunities for *all* students to avail themselves of these alternatives early in their school careers. For example, mainstream children can benefit from early exposure to Trackton's creative highly analogical styles of telling stories and giving explanations . . . to their repertoire of narrative types. (p. 181)

For Black and White working-class children and adults, this means that more attention should be directed to building on their strengths rather than their alleged deficiencies. For White middle-class children, it involves broadening their experience by exposing them to other ways of knowing and using language and literacy (cf. Edwards & Sienkewicz, 1991). It also means *surrendering a privileged position* by acknowledging that something can be learned from other groups. Surrendering the privilege, however, need not be taken as a retreat from high standards nor as imposing a hardship on the children of the middle class, since, as Heath contends, middle-class children can benefit by expanding their own possibilities for understanding and using language. Similarly, adults who have grown up with one set of language and literacy norms can be enriched by learning from the practices of others. Educational encounters with alternative ways of using language could do much to break down linguistic prejudice across groups.

In order for incorporation to occur, teachers need knowledge of the language, communication styles, and literacy practices of their students. A number of authors identify the kinds of knowledge needed (e.g., Camitta, 1993; Dandy, 1992), but there are limits to how far such approaches can take us. As Shuman (1993) warns, the "issue is not only varieties of writing, standard and local, but privileged channels and genres of communication" (p. 267).

Incorporation obviously poses logistical problems for schools and classroom practice. First, schools face the problem that a disproportionate number of teachers, even in racially and linguistically diverse areas of the country, come from the White middle class. There is a need to find ways to recruit and train teachers from the same communities as their students.

As a second strategy for incorporation, Heath (1983) suggests turning teachers into learners and students into ethnographers. This is no simple task; her own efforts involved years of community and school ethnographic work. Short of being able to assign an ethnographer to every school—an anthropologist at school might be at least as useful as a psychologist—there are other possibilities. One is to require ethnographic training within existing teacher education and staff development programs at all levels. Movement in this direction could help to address misunderstandings and ignorance about language use in a diverse society.

Further Reading

Dubin, F., & Kuhlman, N. A. (Eds.). (1992). *Cross-cultural literacy: Global perspectives on reading and writing.* Englewood Cliffs, NJ: Regents/ Prentice Hall.

This work contains case studies of literacy in different national and sociocultural contexts.

Heath, S. B. (1991). *Children of promise: Literate activity in linguistically and culturally diverse classrooms.* Washington, DC: National Education Association.

This small volume provides practical examples of how schools and universities can collaborate to promote literacy within diverse school settings.

8

Rethinking Language: Beyond Dichotomies

In societies such as ours, where literacy is ever present, expectations regarding appropriate language use for speaking and writing are socially constructed and culturally grounded within schools and other institutions. Thus, we should not lose sight of the fact that all uses of language in academic settings are inherently social and that expectations regarding appropriate language use can reflect the same differential power relations that permeate the larger society in which they reside (Fairclough, 1989). Students often resist expectations for linguistic conformity and academic learning, sometimes productively, sometimes unproductively (Erickson, 1984; see also Chapter 3). To be successful in school, students are often required to understand and display contextually appropriate types of language knowledge and behavior that may be based not only on explicit rules, but often on implicit expectations for appropriate behavior. As illustrated in Chapter 7, language minority children and adults may come from communities with different ways with words than those of the schools (Heath, 1983). Historically, more often than not, these differences have been treated as deficiencies in the cognitive development of learners rather than in the system's capacity to respond to diversity.

This chapter briefly reviews some of the important debates of the past several decades regarding the purported dichotomy between academic and social language, which can perpetuate stigmatizing notions of cognitive deficiency. The chapter also reviews trends in language teaching that attempt to broaden the understanding of language as socially situated both in and out of school, and it notes important ethnographically based studies that have helped to extend the social practices and ideological orientations discussed in Chapter 3.

The Cognitive Divide:
From Semilingualism to "Non-Nons"

The idea of a cognitive divide between literates and nonliterates is based on the assumption that there are qualitative cognitive differences between the two groups. The pioneering works of Scribner and Cole (1981) and Street (1984) have done much to refute the concept of the autonomous orientation (see Chapter 3). However, some of the notions of deficiency have reappeared, particularly in popular theories related to bilingualism and biliteracy.

Hakuta (1986) has chronicled the debate over the purported cognitive advantages and disadvantages of bilingualism. Until the 1960s, bilingualism had either been ignored as a confounding factor in explaining lower levels of IQ across ethnic groups or construed as having negative, or subtractive, consequences for intellectual development. By the 1970s, however, some studies (August & Hakuta, 1998; Hakuta, 1986) began to show that bilinguals outperformed their monolingual peers on various cognitive tasks, which suggested that there were additive effects associated with bilingualism. Lambert (1974) developed a psychosocial model of language acquisition in an attempt to explain positive and negative effects associated with bilingualism. This model became a major influence in the field and on terminology used by educators, as Baker (2001) notes:

> Lambert's (1974) distinction between additive and subtractive bilingualism has been used in different ways. First, additive bilingualism is used to refer to positive cognitive outcomes from being bilingual. . . . Subtractive bilingualism hence refers to the negative affective and cognitive effects of bilingualism (e.g., where both languages are "underdeveloped"). (pp. 114–115)

In the 1970s, some writers claimed that subtractive bilingualism could result in the highly controversial notion of *double semilingualism*. This dubious condition was purported to result from a defective or imperfect command of two languages (see Skutnabb-Kangas, 1981, pp. 251–252). The positive cognitive effects of bilingualism, on the other hand, were held to result from *proficient bilingualism*, i.e., having high levels of proficiency in two languages. Neither the positive nor the negative cognitive effects were associated with *partial bilingualism,* which was on a cognitive par with monolingualism, because one had native-like proficiency in only one language.

Following critiques by those who saw behind these labels notions of deficiency based on limited language proficiency, some scholars (from both the social practices and the ideological orientations) began using the terms *additive bilingualism* and *subtractive bilingualism* to refer to the social contexts of learning that allegedly create the deficiencies. Skutnabb-Kangas (1981), for example, suggested that semilingualism could not "be regarded as a deficiency inherent in the individual but should rather be treated as one result of the (linguistically and otherwise) powerless circumstances of the (linguistic) oppression in which she has lived" (p. 249). Cummins' (1989, 2000) *empowerment approach* emphasizes additive as opposed to subtractive contexts for overcoming linguistic and cultural domination.

Nevertheless, constructs such as subtractive bilingualism imply cognitive deficits for students who have merely lacked an equal chance to learn. Many tests designed to determine language proficiency require literacy and knowledge of test-taking. Students classified as proficient bilinguals are probably biliterate and have been schooled in two languages. Those who have lacked this opportunity and are literate in only one language are likely to be labeled partial bilinguals. Those who have lacked all opportunities for schooling are likely to be labeled as *limited bilinguals,* or—even worse—as *non-nons,* that is, those who purportedly have no language (see Valadez, MacSwan, & Martínez, 2002).

Recent empirical work is helping to illuminate some of the problems related to labeling students based on incorrect assessment, which lends itself to deficit labeling. For example, children assessed on grammatical variables drawn from natural speech samples rather than tests have been found not to differ linguistically in any significant way from other children. This was the finding of a study of 6,800 students in the Los Angeles Unified School District who had been classified based on prescriptive tests in 1996 as non-nons and were held to be *low achievers, semilinguals,* or *clinically disfluent.* In fact, the children were not found to differ in any linguistically significant way (Valadez, MacSwan, & Martínez, 2002). Thus, human beings with normal cognitive abilities have command of their native languages, whether or not they are literate and whether or not they have attended school. To label them as limited bilinguals or semilinguals, as was once the case, or as non-nons, as is more recently the case, only stigmatizes them and misrepresents their linguistic and cognitive abilities.

BICS and CALP:
Social Versus Academic Language

For several decades, Cummins' (1981, 1985, 2000) distinction between two assumed dimensions of language proficiencies has been popular: *Basic Interpersonal Communication Skills (BICS)* and *Cognitive Academic Language Proficiency (CALP)*. This distinction was initially intended to help practitioners understand the importance of developing language that students need to succeed in academic contexts and to explain how they would fall behind their peers, who already spoke the language of school, if they did not have opportunities for bilingual instruction in both their home and school languages.

In early versions of Cummins' (1981, 1983, 1984a, 1984b) theoretical discussions, the terms BICS and CALP were presented as two dimensions of language discourse that differ in cognitive difficulty depending on the extent to which the language is contextualized. BICS refers to so-called contextualized language, which was characterized as usually being less cognitively demanding than CALP, which is considered less contextualized, more abstract, and more cognitively demanding.

BICS and CALP, as two dimensions of language proficiency, were used to counter the view that proficiency in different languages is developed separately, according to the *separate underlying proficiency (SUP)* model. Cummins (1981) rejected this model in favor of a *common underlying proficiency (CUP)* model, where the development of a more demanding language (CALP) in L1 (the native language) is seen as positively influencing the development in L2 (the second language). It was assumed that L1 CALP had to be developed to a threshold level of proficiency that would facilitate transfer to L2.

A number of scholars have criticized these ideas for lending support to a hierarchical view of language that tends to privilege some practices as being cognitively superior (Edelsky, 1996; Edelsky et al., 1983; MacSwan, 1999, 2000; MacSwan & Rolstad, 2003; MacSwan, Rolstad, & Glass, 2002; Romaine, 1995; Spolsky, 1984; Troike, 1984; Valadez, MacSwan, & Martinez, 2002; Wald, 1984; Wiley, 1996; see also Baker, 2001, for a summary of various criticisms). It can be argued (Wiley, 1996, chapt. 8) that such a hierarchical view is consistent with, if not derived from, the notion of a great divide, which presumes the cognitive superiority of literate societies over oral societies and literate individuals over nonliterates (see also Chapter 3). One implication of this idea is that children who fail to reach the threshold of literacy are doomed to be semilinguals who lack CALP. Subsequently, the focus is shifted from semilingualism as an individual deficiency to subtractive bilingualism as an inequitable social and educational system that results in individual cognitive deficiencies. Thus, the reframing seems to have shifted blame from the victim to the system.

Cummins (2000, 2003) has responded to these issues and attempts to clarify his position. With specific reference to BICS and CALP, Cummins (2000) notes that, for a time, he substituted the terms *conversational proficiency* and *academic proficiency* for BICS and CALP, after the latter were critiqued by well-known scholars:

> I have intended to use the terms conversational and academic proficiency in place of BICS and CALP because the acronyms were considered misleading by some commentators (e.g., Spolsky, 1984) and were being misinterpreted by others (e.g., Romaine, 1995). However, the acronyms continue to be widely used in the field and from my perspective are still appropriate to use. (p. 75)

Cummins (2000) clarifies that he has reintegrated the terms BICS and CALP as meaningful constructs. Nevertheless, a continuing concern, which was originally raised by Wald (1984), is that the concepts of BICS and CALP have not been sufficiently delineated so as to avoid confusion. More recently, Petrovic and Olmstead (2001) have also noted that in Cummins' (2000) recent work, terms like *proficient, register,* and *function* are used as if they are interchangeable and synonymous with CALP, when, in fact they have different referents. Readers are encouraged to review the critiques cited and Cummins' (2000, 2003) replies and clarifications.

Teaching Trends: Understanding Language as Socially Situated

Language instruction is still often dominated by an autonomous orientation and by traditional methods that focus on the formal properties of language, with grammar and vocabulary taught as ends in themselves. Yet there are a number of commonly identified social functions of language that language minority learners need to master in both academic and nonacademic contexts. Even within traditionally oriented instruction that focuses more on autonomous skills areas, there has been some attempt in recent years to focus more on the social contextualization of language.

Moving beyond the constructs of BICS and CALP, over the past several decades, there has been a greater emphasis on understanding the communicative functions of language and the heavily contextualized language used in the teaching of academic subjects (e.g., Gillham, 1986; Gumperz, 1992). In the 1970s, Barnes (1973a, 1973b, 1976) did important analyses of how language, particularly *exploratory talk* (open-ended conversations focused on a topic), was used to help students learn academic content in the classroom. In K–12 education, there has been an increased emphasis on understanding specific types of language used to facilitate learning academic content in areas such as math, social studies, and the sciences (Gonzalez & Watson, 1986). At the university level, content-based approaches have received attention since the 1980s, (e.g., Brinton, Snow, & Wesche, 1989; Mohan, 1986; Richard-Amato & Snow, 1992; Tchudi & Huerta, 1983). English for Academic Purposes (EAP; see Hamp-Lyons, 2001) has emerged as a specialized field—much like English for Specific Purposes (ESP; see Dudley-Evans, 2001)—to focus on language needs directly related to students' academic learning contexts.

Other approaches are aimed at helping students understand discourse styles and rhetorical and analytical devices that are specific to various academic writing and speaking tasks (e.g., Green, 1983; Kramsch, 1981a, 1981b, 1983; McCarthy, 1991; Mohan, 1989). These approaches are not monolithic but tend to be somewhat eclectic, reflecting autonomous views of language with increased focus on the social contextualization of language. More ethnographically based approaches appeared in the 1980s (e.g., Cazden, 1988; Cazden, John, & Hymes, 1985; Heath, 1983). More recently, Adger (1998), Adger and Wolfram (2000), and others have analyzed the use of different registers in the classroom and demystified dichotomies in home-school language use.

Early Efforts: Notional-Functional Syllabuses

During the 1970s, as part of a general reaction to behavioralism and audiolingualism, language teaching methodologies looked increasingly to cognitive and sociolinguistic theories of language and learning. Audiolingual approaches, which focused on extensive mimicry, memorization, and "over-learning" language patterns and forms (Brown, 1994), were often criticized for failing to consider "the relationship between language and meaning; and . . . to provide a social context within which the formal features of language could be associated with functional aspects, such as politeness" (Bygate, 2001, p. 15). Functional and communicative syllabuses have sometimes been criticized by prescriptivists for not placing enough emphasis on formal grammar. Endless grammar drills, however, do not by themselves necessarily lead to functional proficiency.

Wilkins (1976) was among the first to suggest that language instruction could emphasize fundamental notions, ideas conveyed by language, and the social functions of language. To illustrate how this could be done, he developed a notional-functional syllabus that concentrates on *semantico-grammatical categories* and *language functions*. Wilkins' syllabus provides an alternative to the traditional syllabus organized around traditional grammar categories.

A focus on notional-functional categories does not necessarily exclude instruction in grammar. Rather, it is based on the assumption that learning grammar becomes more meaningful when it is learned in association with common notions and communicative functions. Grammatical forms are dealt with as they are needed in order to express the concepts and functions taught (see Table 8.1).

Despite the advances of these early communicative attempts to recognize social contexts in language learning, "none were anchored in the study of naturally occurring oral interactive discourse or in the study of oral L2 skills" (Bygate, 2001, p. 14). Recently, learner-centered approaches (e.g.,

Nunan, 1988, 1989, 1991) have attempted to move from an autonomous view of language, in which the focus is language form, to a more socially contextualized one, in which the focus is the language as it is actually used. Learner-centered and task-based approaches that involve negotiation of content go further in the direction of social practices (Richards & Rodgers, 2001).

Communicative Functions of Language in and out of Academic Settings

Along with these developments, there have been attempts to move second language and literacy instruction more overtly toward an emphasis on social and communicative language use, with a greater emphasis on language functions and less focus on specific language skills.

Some of the more common language functions that have been identified are exchanging information, making and declining requests, persuading, evaluating, and expressing feelings and attitudes (Van Ek, 1987). Van Ek's list is useful in identifying language functions that may occur in either academic or nonacademic settings. In an attempt to make social awareness and appropriateness in language learning explicit, Van Ek (1978, 1987) suggests a focus on *social roles* (e.g., stranger/stranger, friend/friend, and teacher/student); *psychological stances* (e.g., neutrality, equality, sympathy, and antipathy); *settings* (formal/informal); and the *topics* used.

While Van Ek's (1978, 1987) schema provides a useful starting point for thinking about language functions, language use involves almost unlimited complexities that are affected by culture, social class, political and religious factors, and differential power between superiors and subordinates. Roles can be viewed as *transactional* (e.g., records clerk to student, customer to salesperson); they can involve *inclusion* and *exclusion* (e.g., insider to outsider, visitor to resident); and they can involve *registers* (degrees of formality and informality) associated with *situation* (e.g., public, private, and intimate).

In most formal language instruction, students are directed toward the conventional use of language. However, the complexity of what students need to know about language is not easily reduced to mere formal propositions. In order to use and function in the language, students need to be aware of both the *locutionary* (literal) meaning of speech acts and the *illocutionary* (intended) meaning of the proposition. For example, if one were to say, "I am tired," it might be interpreted as a physical condition (i.e., locutionary meaning), or it might be interpreted as a request for the other person to quit or leave (i.e., illocutionary meaning).

Obviously, for language minority speakers, especially children, who are new to the culture, the illocutionary meaning may be more difficult to grasp. Many speech acts appear to be one type but are actually indirect forms of another. For example, if a teacher asks a student who arrives late to class, "Do you know what time it is?" the appropriate answer is neither "Yes" nor "10:00 o'clock," but rather something such as, "I'm sorry. I missed my bus." In addition, there are culturally appropriate ways of responding to the question. To determine how this exchange could be interpreted, a number of potential contextual and cultural issues must be explored. Explicitly analyzing language functions provides an excellent opportunity for exploring cultural differences.

These examples demonstrate the difficulties involved in developing formal instruction that can grasp the complexity of appropriately using and understanding English for social communication. While Van Ek (1978, 1987; see also Figure 8.1) was among the first to focus explicitly on language functions, the work of others soon followed, which expanded and refined the emphasis on communication (see Candlin, 1981; Finocchiaro & Brumfit, 1983; Nunan, 1989; Yalden, 1983).

While some of these language functions may occur in only one context—either in school or out of school—many could occur in both. Language proficiencies and behaviors have sometimes been classified as "basic and communicative" or "cognitive and academic." Van Ek's (1978, 1987) approach allows for a metacognitive stance to the functional social aspects of language. In formal instruction, language functions can either be placed in contextualized social settings outside of school or in academic settings in school.

Rhetorical Functions and
Speech Acts in School Contexts

The appropriate use of language in academic settings also requires that language learners understand *discourse functions* and are able to perform speech acts in English. Discourse functions may involve the ability to understand and use simple language acts, such as responding to requests for specific information (see Figure 8.1). They may also involve complex rhetorical functions, such as those required to understand and produce coherent, extended oral discourse or written texts (Figure 8.2). Traditionally, these complex discourse functions have been taught explicitly in composition, rhetoric, and public speaking courses but are taught less frequently, or less explicitly, in courses in which the focus is on the subject matter. However, in many content courses that require sophisticated linguistic and content knowledge, there may be a need to teach discourse functions and speech acts, particularly those required to demonstrate knowledge of the subject.

From prior educational experiences, some immigrant students may already know how to perform the rhetorical functions of instructional tasks in their native languages. However, many may not, if they have never had the opportunity to practice them. Similarly, many native speakers of English may not have learned how to perform these rhetorical functions. If students are to be tested and assessed on their ability to perform rhetorical functions such as these, it is important to underscore that, even as they are made explicit, they cannot be taught in isolation but must be grounded in appropriate contexts (see Trimble, 1985, especially chap. 7).

Making Language and Language Expectations Explicit

Delpit (1992, 1995) has noted that many language minority children have greater difficulty in classrooms where expectations for language behavior are *implicitly* based on middle-class norms assumed to be universal by teachers who do not understand the cultural and linguistic differences of their students. As a result, Delpit (1992) has emphasized the need to make behavioral expectations *explicit*. Her concern might be refocused as a question: What works for different types of students, for what purposes, in what contexts, and at what points in their language development? Some second language instructional approaches are focused on *social communication* and seek to develop a student's communicative competence in a variety of social contexts in and out of school; others are focused more narrowly on highly prescribed curricula. In either case, children who come from social backgrounds very different from those of their teachers may be at a disadvantage unless classroom expectations are made explicit.

Even in skills-based approaches to language instruction, there has been some attempt to focus on the social contexts of language use, as the following examples illustrate.

Grammar

There has been considerable debate and concern over the efficacy of formal grammar and vocabulary instruction as they relate to language acquisition. On the one hand, merely knowing about formal grammar does not ensure that students know how to use language appropriately in or out of the classroom; even students who have a good understanding of conventional rules of grammar may not know how to apply that knowledge in complex academic contexts. On the other hand, students are required to write formal papers that are grammatically correct and to demonstrate knowledge of formal grammar and word meaning on standardized achievement tests and, ultimately, on college admissions exams.

The guiding principle in current research on grammar instruction is that all "language exists in context, and the context and purposes for which language is used will determine the ways in which language is realized at the levels of text and grammar" (Nunan, 1991, p. 151; see also Celce-Murcia & Larsen-Freeman, 1998). Although there has been a renewed interest in more explicit grammar instruction, it is unwise to retreat into grammar instruction as an end in itself, ignoring the contexts and purposes of language use. Unfortunately, many grammar texts tend to reflect a decontextualized view of language. Thus, the question emerges regarding how to contextualize formal grammar instruction. Systemic functional approaches address this issue by emphasizing that grammar awareness begins with whole texts and works top-down. With this approach, the teacher focuses "on a particular grammatical item . . . introduced within

Table 8.1.
Sematico-Grammatical Categories in the Notional-Functional Syllabus

Category	Expressed as	Expressed by	Examples
TIME	Point of time		now, then, on Monday the 23rd of April, yesterday, today, tomorrow, this morning, yesterday afternoon, tomorrow evening, this month, last week, next year
	Duration (inception or termination)		for 5 years, since yesterday, from Monday until Friday, all day, the whole day
	Time relations	(a) Tense (past, present, future)	*We went yesterday, and we will go again tomorrow.*
		(b) Frequency	on Mondays, the first chance you get
		(c) Sequence Ordinals	first, second, third
		Adverbials	then, next, finally, the next step
QUANTITY	Divisible Indivisible Count Noncount Singularity Plurality Pre and post determiners		all, some, a few, none
	Numerals (cardinal numbers)		one book, 15 student
	Operations		mathematical
SPACE	Dimension	Volume Gravity Elasticity Temperature Distance Height Weight Speed	a quart of milk, 6 kilometers
	Location	Verbs	inhabit, stay
		Prepositions	in, on, at, inside, in front of, along, against, underneath
	Motion	Prepositions	to, from, in, on, towards, out of, across, past, through
RELATIONAL MEANING	Sentenial relations	Agent	*Mary hit the ball.*
		Initiator	*He exercised his dog.*
		Object	*The door was opened.*
		Beneficiary	*He received an inheritance.*
		Instrument	*The key opened the door.*
		Prediction and attirbution (X will happen/occur X caused Y. X has Y.)	*The door will be opened.*
DEXIS	Time		then, now, formerly, presently
	Place		*Shut that door.*
	Person		he, she

Category	Expressed as	Expressed by		Examples
MODALITY	Scale of certainty	Impersonal	Certainty	*It is certain to rain.*
			Probability	*It is likely to rain.*
			Possibility	*It may rain.*
			Nil certainty	*There is no way it will rain.*
		Personal	Conviction	*I believe* *I am certain*
			Conjecture	*I presume* *I suppose*
			Doubt	*I am not sure* *I am uncertain*
			Disbelief	*I do not believe* *I cannot imagine*
SCALE OF COMMITMENT	Intention	Expressions of desire, purpose, wish, willingness		*I want to go to Spain.* *I plan to go to Spain.*
	Obligation			*I have to go to Spain.* *You ought to come with me.* *We must leave soon.*
COMMUNICATIVE FUNCTION	Judgment and evaluation	Valuation Committal Release Approval Disapproval Disinterest		*I'm dissatisfied with the results.*
	Suasion	Inducement Compulsion Predication Tolerance	Suggest Advise	*You should leave soon.*
	Argument and information		Assert Seek Deny Agree Disagree	*I don't think I should leave yet.*
	Concession			*Okay, I'll leave soon.*
	Rational inquiry and exposition			*I can't explain what happened.*
	Personal emotions	Positive Negative		*I enjoyed the movie.*
	Emotional relations	Greetings Sympathy Gratitude Flattery Hostility		*It's nice to see you again.*

Note. From *Notional Syllabuses* (pp. 25–54), by D. A. Wilkins, 1976, Oxford, United Kingdom: Oxford University Press. Copyright 1976 by Oxford University Press. Adapted with permission.

a particular context, and the learner works from context to text to sentence and clause, rather than from clauses/sentence to text" (Nunan, 1991, p. 152).

Vocabulary

Second language acquisition researchers believe that the lexicon "may be the most important language component for learners" (Gass & Selinker, 2001, p. 372). At the same time, it is important to emphasize that vocabulary should not be taught as an end in itself. As with grammar instruction, vocabulary instruction should emerge from the subject matter, context, and purpose of the lesson. Table 8.2 provides a selection of instructional approaches for vocabulary development.

Listening Comprehension

Traditionally, listening has been treated as one of the four language skill areas. Even when listening is conceptualized this way, students can be helped to focus on the social functions of language (see Figure 8.3 for some examples of listening skills).

Pronunciation

A major theoretical and instructional shift in the teaching of pronunciation has occurred during the past 2 decades, largely as a result of the shift to communicative instructional approaches. The shift in focus has been "from segmental work [focus on vowel and consonant sounds] to a focus on suprasegmental features of rhythm, stress, and intonation" (Nunan, 1991, p. 115), with a corresponding shift in the instructional goals from the development of native-like pronunciation to "communicative effectiveness and intelligibility" (Nunan, 1991, p. 115).

Pronunciation is also an instructional area where serious reconsideration should be given to the expectation for native-like competency. Some experts suggest that the goal in pronunciation for language minority students should be *communicative competence*, rather than the native-like competence stressed by some ESL curriculum standards frameworks. Language educators with an interest in pronunciation have considered such factors as an individual's language background, identity, motivation, and age, and the influence these have on pronunciation in a second language (see Kenworthy, 1987, for a discussion of these issues). Educators need to also consider *accent discrimination* (see Lippi-Green, 1997) as a form of social bias and how to counter prejudices triggered by accent bias. Standards for accent awareness (see Wolfram, Adger, & Christian, 1999), which would include an understanding of social bias toward stigmatized accents, need to be included in curricula on pronunciation.

Toward Critical Language Awareness in Academic Settings

As a concluding note to this discussion, most language instruction focused on formal properties of language stems from, or is compatible with, an autonomous view of language. Emphases on communicative, learner-centered, negotiated, task-based approaches have moved instruction in the direction of the social practices orientation (Richards & Rodgers, 2001; Willis & Willis, 2001). In addition, *language awareness (*van Lier, 2001) or *critical language awareness* (Pennycook, 1997, 2001) is needed to help students understand how language is used as an instrument of power (Fairclough, 1989). This approach is more consistent with the ideological orientation discussed in Chapter 3.

The Value of Ethnographically Based Perspectives

Even as language teachers attempted to move instructional approaches toward more learner-centered, socially grounded understandings of language, in recent decades, ethnographically based studies of language and literacy have extended the social practices and ideological perspectives. A number of other sociolinguistic analyses of the interrelationships between oral and literate language strategies have helped to debunk the myth of a cognitive divide between orality versus literacy (Edwards & Sienkewicz, 1991; Tannen, 1982, 1987). Work emphasizing social factors in multilingual contexts that affect language development in academic contexts includes Heath (1983) and Troike (1984). Work on the significance of cultural factors that affect language and literacy practices in the schools includes Delgado-Gaitán and Trueba (1991); Philips' (1972, 1983) classic Warm Springs studies; Trueba (1989); Trueba, Jacobs, and Kirton (1990); and Cushman's (1998) studies of literacy practices outside of school.

Figure 8.1.
Common Language Functions

1	**Language functions associated with attaining or imparting factual information may include**

correcting	questioning
identifying	reporting (includes describing and narrating)

2	**Language functions associated with intellectual attitudes may include**

accepting or declining an offer or invitation	inquiring about an agreement or disagreement
denying	inquiring whether an offer or an invitation is accepted or declined
expressing certainty or uncertainty	seeking or giving permission
expressing obligation or lack of obligation (for self or others)	

3	**Language functions associated with emotional attitudes may include**

certainty or uncertainty	pleasure or displeasure
desire	satisfaction or dissatisfaction
fear	surprise
gratitude	sympathy
hope	worry
likes and dislikes, preference	

4	**Language functions associated with moral attitudes may include**

making an apology	asking for approval
showing appreciation	asking for forgiveness
expressing approval or disapproval	indifference
	regret

5	**Language functions associated with accomplishing a task or job (suasion) may include**

advising	requesting
instructing or directing	suggesting
inviting	warning

6	**Language functions used in social interactions may include**

attracting attention	introducing people and being introduced
conversing over a meal	proposing a toast
greeting and meeting people	taking leave

Note. From *The Treshold Level in a European Unit/Credit System for Modern Language Learning by Adults* (pp. 19–21), by J. A. van Ek, 1975, Strasbourg, France: Council of Europe. Copyright 1975 by the Council of Europe. Adapted with permission.

Figure 8.2.
Common Rhetorical Functions

describe to give an account, tell about; to represent by a picture
    x has y; x is (attribute)
    x consists of y, z
    x is characterized by y, z
    x displays y, z

define to give the meaning of a word or concept; to place in a category and set off from other items
    formal definitions
        by simple example
        with synonyms
    extended definitions

compare to bring out points of similarity and points of difference on single attributes; for complex comparisons

summarize to sum up; to give the main points briefly
    first, second, third; next, lastly

discuss to talk over, consider from various points of view, present different sides of
    like, the same as
    both . . . and, similar to
    also, resembles

contrast to bring out the points of difference
    but
    however, unlike
    in contrast

trace to follow the course of, follow the trail; to track the progress of
    follow chronological sequence
    pursue causal sequence

illustrate to use word pictures, diagrams, charts, or concrete examples to clarify a point

explain to make clear, interpret; to tell how to do something; to give the meaning of

analyze to resolve, dissect, break down into components

synthesize to make up or produce from components

interpret to make plain, give the meaning of, give one's thinking about something
    common social practices
    academic essays

evaluate to give the good and the bad points
    appraise give an opinion regarding the value of
    assess the advantages and limitations

criticize to state an opinion on the correctness or merits of an item or issue; to approve or disapprove

justify to show good reasons for; to present facts to support one's position, to provide evidence

argue (advanced-intermediate and advanced) to prove; to demonstrate based on logical reasoning or factual evidence
    refute to disprove based on logical analysis or factual evidence
    dispute to challenge; to show contradictions in a claim or argument
    prove to establish the truth of something by giving factual evidence or logical reasons

debate to advance arguments and attack counter arguments

Note. These functions might be performed orally or in writing in either academic or nonacademic settings and may be subject to different levels of formality or register appropriate to context. The list is suggestive, rather than prescriptive, of the kinds of language students might need in various contexts. See also Fulwiler, T., & Hayakawa, A. R. (1994). *The Blair Handbook.* Englewood Cliffs, NJ: Prentice Hall; Moss, A., & Holder, C. (1988). *Improving Student Writing: A Guidebook for Faculty in All Disciplines.* Dubuque, IA: Kendall/Hunt.

Table 8.2.
A Sample of Instructional Approaches for Vocabulary Development

Instructional approach	Description
Word morphology	Learners can be taught to extend their vocabulary by mixing and matching word stems, suffixes, and affixes.
Loci	This is a form of mnemonics, in which a list of vocabulary words is associated with a familiar visual image such as a room or a well-known tourist spot. Each word is associated in some way with one of the items in the visual image, and the image is used to assist in the recall of the words.
Paired associates	In this technique, which is similar to the use of loci, words in the first and second language that share some similarity in sound and meaning are associated.
Cognitive depth	Students are asked questions about specific words, including words they rhyme with and their acceptability within sentences.
Formal groupings	Students are taught to recognize basic forms of words and how they combine with certain affixes.
Word families	Students are taught how to recognize families of words with a single root.

Note. From *Language Teaching Methodology: A Textbook for Teachers* (1 ed., pp. 134–136), by D. Nunan, 1992, New York: Prentice Hall. Copyright 1992 by Pearson Education, 10 Bank Street, New York. Adapted with permission.

Other works have addressed the instructional implications of language varieties in literacy instruction: Delpit (1995), Penfield (1982), and Trueba (1984). Valadez (1981) has addressed both issues as they apply to writing. She maintains that before effective literacy instruction can be planned for language minority students, it is necessary to understand the significance of literacy outside the classroom for members of these groups. In order to motivate students to write in an alien environment (i.e., the classroom), it may be necessary, at least initially, to allow them to write in the language or dialect in which they are most comfortable (see Chapter 6). Valadez also contends that students' motivation to write must be nurtured. She concludes that

> [there are] benefits which accrue to those who discover that they can write, who feel the power that the written word gives, (as

Figure 8.3.
Taxonomy of Listening Skills

Ability to recognize the communicative functions of utterances, according to situations, participants, and goals

Ability to reconstruct or infer situations, goals, participants, and procedures

Ability to use real-world knowledge and experience to work out purposes, goals, settings, and procedures

Ability to predict outcomes from events described

Ability to infer links and connections between events

Ability to deduce causes and effects from events

Ability to distinguish between literal and implied meanings

Ability to reconstruct topics and coherent structures from ongoing discourse involving two or more speakers

Ability to adjust listening strategies to different kinds of listener purposes or goals

Ability to identify topic of lecture and follow topic development

Ability to identify relationships among units within discourse, such as major ideas

Ability to identify role of discourse markers in signaling the structure of a lecture (e.g., conjunctions, adverbs, gambits, routines)

Ability to infer relationships (e.g., cause, effect, conclusion)

Ability to detect attitude of speakers toward subject matter

Familiarity with different styles of lecture: formal, conversational, read, and unplanned

Familiarity with different registers: written versus colloquial

Ability to recognize irrelevant matter: jokes, digressions, and meanderings

Ability to recognize functions of nonverbal cues as makers of emphasis and attitude

Knowledge of classroom conventions (e.g., taking turns, requesting clarification)

Ability to recognize instructional/learner tasks (e.g., warnings, suggestions, recommendations, advice, instructions)

Note. Although Richards' (1987) inventory of listening skills represents an autonomous orientation and focus on phonological features of communication, the items here focus on social judgments.

From "Listening Comprehension," by J. C. Richards, in M. H. Long and J. C. Richards (Eds.), *Methodology in TESOL: A Book of Readings*, 1 ed. (pp. 167–169), 1987, Boston: Heinle & Heinle. Adapted with permission of Heinle, a division of Thomson Learning (www.thomsonrights.com; fax 800-730-2215).

Paulo Freire teaches, and as our graffiti writers express), and [this] will improve academic achievement in the language arts and in other areas of the school curriculum. (p. 177)

The Need for More Focus on Adult ESL Issues

Over the past several decades, much of the available research on language minority status and literacy acquisition has focused more on school-age children and adolescents than on adults (August & Hakuta, 1998). This is due in part to researchers' easier access to children and adolescents as research subjects and to the fact that this age group stays in school for long and continuous periods of time. In addition, funding for research has also focused on children. While it is likely that many issues related to second language and literacy acquisition among children are of relevance to adults, much more research needs to be done with adults. This is beginning to occur (see, for example, Adams & Burt, 2002; Bos, Comings, Cuban, & Porter, 2003; Burt, Peyton, & Adams, 2003; Condelli, Wrigley, Yoon, Seburn, & Cronen, 2003; Reder, Harris, & Seltzer, 2003; Strucker & Davidson, 2003).

A Variety of Populations

Not only is there insufficient research on adult second language learners, but much of the literature that does exist is based on studies of adults who are literate in their native languages, for example, university ESL students who have already received extensive schooling in their countries. A much smaller body of literature exists on the acquisition of language and literacy by adult second language learners in noncollege environments. Studies of a variety of populations are necessary, since groups vary according to language and cultural background, social class, immigrant status, and age (see Burt, Peyton, & Adams, 2003; Weinstein-Shr, 1995). The studies and other qualitative investigations that have been done are useful, because they describe actual literacy practices of adults and the treatment of adult language minorities by the majority. Important examples include Condelli et al.'s (2003) study of low-literate English language learners; Auerbach's (1989) and Weinstein-Shr and Quintero's (1995) work on family literacy; Miller's (1991) study of access issues faced by

Hmong adults in California; Klassen and Burnaby's (1993) work on adult immigrants in Canada; Weinstein's (1984) and Weinstein-Shr's (1993a) studies on the Hmong in Philadelphia; and Reder's (1999) cross-ethnic group analysis. Additional work on biliteracy has been published by Farr (1994), Hornberger (1989), and Hornberger and Hardman (1994).

Many issues need to be addressed on adult second language and literacy education, including language learning and the older learner, adult learners' reasons for entering and continuing in ESL programs, and learners' involvement in their education.

Language Learning and the Older Learner

What are the effects of prior schooling, life experience, and aging on literacy development? In most controlled studies to date, *older* means subjects in their teens (Hatch, 1983). Thus, the role of age and the aging process in second language learning is uncertain. Aging seems to have some relationship to language loss. However, its relationship to ability and motivation to learn a second language and to develop literacy in a first or second language (within the contexts of normal adult life) is not fully known (Wiley, 1986).

Adult Learners' Reasons for Entering and Staying in Programs

It is important to consider the reasons why adult learners enter and stay in programs. Program design and curricula need to be matched with learners' aims and needs. Learner profiles and needs assessments are essential in program, curriculum, and instructional planning. According to Wrigley and Guth (1992), adult learners have many reasons for enrolling in programs. In one survey, students were asked, "Why would an adult want to go (back) to school and learn to read and write in English?" Responses from students indicated what they wanted:

- To become more independent: to not have to rely on friends and family to translate, to not be at the mercy of kids who "interpret" school notices and report cards creatively, to be able to go to appointments alone

- To better their own and their families' economic and educational circumstances: to gain access to better jobs, to help children succeed, to teach children how to make it through the school system

- To give something back to the community: to help others, to support the school by becoming a teacher or an aide

- To feel like "somebody" and get some respect: to have others realize that they are dealing with someone who is smart and has ideas, to avoid feeling that all communication breakdown is the fault of the speaker

- To be involved in education for its own sake: to do something worthwhile for themselves (p. 10)

The National Center for the Study of Learning and Literacy (NCSALL), in a study of attendance rates among adult basic education students (native English speakers), identified three factors that positively affect participation: personal goals for attending the program, support from the teacher and fellow students in the class, and strong determination. Three negative factors mentioned were life demands (e.g., home, child care, and work obligations), relationships that impede participation, and poor determination (Comings, Parrella, & Soricone, 1999). Similar factors probably affect participation rates for adult English language learners.

Learners' Involvement in Their Education

When programs work with learners to develop a curriculum, the curriculum will better reflect the learners' needs, goals, and interests, and learners can exercise language choices. Instead of making English the sole language used in literacy instruction, programs should allow adult learners to have a say in the language of instruction, if possible. Programs for adults need to be concerned with which language provides the most immediate access to the knowledge they need and the best foundation for continued learning. The choice of one language of instruction does not preclude the development of another; it may, in fact, enhance it (Wrigley & Guth, 1992).

There are, however, some limitations to involving students in decisions about literacy curricula. As Crandall (1979) maintains, curriculum choices are constrained by the availability of trained teachers and materials, the language and literacy practices that need to be learned and the situations in which they will be used, the difficulty or ease of transferring prior literacy skills from the first to the second language, and the amount of time allowed for literacy training (see also Chisman, Wrigley, & Ewen, 1993).

Conclusion

As Dumont (1972) observed many years ago, in the absence of linguistically and culturally appropriate instruction, "education for most students is an either-or proposition: Participate by teacher-school established norms or withdraw. It is being able to speak English or be silence" (p. 368). If students are to benefit from educational programs, they must also have opportunities to develop their literacy skills by building on their linguistic, literacy, and cultural resources.

To develop children's and adults' literacy, educators need to understand which aspects of instruction reflect the autonomous orientation (focusing on learner characteristics), the social practices orientation (focusing on language in social and cultural contexts), and the ideological orientation (focusing on systemic inequities). They also need to keep in mind that language and literacy development in schools is always carried out in specific social contexts involving specific literacy practices that differentially build on students' prior knowledge and affect their motivation, involvement, and success. Because much of what falls under the rubric of *academic language proficiency* involves academic socialization to specific literacy practices, we need to concentrate explicitly on those practices rather than on levels of proficiency that are not specific to any particular context.

A rationale for building upon students' first language can be provided in relatively straightforward terms. Students need to develop school-based literacy in a language that they understand if they are to keep pace academically with their peers who already understand the language of instruction. If they must spend all of their instructional time learning the dominant language of instruction before they are allowed to study academic content, they will fall behind those who already understand the language of instruction. For language minority children and adults, the native language usually provides the most immediate means for participating in school literacy practices. While school literacy, content knowledge, and other language skills are being developed in the native language, students can also learn the second language. When their oral language is sufficiently developed, they can develop academic language skills in the second language, if they have practiced parallel activities in their first language. Reframing the issues in this way shifts the focus from academic language as an autonomous entity to language and literacy practices as context-specific activities.

Further Reading

Martin-Jones, M., & Romaine, S. (1986). Semilingualism: A half-baked theory of communicative competence. *Applied Linguistics, 7*(1), 26–38.

This article raises concerns related to those of Edelsky et al. (1983).

Rivera, C. (Ed.). (1984). *Language proficiency and academic achievement.* Clevedon, England: Multilingual Matters.

This collection includes responses by a number of well-known researchers to Cummins's earlier work. Contributions by Cummins, Saville-Troike, and Wald have particular relevance for the issues raised in this chapter.

The Standards Movement: Considerations for Language Minority Students

In recent years, many educators, parents, and politicians have argued for high academic standards across the curriculum for all students, particularly in the area of English language arts. There is also a common perception, as noted in Chapter 5, that recent educational standards and student performance levels have fallen dramatically from those of the past. This drop is largely because higher standards for literacy are being applied to larger numbers of students, or, stated differently, literacy expectations tend to inflate over time, because higher expectations are being applied to the entire population rather than to just a small elite portion (Resnick & Resnick, 1988).

Nevertheless, serious problems exist for many people as the result of "savage inequalities," to borrow Kozol's (1991) phrase, among groups based on their educational opportunities. Many language minority students, particularly those who are recent immigrants, tend to be located in schools and districts where problems of inequity persist (McDonnell & Hill, 1993). Thus, high standards for literacy and academic achievement should not be seen as a panacea for what may be a breakdown in the political will to provide equitable opportunities for all to learn.

Similarly, since the publication in 1983 of the highly publicized *A Nation at Risk: The Imperative for Educational Reform* (National Commission on Excellence in Education), there has been considerable ado over the purported lower achievement of students in the United States compared to those of other countries. Such comparisons, however, are often dubious because, for one of many reasons, they ignore local contexts and the important characteristics of the specific groups being compared (Berliner

& Biddle, 1995; Bracey, 1997). When these differences are noted, language minority students' lack of English literacy is often blamed for the low comparative performance, and educators are blamed for not promoting higher standards.

This chapter considers the implications on language minority students of the recent push for English language standards. The chapter identifies potential areas of focus in language development for which standards may be developed and identifies some potential difficulties that can result when the formal curriculum is overly prescribed and other factors that influence learning are ignored.

Language Minority Students and the Law

The U.S. Supreme Court has recognized the importance of English literacy for language minorities but with the important qualification that language minority students need to learn English not only for its own sake, but also because it is the language in which school subjects are taught. This fact was recognized in the landmark decision of *Lau v. Nichols* (1974), where the U.S. Supreme Court concluded,

> Basic English skills are at the very core of what these public schools teach. Imposition of a requirement that, before a child can effectively participate in the educational program, he must have already acquired those basic skills is to make a mockery of public education. We know that those who do not understand English are certain to find their classroom experiences wholly incomprehensible and in no way meaningful.

The fundamental concern is that students cannot be expected to participate in content instruction taught in English if they have not had opportunities to learn the language of instruction to promote the further development of literacy and learning at school. It follows that beyond setting general academic standards, there is also a need for *developmental standards* for learning the language of school and *professional standards* for those who teach. Developmental language and academic content standards attempt to make explicit what students are expected to know at different levels of development. Standards are only effective, however, when they are both challenging and achievable, and when they are part of a well-defined curriculum that incorporates a developmental perspective and provides a plan for articulating the developmental language curriculum with the rest of the academic curriculum.

Ensuring Equity

In the past, when school dropout rates were much higher, maintaining high standards was relatively easy, because they were applied only to the small section of the population that completed school (Resnick & Resnick, 1988). Today, the good news is that there are higher expectations for all students. However, if these standards are to be equitably met, they need to be developed for all segments of the population and not just a privileged portion of it. Toward that end, standards need to be scrutinized to ensure that they are not implicitly or unwittingly biased.

All students develop their language and literacy skills within the social contexts of their homes, communities, schools, and the larger society. An understanding of learners' home and community language and literacy practices can usefully inform instruction at school. However, when teachers are unaware of the language and literacy practices of the home and community, students may be at a disadvantage. Teachers' expectations regarding language are almost always based on their own socialization and formal training. As noted in Chapter 8, language minority students do not always understand these expectations, unless they are made explicit. This is equally true for English language learners and for native English speakers whose variety of language differs from that taught in the classroom (Delpit, 1992, 1995). Thus, clearer expectations are beneficial to all students. Failure to clarify expectations results in the *communicative burden* being placed on the student (Lippi-Green, 1997). To the extent that formal standards help to make expected language behaviors explicit for both the child and the adult teacher, they are useful.

However, given the complexities and subtleties of language behavior, much of learning is implicit and contextual; there is a limit to what can be taught formally. Thus, language minority students need access to and interaction with students and adults who can model and extend their learning. Merely requiring that language minority students meet the same academic standards as students who already speak English is not enough, unless they have an equal chance to use and develop their English in a wide variety of social contexts, including those at school and in the classroom.

Most children, regardless of their language background, know something about the uses and functions of print before they come to school. Nevertheless, school is where most children acquire and develop their literacy, and most schools in the United States use only English as the medium of instruction. In schools that do not have bilingual programs, language minority students face a major developmental challenge with regard to English in that they must use it in a variety of contexts, including those directly related to academic subjects.

Given the national push for higher standards for all students, this question may be asked: To what extent do standards adequately reflect the language needs of all students? Students come to schools with different resources and needs. Language minority students can be disadvantaged by standards if their home and community linguistic and cultural resources are ignored or misunderstood, or if they must compete with students who have systematic or privileged advantages over them. Thus, standards must be equitable for all students. To do this, schools seeking to promote standard English and English language arts need to develop standards with an understanding of the specific linguistic and cultural resources all students bring with them to school.

Failure to take the resources that students bring with them into consideration can result in an implicit *monocultural bias,* whereby members of the dominant culture come to believe that their standards and practices represent common sense or universal norms for behavior. Monocultural bias has been defined as "the practice of catering to the dominant or mainstream culture, providing second class treatment or no special consideration at all to persons of non-mainstream cultures" (Hass, 1992, p. 161). Monocultural bias can create a false image of deficiency for language minority students as they enter the educational process. As a result, they may be labeled "at risk" even before they enter the system.

Finally, schools need to be mindful of the interpersonal relations between the language minority groups and the native English speakers; these relations can affect the language minority students' ability to acquire the English they need to interact with their peers and teachers and to perform academic tasks. These interpersonal factors include the following:

- The proportionate balance of language minority students to native speakers of English in the school

- The presence of students who already know English with whom language minority students can interact

- The nature and quality of the interaction between language minority students and native English speakers in the school

- The relative status of language minority students and native English speakers

- The extent to which language minority students are stigmatized, based either on their language backgrounds or on their lack of English proficiency

- The extent to which language minority students are fully integrated into the social life of the school

In schools where the majority of students are of language minority backgrounds, promoting English literacy is a major challenge. In such schools, the English as a second language (ESL) curriculum may face the same problem as programs for English as a foreign language (EFL): Finding opportunities for learners to interact with native English speakers is limited. In schools where the majority of students are native speakers of English, administrators and teachers face a different kind of challenge: breaking down social barriers, often rooted in prejudice, between those who are learning English and those who already know it.

Standards for English Language and Literacy Development

Advocates of national standards argue that such standards would provide a clear basis for comparing student progress in one district with national norms. Local student demographics, resources, and materials, however, vary greatly across the nation. Developing standards that are custom-tailored for the local district has obvious advantages, because the standards may be more sensitive to the local context; however, comparisons of local standards with intranational or intrastate standards cannot be made without some difficulty.

Two model standards are reviewed in this section: *Standards for the English Language Arts*, developed by the International Reading Association (IRA) and the National Council of Teachers of English (NCTE) and *ESL Standards for Pre-K–12 Students*, developed by Teachers of English to Speakers of Other Languages (TESOL).

IRA/NCTE Standards for the English Language Arts

The International Reading Association (IRA) and the National Council of Teachers of English (NCTE) have developed the Standards for the English Language Arts, which is among the more influential publications in the field of English language teaching (see Figure 9.1). Although not developed specifically for language minority students, "the vision guiding these standards is that all students must have the opportunities and resources to develop the language skills they need to pursue life's goals and to participate fully as informed, productive members of society" (IRA/NCTE, 1996, p. 3). By acknowledging that literacy development begins in the home with a variety of literacy-related activities and by emphasizing that schools have an important role in building that knowledge, the IRA/NCTE vision reflects a constructivist approach: Effective teaching builds on the skills and experiences that students bring with them. Importantly, IRA/NCTE recommend,

> The standards provide ample room for the innovation and creativity essential to teaching and learning. They are not prescriptions for particular curriculum or instruction.
>
> Although we present these standards as a list, we want to emphasize that they are not distinct and separable; they are, in fact, interrelated and should be considered as a whole. (p. 3)

Figure 9.1.
IRA/NCTE Standards for the English Language Arts

1. Students read a wide range of print and nonprint texts to build an understanding of texts, of themselves, and of the cultures of the United States and the world; to acquire new information; to respond to the needs and demands of society and the workplace; and for personal fulfillment. Among these texts are fiction and nonfiction, classic and contemporary works.

2. Students read a wide range of literature from many periods in many genres to build an understanding of the many dimensions (e.g., philosophical, ethical, aesthetic) of human experience.

3. Students apply a wide range of strategies to comprehend, interpret, evaluate, and appreciate texts. They draw on their prior experience, their interactions with other readers and writers, their knowledge of word meaning and of other texts, their word identification strategies, and their understanding of textual features (e.g., sound-letter correspondence, sentence structure, context, graphics).

4. Students adjust their use of spoken, written, and visual language (e.g., conventions, style, vocabulary) to communicate effectively with a variety of audiences and for different purposes.

5. Students employ a wide range of strategies as they write and use different writing process elements appropriately to communicate with different audiences for a variety of purposes.

6. Students apply knowledge of language structure, language conventions (e.g., spelling and punctuation), media techniques, figurative language, and genre to create, critique, and discuss print and nonprint texts.

7. Students conduct research on issues and interests by generating ideas and questions, and by posing problems. They gather, evaluate, and synthesize data from a variety of sources (e.g., print and nonprint texts, artifacts, people) to communicate their discoveries in ways that suit their purpose and audience.

8. Students use a variety of technological and informational resources (e.g., libraries, databases, computer networks, video) to gather and synthesize information and to create and communicate knowledge.

9. Students develop an understanding of and respect for diversity in language use, patterns, and dialects across cultures, ethnic groups, geographic regions, and social roles.

10. Students whose first language is not English make use of their first language to develop competency in the English language arts and to develop understanding of content across the curriculum.

11. Students participate as knowledgeable, reflective, creative, and critical members of literacy communities.

12. Students use spoken, written, and visual language to accomplish their own purposes (e.g., for learning, enjoyment, persuasion, and the exchange of information).

Note. From *Standards for the English Language Arts* (p. 3), by International Reading Association and National Council of Teachers of English, 1996, Newark, DE, and Urbana, IL: Authors. Copyright 1996 by the International Reading Association and the National Council of Teachers of English. Reprinted with permission.

This qualification is significant, because students are often evaluated by performance standards that are discrete and separable.

Standards and Educational Equity

The IRA/NCTE *Standards for the English Language Arts* appropriately notes limits to what can be expected from these, or any, standards by themselves. It is not enough for schools to develop challenging standards; they need to take measures to ensure that the standards are implemented equitably so that *all* students receive "equal educational opportunities and meet high expectations for performance" (IRA/NCTE, 1996, p. 9). Specifically, all students must be able to learn how to learn, and they must be provided equal access to school resources, adequately trained and knowledgeable teachers, and safe, well-equipped schools. Consider, for example, Standard 8: "Students use a variety of technological and informational resources (e.g., libraries, databases, computer networks, video) to gather and synthesize information and to create and communicate knowledge" (IRA/NCTE, p. 3). If all students are to have an equal opportunity to achieve this standard, they all must have access to comparable libraries and technology, and their teachers must be comparably prepared to use them.

If these conditions are not met, there is a danger that the standards may become little more than gatekeeping devices that serve to push out rather than fully educate underperforming students. This *New York Times* article points to a link between school dropouts in New York City and high standards:

> Growing numbers of students—most of them struggling academically—are being pushed out of New York City's school system and classified under bureaucratic categories that hide their failure to graduate. Officially the city's dropout rate hovers around 20 percent. But critics say that if the students who are pushed out were included, that number could be 25 to 30 percent.
>
> The city data make it impossible to determine just how many students are being pushed out, where they are going and what becomes of them. But experts who have examined the statistics and administrators of high school equivalency programs say that

the number of "pushouts" seems to be growing, with students shunted out at ever-younger ages.

Those students represent the unintended consequence of the effort to hold schools accountable for raising standards: As students are being spurred to new levels of academic achievement and required to pass stringent Regents exams to get their high school diplomas, many schools are trying to get rid of those who may tarnish the schools' statistics by failing to graduate on time. Even though state law gives students the right to stay in high school until they are 21, many students are being counseled, or even forced, to leave long before then. (Lewin & Medina, 2003)

Among immigrant students, older entrants—students who arrive in the United States in their late teens—are at a particular risk since many have not had full access to education in their home countries (see Chapter 5). Because of their prior lack of educational opportunities, these late-entrant students may have great difficulty in trying to learn enough English to complete their graduation requirements (see Mace-Matluck, Alexander-Kasparik, & Queen, 1998). Adolescent students with limited schooling present significant curricular challenges for both secondary schools and providers of adult education. Programs that lead to meaningful educational outcomes for these students need to be developed and articulated.

Standards and Diversity

For ESL educators, an issue of major interest that the IRA/NCTE standards touch upon is the importance of helping students understand and appreciate linguistic and cultural diversity. Standard 9, for example, says that students will "develop an understanding of and respect for diversity in language use, patterns, and dialects across cultures, ethnic groups, geographic regions, and social roles" (1996, p. 3). The IRA/NCTE standards do not elaborate on how this understanding and respect might actually be instilled. However, the recognition that linguistic and cultural awareness is a necessary part of public school education represents a positive contribution to the development of standards and is consistent with what advocates of language awareness programs propose (see Adger, 1998;

Adger & Wolfram, 2000; Ramírez, Wiley, de Klerk, & Lee, 1999; Wolfram, 1994; Wolfram, Adger, & Christian, 1999).

One issue that emerges relates how language diversity, even among varieties of English, should be addressed. Obviously, schools must promote standard academic English, but what stance should they take toward other varieties of English? Wolfram (1994) argues that it is important for ESL students to develop an understanding of language variations in English for the following reasons:

- The standard version of English provided in most ESL curricula aims unrealistically at a dialect-neutral variety of English identified as the General American Standard.

- ESL learners are surrounded by a rich variety of dialects, including vernacular dialects of English spoken by those who live in economically impoverished conditions.

- ESL learners' socialization in American culture may lead them to adopt the same uncharitable, biased opinion of vernaculars as that so often found among native speakers of English.

- ESL learners may, in fact, speak vernacular varieties of their native languages that are comparable in status to vernacular dialects of English.

- ESL programs have much to gain from adopting a curriculum that includes a healthy understanding of language variation. (p. 85)

The Role of the Home Language

The question may be asked, how important is it to recognize language minority students' home languages? IRA/NCTE Standard 10 addresses this question: "Students whose first language is not English make use of their first language to develop competency in the English language arts and to develop understanding of content across the curriculum" (1996, p. 3). This standard is consistent with constructivist theory, which holds that children build on their prior knowledge and experience. There is a danger, however, that standards that acknowledge the role of the home language can become meaningless declarations unless the schools that subscribe to them have strong multicultural and bilingual programs.

Note also that language use at home may be very different from language expectations in the school (Heath, 1983). In both conventional English-only instruction and bilingual programs, students are not only tapping into their knowledge of their home languages but are further developing them in ways that may be different from their uses in the home. For many students who speak regional and social varieties of language that are different from that of the school, there may be little correspondence between the two.

TESOL's ESL Standards for Pre-K–12 Students

The IRA/NCTE *Standards for the English Language Arts* represents a major advance over previous ones in recognizing the needs of language minority students and language diversity more broadly. However, these standards were not developed specially for language minority learners. To address the specific needs of English as a second language (ESL) learners, the international association Teachers of English to Speakers of Other Languages (TESOL) published *ESL Standards for Pre-K–12 Students* (1997). TESOL offers these reasons why ESL standards are needed:

- Schools and communities throughout the United States are facing increased linguistic and cultural diversity.

- ESOL students vary greatly in proficiency level and academic needs.

- The *ESL Standards* describe the language skills necessary for social and academic purposes.

- The *ESL Standards* provide the bridge to general education standards expected of all students in the United States. (pp. 2–3)

TESOL's standards view learners' English language development as part of a larger goal of achieving grade-level standards. These standards must also be viewed within a broader educational vision that values the development of the learners' native language as well as English (p. 3):

- Effective education for ESOL students includes nativelike levels of proficiency in English.

- Effective education for ESOL students includes the maintenance and promotion of ESOL students' native languages in school and community contexts.

- All educational personnel assume responsibility for the education of ESOL students.

- Effective education also calls for comprehensive provision of first-rate services and full access to those services by all students.

- Knowledge of more than one language and culture is advantageous for all students.

TESOL's stress on the value of learners knowing more than one language and culture affirms the importance of building upon students' knowledge as a resource. Note, too, the emphasis on maintaining and developing the learners' native languages in school and community contexts, a standard that affirms the need for bilingual education programs. Furthermore, TESOL places the responsibility of educating ESL students on the entire school rather than on only the ESL faculty and establishes native-like proficiency in English as a goal. This high threshold of expectation is one that needs to take into account the ages and prior educational experiences of the students.

TESOL (1997) bases its standards on eight principles drawn from research on first and second language acquisition (pp. 6–8):

1. Language is functional.

2. Language varies.

3. Language learning is cultural learning.

4. Language acquisition is a long-term process.

5. Language acquisition occurs through meaningful use and interaction.

6. Language processes develop interdependently.

7. Native language proficiency contributes to second language acquisition.

8. Bilingualism is an individual and societal asset.

Figure 9.2. TESOL's Goals for ESOL Learners

Goal 1: To use English to communicate in social settings

Standards for Goal 1

Students will

    1. use English to participate in social interaction

    2. interact in, through, and with spoken and written English for personal expression and enjoyment

    3. use learning strategies to extend their communicative competence

Goal 2: To use English to achieve academically in all content areas

Standards for Goal 2

Students will

    1. use English to interact in the classroom

    2. use English to obtain, process, construct, and provide subject matter information in spoken and written form

    3. use appropriate learning strategies to construct and apply academic knowledge

Goal 3: To use English in socially and culturally appropriate ways

Standards for Goal 3

Students will

    1. use the appropriate language variety, register, and genre according to audience, purpose, and setting

    2. use nonverbal communication appropriate to audience, purpose, and setting

    3. use appropriate learning strategies to extend their sociolinguistic and sociocultural competence

Note. From *ESL Standards for Pre-K–12 Students* (pp. 8–10), by Teachers of English to Speakers of Other Languages, Inc., 1997, Alexandria, VA: Author. Copyright 1997 by Teachers of English to Speakers of Other Languages, Inc. Reprinted with permission.

TESOL has established three broad goals that relate to the social, academic, and cultural uses of English (see Figure 9.2). Three standards under each goal further delineate the goal.

Note that the social and cultural aspects of acquiring English in Goals 1 and 3 are distinguished from the academic aspects identified in Goal 2.

Nevertheless, it is important to recognize that the academic use of English is sensitive to social and cultural context (see Chapter 8).

Within the field of ESL, considerable progress has been made in the development of functional and communicative syllabuses that would help to further delineate Goals 1 and 3. However, there has been less delineation of academic language functions (see Chapter 8). Works on academic ESL have tended to emphasize the importance of vocabulary, content knowledge, and basic academic skills (Goldenberg, 1991). In addition to our rudimentary knowledge of "instructional conversations"—that is, oral interactions between the teacher and student—we need to know much more about the complexities of instructional registers, student response registers, and what might be termed *speech acts in academic contexts* as they relate to specific content areas.

Recall that one of the reasons that standards are needed is that they place students' English language development needs in the context of their overall academic goal of attaining grade-level standards. To address this need, TESOL (1997) has configured its standards by levels of language proficiency (beginning, intermediate, advanced) and by grade-level clusters. TESOL reasons that using grade-level clusters for ESL parallels accepted practice for other content areas of the curriculum and allows for the alignment of ESL standards with other subject areas. This in turn helps to facilitate collaboration on curriculum planning across grade levels within the cluster. The grade-level clusters loosely correspond to the common cognitive and age divisions of schooling: elementary, middle, and secondary. This approach also assumes that students build on their prior knowledge and that they develop greater proficiency with language as they grow older. Thus, more progress indicators are added for older students with more advanced levels of English proficiency.

Considerations Regarding the Use of Standards

The use of standards, whether for English language arts or for English as a second language, can be a positive tool in achieving equitable instruction for language minority students, particularly when instruction is focused on making academic language explicit and comprehensible to learners. However, the history of curriculum planning suggests some basis for caution in the implementation of standards. The push for standards, while based on a concern for accountability, can unduly shift to overly prescribed curricula. Thus, caution is needed to maintain a balanced focus between the instructional and learning processes and student performance.

In reviewing various standards, such as those developed by IRA/NCTE and TESOL, some may object to the general nature of the standards, especially given the level of detail that could be included. However, keeping standards more general rather than overly specific is wise.

Many years ago, John Dewey (1938/1963) admonished against a heavily prescribed curriculum. He and others, such as Stenhouse (as cited in Redduck & Hopkins, 1985), warned that the attempt to overly control curricular content and student behavior could result in an instrumentalization of the curriculum. Similarly, Barnes (1976), Wells (1986), and, more recently, neo-Vygotskyans, have argued that opportunities for students to engage in open-ended exploratory talk is an essential component of the learning process. Such an element, however, is difficult to regiment and assess. In an effort to promote accountability, some educators are inclined to emphasize only those aspects of student knowledge and behavior that can be easily and discretely measured. Reducing the entire curriculum to only things that can be measured and tested can send the wrong message to learners by making them believe that the "only valid learning is that which takes place when they are engaged in teacher-prescribed tasks" (Barnes, 1976, p. 93).

Others argue against overly prescribing the second language curriculum for the reason that the totality of what needs to be learned through language acquisition cannot be reduced to any isolated set of items, however convenient for instruction that may be (see Chapter 8). As Tumposky (1984) has noted,

> The equation of the knowledge of a language with the mastery of isolated, discrete items would seem to have been disproven by the acknowledged failure of certain methods, such as audiolingual-

ism, which focused almost exclusively on the minutiae of language's building blocks. (p. 303)

Tumposky (1984) further notes that the mastery of a language is far different from the mastery of other subjects such as geometry, in which one concept must be mastered before the next: "Language is creative and, in a certain sense, unpredictable; we as teachers cannot predict that a given set of inculcated behaviors will later be relevant to a student or will necessarily occur in a similar linguistic or extra-linguistic context" (p. 304).

The challenge for the language teacher is to achieve through conscious planning what nature does naturally (Dewey, 1938/1963). An adult teacher may lose sight of how different his or her own model of the world and instructional expectations are from those of a young student (Wells, 1986). No matter how much the curriculum reflects the advanced planning of curriculum designers, textbook writers, and teachers, it is still experienced differently by the learners. Dewey argues that for children, learning involves a continuous process of reconstructing experience. Thus, learning experiences cannot be reduced to the standards of the curriculum designer, because students interpret and reconstruct those plans. To produce outcomes in actual student behavior, instructional plans must be sensitive to how they are understood and reconstructed by the students (Barnes, 1976; Redduck & Hopkins, 1985; Wiley, 1991b).

Making Standards Comprehensible to Students

Even when learners understand English, once they arrive at school or at an adult education center, many experience the social uses of language as new or alien, because how that language is used in the classroom may be very different from how it is used at home (Heath, 1983). For this reason, the instructional process and expectations for appropriate language use in education have to be clear and comprehensible. Standards can do much to help language minority individuals, including those who speak so-called nonstandard dialects of English (Delpit, 1995); nevertheless, there still remains much that is implicit within the language curriculum, no matter how much we attempt to make it clear. Consequently, there is a need to examine both the standards and the instructional processes for potential bias. If certain groups of students consistently fail to achieve a standard, the standard itself should be considered questionable.

Conclusion

What then is the appropriate role of ESL standards in the curriculum? To answer this question, it is necessary to distinguish between an overly specified curriculum and careful planning. Performance-based standards are largely concerned with the specification of content and explicit displays of student knowledge and abilities. Although it is important to make expectations clear and accountable, we must be careful not to reduce every learning opportunity and event into a specific performance. Standards are important tools for curriculum planning, but in using them, we should not lose sight of the students' attempts to understand not only what they are expected to do, but why they are expected to do it. Moreover, instructional planning must also focus on the social and cultural processes and contexts of teaching and learning and on the issues related to equitable instruction for a diverse student population. Many of these issues have been identified in the standards reviewed in this chapter. The responsibility for appropriately implementing them must be developed through comprehensive teacher education and administrative training in both college and university programs and nurtured by professional development within school districts and local programs.

Further Reading

Florez, M. C. (2002, March). *An annotated bibliography of content standards for adult ESL.* From National Center for ESL Literacy Education Web site: www.cal.org/ncle/constanbib.htm

This online bibliography annotates and links to documents on issues of content standards and accountability. Some documents include information on performance standards, i.e., what learners need to do to demonstrate proficiency in a content standard.

Florez, M. C. (2002, March). *An annotated bibliography of program standards for adult ESL.* From National Center for ESL Literacy Education Web site: www.cal.org/ncle/prgstanbib.htm

This online bibliography annotates and links to documents that describe program standards developed by national associations, states, and literacy programs. *Program standards* are defined as the elements of development and delivery that reflect effective and efficient program performance. In other words, program standards are all the issues that programs need to address to provide the context and resources that support learner achievement.

Teachers of English to Speakers of Other Languages, Inc. (TESOL; 2003). *Standards for adult education ESL programs.* Alexandria, VA: Author.

This book describes the key features of nine standards for program quality in adult ESL programs and includes a self-review instrument for program staff to use to assess the quality of their program and to plan improvements. (Available from TESOL, 700 South Washington Street, Suite 200, Alexandria, VA 22314; www.tesol.org)

10

The Impact of Literacy Policies and Practices on Language Minority Learners

What emerges as the key question in examining literacy theories, practices, and research is not whether they recognize variable and contextual aspects of literacy, but whether they consider how . . . diversity positions learners, teachers, and researchers with respect to existing inequities and relations of domination and subordination. (Auerbach, 1991, p. 80)

Policy discussions regarding the education of immigrants and other language minority groups often focus on student outcomes, and ultimately, the financial costs and benefits to the country. Less frequently is public discussion centered on the impact of policy—or its absence—on language minorities themselves.

Consider, for example, the way that public and educational policy issues affecting refugees have been framed. In the early 1980s, a congressional fact-finding committee on refugee affairs met with educators and health-care providers to assess the impact of refugee resettlement on states and communities. A federal policy was initiated to reduce the cost of refugee resettlement to the U.S. government. Subsequently, there was a shift toward English-language and job-training programs designed to get refugees off of public assistance and into entry-level jobs (Wiley, Wrigley, & Burr, 1983).

The impact of the new policy on refugees was considerable: It meant reduced social, health, and educational support. For those who had successfully acquired entry-level jobs, it meant that they would earn only minimum wage. For those with families to support, it often meant the loss of medical treatment for their family members. Thus, the impact of the policy changes on people was increased marginalization and a greater struggle to survive (Wiley, Wrigley, & Burr, 1983).

This chapter reviews societal attitudes, social and educational policies, and pedagogical practices and their impact on language minority groups in the United States. It attempts to locate these attitudes, policies, and practices within the three orientations toward literacy education and research and suggests areas in which further research and reflection on policies and practices related to literacy are needed.

As discussed in Chapter 3, the three orientations (autonomous, social practices, and ideological) differ in several ways: in their emphasis on individual versus group factors, in their emphasis on intergroup power relations, and in their interpretation of the roles of the social scientist and the teacher in the processes of conducting research and teaching (Tollefson, 1991). In Chapters 3 and 7, the influence of these orientations on general literacy theory and ethnographic research, respectively, is noted. This chapter further addresses their implications for educational practice.

The Impact of Societal Attitudes Toward Language Minorities

As discussed in Chapter 5, research on the processes of second language and literacy acquisition has, historically, emphasized individual motivation. Such analyses are consistent with the autonomous orientation. Over the past 2 decades, a number of important studies have contributed to our understanding of societal and economic factors affecting second language and literacy acquisition.

Perdue's (1984) investigation of adult immigrant workers in Europe provided clues on the impact of social obstacles facing adults trying to learn and use a second language. Perdue found that intolerant language attitudes and expectations held by the majority often discouraged adult learners, particularly those of lower socioeconomic status, from attempting to use the language they were trying to learn. He observed that many speakers of a dominant language expected immigrants and language minorities to use the dominant language, and more importantly, to use it as well as a native speaker. Perdue concluded that the inability of language minority adults to do so reinforced the language prejudices of those among the majority who stigmatized the nonnative speakers. Sensing prejudice, the nonnative speakers avoided situations where they might feel less than competent, thereby losing opportunities to use, practice, and experiment with the second language.

In situations with members of the dominant language group, language minorities are frequently in a subordinated social position. Klassen and Burnaby's (1993) analysis of Canadian immigrants and Miller's (1991) study of Hmong refugees in the United States show how social and ideological issues are significantly related to second language and literacy acquisition. Miller explored institutional barriers that discourage adult immigrant students from participating in classroom practices that they perceive as alien and threatening. These studies indicate a need for additional research on how the language attitudes of dominant groups affect the motivation of language minority groups to acquire and use second language and literacy. Similarly, there is a need to study teachers' attitudes toward language minority students to see how their attitudes affect the students' motivation to learn.

Other studies have considered social class tensions that immigrant groups bring with them from their native countries. Klassen and Burnaby (1993) noted tensions among Central American students based on social class conflicts that existed prior to immigration and reappeared in Canadian ESL classrooms. Their work indicates that we need to know more about students than just their national origin and the dominant language in their home country. There are often differences in social class, language background, and ethnicity within the new immigrant communities that are important to understand.

The Impact of Policies and Resources on Adult Immigrants

Immigration and education policies and practices, along with the availability of resources and immigrants' difficulty in accessing them, have profound impacts on language minority adults. This section briefly considers some of these policies, practices, and resources.

Immigration Policies and Educational Resources

Historically, the United States has imported labor for some of its labor needs. Prior to the Civil War, Southern agriculture depended on imported, involuntary (enslaved) laborers and their descendants, particularly in the cotton and tobacco industries. There was no upward mobility for these workers, and mandatory illiteracy, or "compulsory ignorance" laws, were enacted. In California, Chinese immigrants, who were instrumental in developing the state's agriculture, became targets of exclusionary immigration policies in the 1880s and were subsequently replaced by Japanese and Filipino workers, who experienced a similar fate and were ultimately replaced by a predominantly Mexican labor force. As each group toiled in the fields, their children were all too often discriminated against or—at best—relegated to inferior schools (Weinberg, 1997).

Today, the United States benefits from the importation of foreign labor. In fact, some believe that most of the future growth of the U.S. workforce will come from the ranks of immigrant groups (Wrigley, Richer, Martinson, Kubo, & Strawn, 2003). Interestingly, today's immigrants come from opposite ends of the economic scale and educational ladder: While many of our lowest paying jobs are performed by immigrants with little formal education, many highly paid, technical jobs are performed by workers from other countries (U.S. Census Bureau, 2000). Those at the upper end of the economic scale have received most of their education elsewhere, and their educational costs to this country are negligible. In contrast, those at the lower end of the scale have extensive needs for English language and literacy development, as well as job-skills training (Greenberg, Macías, Rhodes, & Chan, 2001). Currently, however, the opportunities for such training are limited. For example, few educational opportunities exist for immigrant and migrant agricultural workers with little formal education; as a result, there is little in the way of job mobility for them (Wiley, 2001).

The amnesty program in the middle and late 1980s illustrates the impact of inadequate resources for immigrants. Under the 1986 Immigration Reform and Control Act (IRCA), undocumented immigrants and refugees who met certain conditions were entitled to legal permanent resident status that would eventually lead to U.S. citizenship. These conditions included participating in 40–60 hours of ESL and U.S. history classes (Spener, 1994). Thousands of people responded, swamping adult education programs with new students that the programs "were not adequately prepared to serve. . . . Regardless of its quality, 60 hours of instruction . . . is an impossibly short amount of time to achieve significant gains in spoken English proficiency, much less English literacy" (Spener, pp. 5–6). Consequently, students who had completed the program often sought further education; many had lacked opportunities for schooling in their native countries and as therefore lacked a foundation in literacy.

Today, nearly 2 decades after the amnesty program, the problem of inadequate resources persists in ESL programs. An analysis sponsored by the Center for Law and Social Policy (Wrigley et al., 2003) reviewed existing ESL and workplace literacy programs and found them inadequate in meeting the needs of adult immigrant students. The report details serious limitations in program design and delivery and in the requirements for eligibility that often restrict participation, thereby working against the efforts of adult learners to attain equitable employment and self-sufficiency. In addition to a lack of language and job training programs, immigrants face difficulties accessing available classes because of constraints such as time, transportation, and childcare needs (Greenberg et al., 2001). As a result of these limitations and constraints, immigrants are likely to remain among the poorest of the working poor.

The Language of Instruction

Additionally, the choice of the language of instruction has an impact on individuals wanting to learn English language and literacy. Which languages are used for instruction depends on a number of factors, including the availability of native language teachers and materials and the goals of the students. There are sound pedagogical reasons for developing literacy in the native language when learning English:

If an individual who is literate in his or her mother tongue is more likely to become a proficient speaker, reader, and writer of English than one who is illiterate in the mother tongue, and if in turn such proficiency and literacy in the English language increases that individual's potential to be a skilled and productive worker in the U.S. economy, then a rationale for biliteracy as both an educational goal and an instructional approach for language minority adults can be conscientiously made. (Spener, 1994, p. 7)

Spener (1994) further observes that in spite of their strong motivation to learn English, immigrants working in low-skilled and semiskilled jobs are often required to learn under conditions that are far from conducive for learning a new language.

In addition to the difficulty of finding time to study English each day after family and work responsibilities are taken care of, both immigrants and U.S.-born limited English speakers too often find themselves working low-skill, low-wage jobs where they either work primarily alongside other immigrants (with whom they interact in their shared native language or in their limited English) or at jobs where they are required to engage in only limited verbal communication with anyone. The potential for them to acquire English informally through interaction with native English speakers is thus limited as well. Denying access to job-related training by making it available only to literate, proficient English speakers (native or not) only compounds the problem of lack of contact with English by making it more difficult for language minority adults to break into higher skill jobs where they are more likely to interact with native English speakers. (p. 8)

The Impact of Policies and Resources on Language Minority Youth

The next generation of language minority workers is now enrolled in U.S. schools. These students, along with a large number of English-speaking students, are frequently receiving an inadequate education in under-funded schools with scarce resources and inappropriate educational programs. In this regard, McDonnell and Hill (1993) note, "Problems of these districts are geographically localized" (p. 107). They observe that Latino and African American youth are heavily concentrated in a small number of urban areas. For example, nearly 75% of all Latino immigrant youth are concentrated in just 11 cities, and 40% of all African Americans live in 5 cities (Chicago, Houston, Los Angeles, Miami/Dade County, and New York) that together educate nearly 1 in 20 U.S. students of school age (McDonnell & Hill). While language minorities remain largely concentrated in urban areas, over the past 10 years, a significant number of immigrants have migrated to less urbanized areas of the United States (Wrigley et al., 2003), where educators have previously had little experience meeting the needs of immigrant youth.

National agendas fail to address the special needs of students in these areas. As McDonnell and Hill (1993) note, national agendas for school reform, which began during the presidency of George H.W. Bush (1989–1993), fail because they assume that schools have enough money "to improve their own performance, if only efforts are properly focused by means of goals, standards, and accountability measures" (p. 107). The current push for national standards and accountability measures may increase the perception of widespread educational failure and of a national literacy crisis, because the resources are not available to make meaningful reforms possible. McDonnell and Hill also note that school efforts have not contemplated the creation of new curricula for students who cannot profit from full-time instruction in English, nor do they remedy the shortages of teachers and texts that can provide a bridge between immigrant students' native languages and English.

Since 1998, problems facing K–12 immigrant students have been exacerbated by the antibilingual education movement, manifested in California's Proposition 227, Arizona's Proposition 203, and Massachusetts' Question Two. These propositions have resulted in the reduction of instructional options available to educators (Ovando & Wiley, 2003; Wiley, 2004; Wiley & Wright, in press). From a policy perspective, there has been a partial return to the sink-or-swim, English-only approaches of the past, which made little distinction between the needs of English-speaking students and immigrant students. It is dubious that 180-day English immersion programs mandated by Propositions 227 and

203 can begin to address the needs of all students learning English. Nevertheless, if access to academic content is to be provided equally to all students, there is also a need for native language instruction for those who cannot benefit from specially designed academic instruction in English and a need for increased funding if these new initiatives are to have a positive impact.

However, as important as the issue is of appropriate language of instruction, instruction by itself is not sufficient to address all problems associated with educational inequities. Even students whose native language is English cannot get an equal chance to learn in inadequately funded schools whose teachers lack appropriate training. Thus, reform efforts that merely emphasize raising standards, as discussed in Chapter 9, will not lead to meaningful change when "students have only limited access to relevant curricula" (McDonnell & Hill, 1993, p. 110).

The larger issue of accountability also needs to be addressed. Typically, accountability refers to holding schools responsible for meeting standards. However, as McDonnell and Hill (1993) contend,

> Accountability implies a reciprocal relationship between schools and the broader community. Schools are to produce educational outcomes desired by the community, but in return, the community needs to provide the legitimacy and support to make those outcomes possible. In its highest form, accountability is a social contract—an acceptance of shared responsibility between schools and the larger society. (p. 110)

Ideally, reform efforts should involve equal access to meaningful curricula and equitable funding. However, if such access were achieved, some questions would have to be raised: First, if dropout rates were substantially reduced, would schools in many areas of the nation be able to accommodate all the students they would need to serve? Second, if the literacy and educational achievement of high school students and adult learners increased dramatically, would all those qualified to work find jobs and be paid at levels that would allow them to live their lives with dignity? Frank answers to these questions should specify that merely raising literacy standards and improving the quality of education is not enough. Social and economic conditions must also be improved.

The Impact of Pedagogy

Instructional practices also affect students' literacy development. Whether consciously or not, instructional practices are guided by the three orientations (autonomous, social practices, and ideological) discussed in Chapter 3. These orientations are reflected in various instructional trends. For example, Auerbach (1991) has identified four recent trends in adult literacy pedagogy that reflect these orientations.

The first involves educators using ethnographic methods to determine which literacy practices should be taught. For example, in workplace literacy programs, it is common to teach adults specific practices and skills that will enable them to do their jobs more efficiently. Auerbach (1991) notes that this approach, which reflects an autonomous orientation, "has, in some cases, given rise to a new prescriptivism" (p. 77). Thus, using ethnographic techniques to first describe and then prescribe literacy practices for instruction without allowing learners to critically analyze those practices has little advantage over merely prescribing a set of skills for learners to acquire.

A second pedagogical trend that Auerbach (1991) observes is the attempt to involve adults more in curricular decisions. She notes that some educators mistakenly equate learner involvement in curricular choices with empowerment. However, a focus on personal learning goals alone as a means to empower learners who are generally marginalized in this country "may undermine the possibilities for collective action and obscure the limitations on their power as isolated individuals to shape their environment, thus leading to self-blame" (p. 78).

A third trend has been to overemphasize the transformative and empowering aspects of literacy. Auerbach (1991) cites, as an example, early interpretations of Freire's work in developing countries, where rapid social change was occurring. Such interpretations, with superficial applications to U.S. contexts, tended to become simplistic and dogmatic and to leave learners with an "idealized and mystified view of literacy that can only lead to disillusionment when learners discovered that literacy alone doesn't open up new political possibilities" (pp. 78–79; see Mayo, 1999, which provides a more recent theoretical synthesis aimed at transformative possibilities for adult education).

By contrast, the fourth pedagogical trend identified by Auerbach (1991) involves integrating learners' voices and experiences into the curriculum while at the same time developing their abilities to undertake critical social analysis. She summarizes this approach:

> It focuses on transforming both the content and the process of literacy education in order to challenge inequities in the broader society. In terms of content, this means centering instruction on lived reality of learners as it relates to the broader social context. . . . In terms of process, it means problematizing reality as the basis for dialogue, critical analysis, the collaborative construction of knowledge, and action outside the classroom. (p. 79)

For socially and economically marginalized students, this trend can have a positive impact in programs that have been able to implement it (see Nash, Cason, Rhum, McGrail, & Gomez-Sanford, 1992; and Smoke, 1998, for descriptions of its implementation).

Policy Needs and Recommendations

For decades, programs serving adult immigrants have been substantially underfunded. With the exception of the Title IX refugees services in the late 1970s and early 1980s, English language development and job training have usually not been linked. As Wrigley et al. (2003) argue, conventional English language and job training models have not met the needs of language minorities whose goals are to improve their long-term job opportunities and economic well-being.

Among the recommendations that Wrigley et al. (2003) make to remedy this situation is the integration of job training that builds on students' prior knowledge and skills to promote their English language and literacy development. Job training should occur in authentic work-like environments, where staff have an in-depth understanding of the local job market and can provide training in job-specific skills. Such programs must include a range of social support services that include literacy instruction. For many language minority students, the most immediate path to literacy is through native language instruction and bilingual/biliteracy programs staffed by trained, competent personnel. Because adult ESL and basic education programs are often poorly articulated with job training and higher education opportunities, there is a need for short-term bridge programs that transition language minorities to specific job training and higher education more quickly.

In terms of specific policy recommendations aimed at legislation, Wrigley et al. (2003) argue that there is a need for specific changes in the Workforce Investment Act (WIA), which currently fails to adequately link language, literacy, and job training services for adult immigrants. Wrigley et al. (2003) recommend that adult vocational ESL should become fundable activities for local programs under Title I and Title II, and that funding for research and demonstration and for evaluation should be provided for projects that combine job training with ESL literacy services.

Conclusion: From Crisis to Opportunity

To more positively impact the education of language minority students, policy makers, program designers, and teachers must work together to expand practices that integrate the languages and knowledge of learners into educational programs and curricula. By engaging in discussions and debates with others outside the domains of our daily work, we may find that, in addition to voicing our common frustrations, we can improve the educational experiences and opportunities of our students. For teachers working within the constraints of declining resources and limited opportunities for professional development and collaboration, the task is wearisome. Change is slow and meandering, and those committed to it must be in it for the long haul (see Fullan, 1994).

In concluding this discourse on literacy and language diversity in the United States, there is one guiding principle against which theory, policy, and practice can be evaluated: *All normal people can learn to do what they have the opportunity, need, and desire to do in a language they understand.* Since most language minorities are normal people, if a disproportionate number appear to have literacy problems, we must reexamine our literacy theories, research, policies, and practices to determine why this is so.

As stressed in Chapter 2, literacy problems do not result from language diversity. Rather, the perception of a literacy crisis is magnified by ignoring literacy in languages other than English and by blaming those who have not had an opportunity for a meaningful education (see Chapter 5). The so-called literacy crisis in the United States is largely invented and reinvented as cover for an economic system that is unable to employ all who can work and for the failings of an educational system that is neither adequately funded nor designed to meet the educational needs of all its students.

Given the importance of educational credentials, which are acquired through formal instruction, lack of schooling is a problem for many people. Schooling documents one's literacy; therefore, schooling is important not merely for its purported cognitive effects, but also for its social effects. Given this importance of schooling, there is a need to improve access to it and to incorporate diverse languages, language styles and varieties, and literacy practices into it. The most direct way to achieve this is to promote two-way bilingual immersion programs for all students and special heritage language programs for those whose family backgrounds include another language. Beyond this, there is a need to recognize the value of literacies developed and nurtured outside of school (Hull & Schultz, 2002) so that we can appreciate and build on the richness of our language diversity.

Even as developing literacy in languages other than English remains controversial and the target of those opposed to bilingual education (Crawford, 2000; Tse, 2001; Wiley 2002a), there has been, in recent years, increased interest and support to help linguistically diverse students acquire speaking, reading, and writing abilities in their home languages. Building on the linguistic backgrounds of language minorities in the United States moves us from regarding language diversity as a personal deficiency to viewing it as a rich national resource to be fully developed.

Further Reading

Crandall, J., & Peyton, J. K. (Eds.). (1993). *Approaches to adult ESL literacy instruction*. Washington, DC, and McHenry, IL: Center for Applied Linguistics and Delta Systems.

This collection provides contributions from well-known specialists in adult ESL literacy education. The work reflects a broad range of orientations toward literacy education.

Rodby, J. (1992). *Appropriating literacy: Writing and reading in English as a second language*. Portsmouth, NH: Heinemann-Boynton/Cook.

This theoretical, interdisciplinary work draws on practical examples from university and adult ESL contexts.

Notes

Chapter 1

1. The term *illiteracy* is used in this book because it is a term that is commonly used to describe people who do not read and write. Unfortunately, the term is also used to stigmatize and ascribe low social status to individuals and groups. Use of the term here does not endorse this status-ascribing function.

2. The expression *linguistic minority* refers to a "social subgroup (e.g., a conquered indigenous people, or an immigrant group), the identity of which is defined in terms of language" (Bright, 1992, p. 313). *Language minority* is used as an equivalent expression in this text. In the United States, I would add to this group African Americans, most of whose ancestors were involuntary immigrants (see Gibson & Ogbu, 1991; Ogbu & Matute-Bianchi, 1986), who developed a distinct language variety variously called *Ebonics, Black English,* or *African American language* (see Chapter 6).

3. The notion of *mainstream* needs scrutiny and explication, because it often masks the ethnic and linguistic identity and gender of those whose behaviors are implicitly being taken as normative. Sometimes the word *majority* is used synonymously with mainstream. Because in some regions of the country, White, middle-class, old-immigrant-background individuals are in the minority, the notion of *mainstream* can be seen as carrying a connotation of dominance rather than of simple majority.

Chapter 2

1. The role of age in language and literacy acquisition is complex. See Singleton (1989) for a survey and critique of the major theoretical views and research on the age factor.

Chapter 3

1. Whereas Street (1984) locates Scribner and Cole's and Heath's work within the ideological approach, I find their work and conclusions less self-consciously ideological and more related to social practice concerns.

However, it is largely through the work of Gee (1986, 1991, 2000); Street (1984, 1993, 1995, 1999); and others that the relevance of this research has come to be appreciated for those operating from an ideological perspective.

2. Interestingly, distancing is a stylistic characteristic of much scientific writing and academic writing generally, where it is often considered inappropriate to use a personal pronoun. But is it really more objective to write, "The conclusions are. . . ." or "It is concluded. . . ." rather than "I think that. . . ."? Those working from the social practices orientation think not.

3. Erickson's use of resistance theory to explain self-defeating failure retains some sense that individuals—even if subordinated—still exercise some degree of choice in determining their fate. Such choice appears lost in more deterministic reproduction theory explanations (e.g., Bowles & Gintis, 1976, critiqued by Giroux, 1983a). Erickson's position bears some resemblance to what Ogbu and Matute-Bianchi (1986) have called the "expressive response" of minorities to their "perceived ascribed status" (see also Gibson & Ogbu, 1991).

4. Erickson seems to be referring to overt and intentional discrimination more than to systematic institutional bias. Prior to the civil rights movement and basic changes in the law, it is arguable that discrimination was a major cause of poor educational performance among groups who were its victims. Because African Americans are more segregated in education today than they were 25 years ago (Kozol, 1991), it is arguable that discrimination, at least in terms of implicit institutional practices, is still an important factor, explaining the persistent and disproportionate failure among some groups.

Chapter 4

1. In addition to the test data, some demographic data were collected that allow for the construction of a biliteracy variable. Further secondary data analysis provides useful information based on self-reported data (Greenberg, Macías, Rhodes, & Chan, 2001).

2. The NCS used a household survey of individuals of Mexican descent living in Arizona; California; Colorado; Texas; and Chicago, Illinois. Although the other states were excluded, the geographical scope of the study exceeded that of any previous study on Chicanos, and the survey covered a geographical area that included about 90% of the Mexican-origin population in the United States (Santos, 1985). In defining its sample population, the NCS treated "person of Mexican origin/descent" and "Chicano" as operationally synonymous. These terms were treated as encompassing the native born, immigrants, and undocumented persons.

The survey was conducted from February through August 1979. The sample design produced 12,000 eligible housing units, of which 11,000 were actually screened using a 5-minute screening instrument. Of these, 1,360 had at least one eligible member. Interviews were obtained from 991 respondents, thereby yielding a response rate of 73%. Of the respondents, 44% were residents of California, about 35% were from Texas, 16% were from the Southwest, and just over 5% were from the Chicago area. Face-to-face interviews were conducted in either English or Spanish (Santos, 1985). Approximately 60% of the respondents were female, which reflects both a disproportionate representation in the population and a slightly higher refusal rate among men. Of the respondents, 62% were born in the United States compared with 38% who were born in Mexico. The mean age of the respondents was 40.1 years for females and 39.6 years for males (Santos). Slightly more than half (52%) of the interviews were conducted in Spanish; 48% were conducted in English (Arce, 1985).

The survey questionnaire included a number of items useful in the analysis of educational achievement and literacy among Chicanos. These include years-of-schooling data and self-assessment measures of literacy in both English and Spanish. By allowing for literacy assessment in both languages, the NCS facilitated a broader assessment of literacy than do most national surveys and allowed for a biliteracy comparison to educational achievement. In the survey, at the beginning of each interview, the respondents were given the option to use English or Spanish.

Chapter 5

1. The decline for African Americans at 8.6% was also high and can be interpreted as reflecting the continued neglect and segregation found in many urban schools, documented in Kozol's (1991) *Savage Inequalities*.

2. According to a study by Catteral of UCLA, a preponderance of jobs at the turn of the century "will be in areas that typically require only a high school education. And although only 25% of available jobs are likely to require a college degree, about 35% of students will have a diploma from a four-year institution" (as cited in Goldman, 1994, p. B1). Moreover, during the 1990s, federal policy makers openly acknowledged their willingness to accept a "natural" 6% jobless rate in an effort to thwart inflation (Risen, 1994).

Chapter 6

1. Sometimes language background is used as a substitute for race and ethnicity. In December 1993, the *Los Angeles Times* (Carvajal, 1993), for example, carried the headline, "When Languages Collide." Immediately below the headline there were two pie charts on demographic changes in the ethnic/racial composition of Orange County. The charts were introduced by the subheading, "Changing Ethnicity." Although language was identified in the headline as the subject of discussion, it was really only a surrogate for race and ethnicity.

2. Meyer Weinberg has argued convincingly in several faculty seminars on racism at California State University, Long Beach, that related "isms" (racism, sexism, ageism) share the common characteristic of denying equal human worth.

3. In order to define *creole*, it is first necessary to define *pidgin*. A pidgin is a language with "limited vocabulary, and a reduced grammatical structure, and a narrow range of functions, compared to the languages which gave rise to [it]" (Crystal, 1987, p. 334). It is "the native language of no one" and develops "when members of two mutually unintelligible" languages attempt to communicate (Bright, 1992, p. 325). Typically, language contact occurs in connection with some form of colonization. Many pidgins are derived from politically and economically dominant

European colonial languages; however, non-European derived pidgins can be found in areas where cross-linguistic contact has been common (Crystal, 1987). When the next generation is born, the pidgin has its first native speakers, and it becomes more complex; it becomes a creole. A creole then, unlike a pidgin, is a mother tongue. The process of a pidgin becoming a creole is called *creolization*. When a standard language begins to influence a creole, the process is called *decreolization* (Bright, 1992).

4. *Diglossia* refers to a "sociolinguistic situation where two very different varieties of a language co-occur throughout a speech community, each standardized to some degree, and each performing an individual range of social functions. The varieties are usually described as high (H) and low (L), corresponding broadly to a difference in formality" (Bright, 1992, p. 292).

5. *Markedness* is an "analytic principle" used by linguistics "whereby pairs of linguistic features, seen as oppositions, are given values of positive or marked vs. neutral, negative, or unmarked" (Bright, 1992, p. 314). When a language variety is marked, it may be seen as having either high (H) or low (L) status. In the context of Roy's statement, for successive generations to receive a less marked form of language means that it had fewer characteristics that contrasted with those of so-called standard English.

References

Adams, R., & Burt, M. (2002). *Research on reading development of adult English language learners: An annotated bibliography* [Online bibliography]. Available from Center for Applied Linguistics Web site, www.cal.org/ncle/readingbib

Adger, C. T. (1998). Register shifting with dialect resources in instructional discourse. In S. Hoyle & C. T. Adger (Eds.), *Kids talk: Strategic language use in later childhood* (pp. 151–169). New York: Oxford University Press.

Adger, C. T., Snow, C. E., & Christian, D. (2002). *What teachers need to know about language*. Washington, DC, and McHenry, IL: Center for Applied Linguistics and Delta Systems.

Adger, C. T., & Wolfram, W. (2000). Demythologizing the home-school language dichotomy: Sociolinguistic reality and instructional practice. In J. K. Peyton, P. Griffin, W. Wolfram, & R. Fasold (Eds.), *Language in action: New studies of language in society* (pp. 391–407). Cresskill, NJ: Hampton Press.

Arce, C. H. (1985). *Mexican origin people in the United States: The 1979 Chicano survey*. Ann Arbor, MI: Inter-University Consortium for Political and Social Research.

Aronowitz, S., & Giroux, H. (1985). *Education under siege: The conservative, liberal, and radical debate over schooling*. South Hadley, MA: Bergin & Garvey.

Auerbach, E. R. (1989). Toward a social-contextual approach to family literacy. *Harvard Educational Review, 59,* 165–182.

Auerbach, E. R. (1991). Literacy and ideology. *Annual Review of Applied Linguistics, 12,* 71–86.

Auerbach, E. R. (1992). *Making meaning, making change: Participatory curriculum development for adult ESL literacy*. Washington, DC, and McHenry, IL: Center for Applied Linguistics and Delta Systems.

August, D., & Hakuta, K. (Eds.). (1998). *Educating language-minority children*. Washington, DC: National Academy Press.

Bailey, R. W., & McArthur, T. (1992). Illiteracy. In T. McArthur (Ed.), *The Oxford companion to the English language* (pp. 498–499). Oxford, United Kingdom: Oxford University Press.

Baker, C. (2001). *Foundations of bilingual education and bilingualism* (3rd ed.). Clevedon, England: Multilingual Matters.

Baratz, J. C. (1973). Teaching reading in an urban Negro school system. In R. H. Bentley & S. D. Crawford (Eds.), *Black language reader* (pp. 154–171). Glenview, IL: Scott Foresman.

Barnes, D. (1973a). Classroom contexts for language and learning. *Educational Review, 23*, 235–247.

Barnes, D. (1973b). *Language in the classroom*. Berkshire, United Kingdom: Open University Press.

Barnes, D. (1976). *From communication to curriculum*. London: Penguin.

Barton, D., Hamilton, M., & Ivanic, R. (Eds.). (2000). *Situated literacies: Reading and writing in context*. London: Routledge.

Barton, D., & Ivanic, R. (Eds.). (1991). *Writing in the community*. London: Sage.

Baugh, J. (1997). Linguistic discrimination in educational contexts. In R. Wodak & D. Corson (Eds.), *Encyclopedia of language and education: Vol. 1* (pp. 33–41). Norwell, MA: Kluwer.

Baugh, J. (1999). *Out of the mouths of slaves: African American language and educational malpractice*. Austin: University of Texas Press.

Baugh, J. (2000). *Beyond Ebonics: Linguistic pride and racial prejudice*. Oxford, United Kingdom: Oxford University Press.

Baugh, J. (2001). Coming full circle: Some circumstances pertaining to low literacy achievement among African Americans. In J. L. Harris, A. G. Kamhi, & K. E. Pollock (Eds.), *Literacy in African American communities* (pp. 277–278). Mahwah, NJ: Erlbaum.

Berliner, D. (1996). Nowadays, even the illiterates read and write. *Research in the Teaching of English, 30*(3), 334–351.

Berliner, D., & Biddle, B. (1995). *The manufactured crisis: Myths, fraud, and the attack on America's schools.* Boston: Addison-Wesley.

Bhatia, T. K. (1983). Literacy in monolingual societies. *Annual Review of Applied Linguistics, 4,* 23–38.

Boone, E. H., & Mignolo, W. D. (1994). *Writing without words: Alternative literacies in Mesoamerica and the Andes.* Durham, NC: Duke University Press.

Bos, J., Comings, J. T., Cuban, S., & Porter, K. (with Doolittle, F. C.). (2003). *"As long as it takes": Responding to the challenges of adult student persistence in library literacy programs.* New York: Manpower Demonstration Research Corporation. Available from MDRC Web site, www.mdrc.org

Bowles, S., & Gintis, H. (1976). *Schooling in capitalist America.* New York: Basic Books.

Bracey, G. (1997). *Setting the record straight: Responses to misconceptions about public education in the United States.* Alexandria, VA: Association for Supervision and Curriculum Development.

Brecht, R. D., & Rivers, W. P. (2000). *Language and national security in the 21st century: The role of Title VI/Fulbright-Hays in supporting national language capacity.* Dubuque, IA: Kendall/Hunt.

Brigham, C. C. (1923). *A study in American intelligence.* Princeton, NJ: Princeton University Press.

Bright, W. (Ed.). (1992). *International encyclopedia of linguistics: Vol. 4.* New York: Oxford University Press.

Brinton, D. M., Snow, M. A., & Wesche, M. B. (1989). *Content-based second language instruction.* Boston: Heinle & Heinle.

Brodkey, L. (1991). Tropics of literacy. In C. Mitchell & K. Weiler (Eds.), *Rewriting literacy: Culture and the discourse of the other* (pp. 161–168). New York: Bergin & Garvey.

Brown, H. D. (1994). *Teaching by principles: An interactive approach to language pedagogy.* Englewood Cliffs, NJ: Prentice Hall Regents.

Burt, M., Peyton, J. K., & Adams, R. (2003). *Reading and adult English language learners: A review of the research.* Washington, DC: Center for Applied Linguistics.

Bygate, M. (2001). Speaking. In R. Carter & D. Nunan (Eds.), *The Cambridge guide to teaching English to speakers of other languages* (pp. 14–20). Cambridge, United Kingdom: Cambridge University Press.

Camitta, M. (1993). Vernacular writing: Varieties of literacy among Philadelphia high school students. In B. Street (Ed.), *Cross-cultural approaches to literacy* (pp. 228–246). Cambridge, United Kingdom: Cambridge University Press.

Candlin, C. (Ed. & Trans.). (1981). *The communicative teaching of English: Principles and exercise typology.* Harlow, Essex, United Kingdom: Longman.

Carter, T. P., & Segura, R. D. (1979). *Mexican Americans in school: A decade of change.* New York: College Entrance Examination Board.

Carvajal, D. (1993, December 19). When languages collide. *Los Angeles Times*, p. A1.

Cazden, C. (1988). *Classroom discourse: The language of teaching and learning.* Portsmouth, NH: Heinemann.

Cazden, C. B., John, V. P., & Hymes, D. (1985). *Functions of language in the classroom.* Long Grove, IL: Waveland Press.

Celce-Murcia, M., & Larsen-Freeman, D. (with Williams, H.). (1998). *The grammar book: An ESL/EFL teacher's course* (2nd ed.). Boston: Heinle & Heinle.

Chermayeff, I., Wasserman, F., & Shapiro, M. J. (1991). *Ellis Island: An illustrated history of the immigrant experience.* New York: Macmillan.

Chisman, F. P., Wrigley, H. S., & Ewen, D. T. (1993). *ESL and the American dream.* Washington, DC: Southport Institute for Policy Analysis.

Clark, M. M. (1976). *Young fluent readers*. London: Heinemann.

Clark, M. M. (1984). Literacy at home and at school: Insights from young fluent readers. In A. Oberg, H. Goelman, & F. Smith (Eds.), *Awakening to literacy* (pp. 122–130). Portsmouth, NH: Heinemann.

Clifford, G. J. (1984). Buch und lesen: Historical perspectives on literacy and schooling. *Review of Educational Research, 54,* 472–500.

Collins, J. (1991). Hegemonic practice: Literacy and standard language in public education. In C. Mitchell & K. Weiler (Eds.), *Rewriting literacy: Culture and the discourse of the other* (pp. 229–253). New York: Bergin & Garvey.

Collins, R. (1979). *Credential society: A historical sociology of education and stratification.* New York: Academic Press.

Comings, J. P., Parrella, A., & Soricone, L. (1999, December). *Persistence among adult basic education students in pre-GED classes* (NCSALL Reports No. 12). Cambridge, MA: National Center for the Study of Adult Learning and Literacy. Retrieved October 28, 2003, from www.gse.harvard.edu/~ncsall/research/report12.pdf

Condelli, L., Wrigley, H., Yoon, K., Seburn, M., & Cronen, S. (2003). *"What Works" study for adult ESL literacy students.* Unpublished manuscript, U.S. Department of Education.

Cook-Gumperz, J. (Ed.). (1986). *The social construction of literacy.* Cambridge, United Kingdom: Cambridge University Press.

Cook-Gumperz, J. (1993). Dilemmas of identity: Oral and written literacies in the making of a basic writing student. *Anthropology & Education Quarterly, 24,* 336–356.

Cook-Gumperz, J., & Keller-Cohen, D. (Eds.). (1993). Alternative literacies: In school and beyond [Theme issue]. *Anthropology & Education Quarterly, 24*(4).

Cooper, M. L. (1999). *Indian school: Teaching the white man's way.* New York: Clarion Books.

Cope, B., & Kalantzis, M. (Eds.). (2000). *Multiliteracies: Literacy learning and the design of social futures.* London: Routledge.

Coulmas, F. (1992). *Language and economy.* Oxford, United Kingdom: Blackwell.

Crandall, J. (1979). *Adult vocational ESL.* Arlington, VA: Center for Applied Linguistics.

Crandall, J., & Imel, S. (1991). Issues in adult literacy education. *The ERIC Review, 1*(2), 2–7.

Crawford, J. (1992a). *Hold your tongue: Bilingualism and the politics of "English Only."* Boston: Addison-Wesley.

Crawford, J. (Ed.). (1992b). *Language loyalties: A source book on the Official English controversy.* Chicago: University of Chicago Press.

Crawford, J. (1998, June). *The bilingual education story: Why can't the news media get it right?* Paper presented at the National Association of Hispanic Journalists, Miami, FL. Retrieved December 7, 2003, from http://ourworld.compuserve.com/homepages/jwcrawford/nahj.htm

Crawford, J. (1998/1999, Winter). Does bilingual education work? *Rethinking Schools, 13*(2). Retrieved July 28, 2003, from www.rethinkingschools.org/archive/13_02/biside.shtml

Crawford, J. (1999). *Bilingual education: History, politics, theory, and practice* (4th ed.). Los Angeles: Bilingual Education Services.

Crawford, J. (2000). *At war with diversity: U.S. language policy in an age of anxiety.* Clevedon, England: Multilingual Matters.

Crystal, D. (1987). *The Cambridge encyclopedia of language.* Cambridge, United Kingdom: Cambridge University Press.

Cummins, J. (1981). The role of primary language development in promoting educational success for language minority students. In California State Department of Education, Office of Bilingual Education (Ed.), *Schooling and language minority students: A theoretical framework* (pp. 3–49). Los Angeles: California State University, Evaluation, Dissemination, and Assessment Center.

Cummins, J. (1983). Analysis-by-rhetoric: Reading the text or the reader's own projections? A reply to Edelsky et al. *Applied Linguistics, 4*(1), 23–41.

Cummins, J. (1984a). Language proficiency and academic achievement revisited: A response. In C. Rivera (Ed.), *Language proficiency and academic achievement* (pp. 71–76). Clevedon, England: Multilingual Matters.

Cummins, J. (1984b). Wanted: A theoretical framework for relating language proficiency to academic achievement among bilingual students. In C. Rivera (Ed.), *Language proficiency and academic achievement* (pp. 2–19). Clevedon, England: Multilingual Matters.

Cummins, J. (1985). *Bilingualism and special education: Issues in assessment and pedagogy.* San Diego, CA: College-Hill Press.

Cummins, J. (1989). *Empowering minority students.* Sacramento: California Association for Bilingual Education.

Cummins, J. (2000). *Language, power, and pedagogy: Bilingual children in the crossfire.* Clevedon, England: Multilingual Matters.

Cummins, J. (2003). BICS and CALP: Origins and rationale for the distinction. In C. B. Paulston & R. Tucker (Eds.), *Essential readings in sociolinguistics* (pp. 322–328). Oxford, United Kingdom: Blackwell.

Cushman, E. (1998). *The struggle and the tools: Oral and literate strategies in an inner city community.* Albany: State University of New York Press.

Dandy, E. B. (1992). Sensitizing teachers to cultural differences: An African American perspective. In D. E. Murray (Ed.), *Diversity as resource: Redefining cultural literacy* (pp. 87–112). Alexandria, VA: Teachers of English to Speakers of Other Languages.

Darder, A. (1991). *Culture and power in the classroom: A critical foundation for bicultural education.* New York: Bergin & Garvey.

de Castell, S., & Luke, A. (1983). Defining "literacy" in North American schools: Social and historical consequences. *Journal of Curriculum Studies, 15,* 373–389.

de Castell, S., & Luke, A. (1986). Models of literacy in North American schools: Social and historical conditions and consequences. In S. de Castell, A. Luke, & K. Egan (Eds.), *Literacy, society, and schooling* (pp. 87–109). Cambridge, MA: Cambridge University Press.

Delgado-Gaitán, C. (1990). *Literacy for empowerment: The role of parents in children's education.* New York: Falmer Press.

Delgado-Gaitán, C., & Trueba, H. T. (1991). *Crossing cultural borders: Education for immigrant families in America.* New York: Falmer Press.

Delpit, L. (1992, March/April). Teachers, culture, and power. *Rethinking Schools 6*(3), 14–16.

Delpit, L. (1995). *Other people's children: Cultural conflict in the curriculum.* New York: New Press.

Delpit, L., & Dowdy, J. K. (Eds.). (2002). *The skin that we speak: Thoughts on language and culture in the classroom.* New York: New Press.

Dewey, J. (1963). *Experience and education.* New York: Macmillan. (Original work published 1938)

Dillard, J. L. (1972). *Black English: Its history and usage in the United States.* New York: Random House.

Dudley-Evans, T. (2001). English for specific purposes. In R. Carter & D. Nunan (Eds.), *The Cambridge guide to teaching English to speakers of other languages* (pp. 131–136). Cambridge, United Kingdom: Cambridge University Press.

Dumont, R. V., Jr. (1972). Learning English and how to be silent in Sioux and Cherokee classrooms. In C. Cazden, V. John, & D. Hymes (Eds.), *Functions of language in the classroom* (pp. 344–369). Prospect Heights, IL: Waveland Press.

Edelsky, C. (1996). *With literacy and justice for all: Rethinking the social in language and education* (2nd ed.). London: Taylor & Francis.

Edelsky, C., & Hudelson, S. (1991). Contextual complexities: Written language policies for bilingual programs. In S. Benesch (Ed.), *ESL in America: Myths and possibilities* (pp. 75–90). Portsmouth, NH: Heinemann-Boynton/Cook.

Edelsky, C., Hudelson, S., Flores, B., Barkin, F., Altweger, B., & Kristina, J. (1983). Semilingualism and language deficit. *Applied Linguistics, 4*(1), 3–22.

Edwards, V., & Sienkewicz, T. J. (1991). *Oral cultures past and present: Rappin' and Homer.* Oxford, United Kingdom: Blackwell.

Erickson, F. (1984). School literacy, reasoning, and civility: An anthropologist's perspective. *Review of Educational Research, 54,* 525–546.

Fairclough, N. (1989). *Language and power.* New York: Longman.

Farr, M. (1994). Biliteracy in the home: Practices among *Mexicano* families in Chicago. In D. Spener (Ed.), *Adult biliteracy in the United States* (pp. 89–110). Washington, DC, and McHenry, IL: Center for Applied Linguistics and Delta Systems.

Ferreiro, E., & Teberosky, A. (1982). *Literacy before schooling* (K. G. Castro, Trans.). Portsmouth, NH: Heinemann.

Field, M. L. (1992). Reading for cross-cultural literacy. In F. Dubin & N. A. Kuhlman (Eds.), *Cross-cultural literacy: Global perspectives on reading and writing* (pp. 163–173). Englewood Cliffs, NJ: Prentice Hall.

Finocchiaro, M., & Brumfit, C. (1983). *The functional-notional approach: From theory to practice.* New York: Oxford University Press.

Fishman, A. (1988). *Amish literacy: What and how it means.* Portsmouth, NH: Heinemann.

Fishman, J. A. (1966). *Language loyalty in the United States: The maintenance and perpetuation of non-English mother tongues by American ethnic and religious groups.* Berlin, Germany: Mouton.

Fishman, J. A. (1967). Bilingualism with and without diglossia: Diglossia with and without bilingualism. *Journal of Social Issues, 23*(2), 29–38.

Fishman, J. A. (1980a). Ethnocultural dimensions in the acquisition and retention of biliteracy. *Basic Writing, 3*(1), 48–61.

Fishman, J. A. (1980b). Language maintenance. In S. T. Thernstrom, et al. (Eds.), *Harvard encyclopedia of American ethnic groups* (pp. 629–638). Cambridge, United Kingdom: Cambridge University Press.

Fishman, J. A. (1991). *Reversing language shift: Theoretical and empirical foundations of assistance to threatened languages.* Philadelphia: Multilingual Matters.

Freebody, P., & Welch, A. R. (Eds.). (1993). *Knowledge, culture, and power: International perspectives on literacy as policy and practice.* Pittsburgh, PA: University of Pittsburgh Press.

Freire, P. (1970a). *Cultural action for freedom.* Cambridge, MA: Harvard Educational Review.

Freire, P. (1970b). *Pedagogy of the oppressed* (M. B. Ramos, Trans.). New York: Herder & Herder.

Freire, P., & Macedo, D. (1987). *Literacy: Reading the word and the world.* New York: Seabury Press.

Fullan, M. (1994). *Change forces: Probing the depths of educational reform?* Bristol, PA: Falmer Press.

Galbraith, J. K. (1992). *The culture of contentment.* Boston: Houghton Mifflin.

Gardner, R. C. (1985). *Social psychology and second language learning.* London: Edward Arnold.

Gass, S. M., & Selinker, L. (2001). *Second language acquisition: An introductory course* (2nd ed.). Mahwah, NJ: Erlbaum.

Gee, J. P. (1986). Orality and literacy: From the savage mind to ways with words. *TESOL Quarterly, 20,* 719–746.

Gee, J. P. (1991). Socio-cultural approaches to literacy (literacies). *Annual Review of Applied Linguistics, 12,* 31–48.

Gee, J. P. (1996). *Social linguistics and literacies: Ideology and discourses* (2nd ed.). London: Taylor & Francis.

Gee, J. P. (2000). New people in new worlds: Networks, the new capitalism and schools. In B. Cope & M. Kalantzis (Eds.), *Multiliteracies: Literacy learning and the design of social futures* (pp. 43–68). London: Routledge.

Gee, J. P. (2001). Forward. In T. M. Kalmar, *Illegal alphabets and adult biliteracy: Latino migrants crossing the linguistic border* (pp. iii–iv). Mahwah, NJ: Erlbaum.

Gibson, M. A., & Ogbu, J. U. (Eds.). (1991). *Minority status and schooling: A comparative study of immigrant and involuntary minorities.* New York: Garland.

Gillham, B. (Ed.). (1986). *The language of school subjects.* London: Heinemann.

Giroux, H. A. (1983a). Theories of reproduction and resistance in the new sociology of education: A critical analysis. *Harvard Educational Review, 53,* 257–293.

Giroux, H. A. (1983b). *Theory and resistance in education: A pedagogy for the opposition.* South Hadley, MA: Bergin & Garvey.

Giroux, H. A. (1988). *Teachers as intellectuals.* New York: Bergin & Garvey.

Goldenberg, C. (1991). *Instructional conversations and their classroom application* (Educational Practice Report No. 2). Santa Cruz, CA: The National Center for Research on Cultural Diversity and Second Language Learning.

Goldman, A. (1994, September 6). Schools tackling job training needs. *Los Angeles Times,* p. B1.

Gonzales, L. N., & Watson, D. (1986). *Sheltered English teaching handbook.* San Marcos, CA: AM Graphics & Printing.

Goody, J. (1986). *The logic of writing and the organization of society.* New York: Cambridge University Press.

Goody, J. (1987). *The interface between the written and the oral.* Cambridge, United Kingdom: Cambridge University Press.

Goody, J. (1999). The implications of literacy. In D. A. Wagner, R. L. Venezky, & B. V. Street (Eds.), *Literacy: An international handbook* (pp. 29–33). Boulder, CO: Westview Press.

Goody, J., & Watt, I. (1988). The consequences of literacy. In E. R. Kintgen, B. M. Kroll, & M. Rose (Eds.), *Perspectives on literacy* (pp. 3–27). Carbondale: Southern Illinois University Press. (Reprinted from *Comparative Studies in Society and History, 5,* 304–326, 1963)

Gould, S. J. (1981). *The mismeasure of man.* New York: Norton.

Graff, H. J. (1979). *The literacy myth: Literacy and social structure in the nineteenth-century city.* New York: Academic Press.

Graff, H. J. (1987). *The labyrinths of literacy: Reflections on literacy past and present.* New York: Falmer Press.

Green, J. (1983). Exploring classroom discourse: Linguistic perspectives on teaching-learning processes. *Educational Psychologist, 18,* 180–199.

Greenberg, E., Macías, R. F., Rhodes, D., & Chan, T. (2001, August). *English literacy and language minorities in the United States: Results from the National Adult Literacy Survey* (NCES Publication No. 2001464). Washington, DC: National Center for Education Statistics, U.S. Department of Education. Retrieved from http://nces.ed.gov/pubsearch

Greenfield, P. (1972). Oral or written language: The cognitive consequences of literacy development in Africa, United States, and England. *Language and Speech, 15*(1), 169–178.

Grillo, R. D. (1989). *Dominant languages.* Cambridge, United Kingdom: Cambridge University Press.

Gumperz, J. (1992). Contextualization and understanding. In A. Duranti & C. Goodwin (Eds.), *Rethinking context* (pp. 229–252). New York: Cambridge University Press.

Haas, M. (1992). *Institutional racism: The case of Hawai'i.* Westport, CT: Praeger.

Hakuta, K. (1986). *Mirror of language: The debate on bilingualism.* New York: Basic Books.

Hall, E. T. (1959). *The silent language.* Garden City, NY: Anchor Books.

Hamp-Lyons, L. (2001). English for academic purposes. In R. Carter & D. Nunan (Eds.), *The Cambridge guide to teaching English to speakers of other languages* (pp. 126–130). Cambridge, United Kingdom: Cambridge University Press.

Harklau, L. (2003, October). *Generation 1.5 students and college writing.* ERIC Digest. Washington, DC: Center for Applied Linguistics. Retrieved from www.cal.org/resources/digest/0305harklau.html

Harklau, L., Losey, K. M., & Siegal, M. (Eds.). (1999). *Generation 1.5 meets college composition: Issues in the teaching of writing to U.S.-educated learners of ESL.* Mahwah, NJ: Erlbaum.

Harste, J. C., & Mikulecky, L. J. (1984). The context of literacy in our society. In A. C. Purves & O. Niles (Eds.), *Becoming readers in a complex society* (pp. 47–78). Chicago: University of Chicago Press.

Hatch, E. (1983). *Psycholinguistics: A second language perspective.* Rowley, MA: Newbury House.

Havelock, E. A. (1963). *Preface to Plato.* Cambridge, MA: Harvard University Press.

Havelock, E. A. (1988). The coming of literate communication to Western culture. In E. R. Kintgen, B. M. Kroll, & M. Rose (Eds.), *Perspectives on literacy* (pp. 127–134). Carbondale: Southern Illinois University Press.

Heath, S. B. (1980). The functions and uses of literacy. *Journal of Communication, 30*(1), 123–133.

Heath, S. B. (1983). *Ways with words: Language, life, and work in communities and classrooms.* Cambridge, United Kingdom: Cambridge University Press.

Heath, S. B. (1986). Social contexts of language development. In California State Department of Education (Ed.), *Beyond language: Social and cultural factors in schooling* (pp. 143–186). Los Angeles: California State University, Evaluation, Dissemination, and Assessment Center.

Heath, S. B. (1988a). Protean shapes in literacy events: Ever-shifting oral and literate traditions. In E. R. Kintgen, B. M. Kroll, & M. Rose (Eds.), *Perspectives on literacy* (pp. 348–370). Carbondale: Southern Illinois University Press.

Heath, S. B. (1988b). What no bedtime story means. In J. S. Wurzel (Ed.), *Toward multiculturalism: A reader in multiculturalism* (pp. 162–184). Yarmouth, MA: Intercultural Press.

Hewitt, R., & Inghilleri, M. (1993). Oracy in the classroom: Policy, pedagogy, and group oral work. *Anthropology & Education Quarterly, 24,* 308–317.

Hirsch, E. D., Jr. (1987). *Cultural literacy: What every American needs to know.* Boston: Houghton Mifflin.

Hirsch, E. D., Jr., Kett, J. F., & Trefil, J. (1988). *The dictionary of cultural literacy: What every American needs to know.* Boston: Houghton Mifflin.

Hornberger, N. H. (1989). Continua of biliteracy. *Review of Educational Research, 59*(3), 271–296.

Hornberger, N. H. (1990). Creating successful learning contexts for biliteracy. *Penn Working Papers in Educational Linguistics, 6*(1), 1–21.

Hornberger, N. H., & Hardman, J. (1994). Literacy as cultural practice and cognitive skill: Biliteracy in an ESL class and a GED program. In D. Spener (Ed.), *Adult biliteracy in the United States* (pp. 147–169). Washington, DC, and McHenry, IL: Center for Applied Linguistics and Delta Systems.

Hull, G. (1997). *Changing work: Critical perspectives on language, literacy, and skills.* Albany: State University of New York Press.

Hull, G., & Schultz, K. (Eds.). (2002). *School's out: Out-of-school literacies with classroom practice.* New York: Teachers College Press.

Hunter, C., & Harman, D. (1979). *Adult illiteracy in the United States.* New York: McGraw-Hill.

Illich, I. (1979). Vernacular values and education. *Teacher's College Record, 81*(1), 31–75.

International Reading Association, & National Council of Teachers of English. (1996). *Standards for the English language arts.* Newark, DE, and Urbana, IL: Author.

Kalmar, T. M. (1994). ¿Guariyusei? Adult biliteracy in its natural habitat. In D. Spener (Ed.), *Adult biliteracy in the United States* (pp. 123–146). Washington, DC, and McHenry, IL: Center for Applied Linguistics and Delta Systems.

Kalmar, T. M. (2001). *Illegal alphabets and adult biliteracy: Latino migrants crossing the linguistic border.* Mahwah, NJ: Erlbaum.

Kaplan, D. A. (1993, September 20). Dumber than we thought. Literacy: A new study shows why we can't cope with everyday life. *Newsweek,* 44–45.

Kaplan, R. B. (1983). Introduction. *Annual Review of Applied Linguistics, 4,* vii–xv.

Karier, C. (1973). Testing for order and control in the corporate liberal state. In C. J. Karier, P. Violas, & J. Spring (Eds.), *Roots of crisis: American education in the twentieth century* (pp. 108–137). Chicago: Rand McNally.

Kenworthy, J. (1987). *Teaching English pronunciation.* London: Longman.

Kirsch, I., & Guthrie, J. T. (1977–1978). The concept and measurement of functional illiteracy. *Journal of Education, 13*(4), 486–507.

Kirsch, I. S., & Jungeblut, A. (1986). *Literacy: Profiles of America's young adults* (ETS Report No. 16-PL-02). Princeton, NJ: Educational Testing Service.

Kirsch, I. S., Jungeblut, A., Jenkins, L., & Kolstad, A. (1993, September). *Adult literacy in America: A first look at the findings of the National Adult Literacy Survey.* Washington, DC: National Center for Education Statistics, U.S. Department of Education.

Klassen, C., & Burnaby, B. (1993). "Those who know": Views on literacy among adult immigrants in Canada. *TESOL Quarterly, 27,* 377–397.

Kloss, H. (1971). Language rights of immigrant groups. *International Migration Review, 5,* 250–268.

Kloss, H. (1998). *The American bilingual tradition.* Washington, DC, and McHenry, IL: Center for Applied Linguistics and Delta Systems.

Kozol, J. (1991). *Savage inequalities: Children in America's schools.* New York: Crown.

Kramsch, C. J. (1981a). *Discourse analysis and second language teaching.* Washington, DC: Center for Applied Linguistics.

Kramsch, C. J. (1981b). Teaching discussion skills: A pragmatic approach. *Foreign Language Annals, 14,* 93–104.

Kramsch, C. J. (1983). Interaction in the classroom: Learning how to negotiate roles and meaning. *Unterrichtspraxis, 2,* 175–190.

Krashen, S. (1981). Bilingual education and second language acquisition theory. In California State Department of Education, Office of Bilingual Education (Ed.), *Schooling and language minority students: A theoretical framework* (pp. 51–116). Los Angeles: California State University, Evaluation, Dissemination, and Assessment Center.

Labov, W. (1970). The study of language in social context. *Studium Generale, 23,* 66–84.

Labov, W. (1973). The logic of non-standard English. In N. Keddie (Ed.), *Tinker, tailor: The myth of cultural deprivation* (pp. 21–66). London: Penguin.

Labov, W. (1982). Objectivity and commitment in linguistic science: The case of the Black English trial in Ann Arbor. *Language and Society, 11,* 165–201.

Lambert, W. E. (1974). Culture and language as factors in learning and education. In F. E. Aboud & R. D. Meade (Eds.), *Cultural factors in learning and education.* Bellingham, WA: Fifth Western Washington Symposium on Learning.

Langer, J. A. (Ed.). (1987). *Language, literacy, and culture: Issues of society and schooling.* Norwood, NJ: Ablex.

Lankshear, C., & Lawler, M. (1989). *Literacy, schooling and revolution.* New York: Falmer Press.

Lau v. Nichols, 414 U.S. 563 (1974).

Leacock, E. B. (1972). Abstract versus concrete speech: A false dichotomy. In C. B. Cazden, V. P. John, & D. Hymes (Eds.), *Functions of language in the classroom* (pp. 111–134). Prospect Heights, IL: Waveland Press.

LeBlanc, R., & Painchaud, G. (1986). Self-assessment as a second language placement instrument. *TESOL Quarterly, 19,* 673–687.

Leibowitz, A. H. (1969). English literacy: Legal sanction for discrimination. *Notre Dame Lawyer, 25*(1), 7–66.

Leibowitz, A. H. (1971). *Educational policy and political acceptance: The imposition of English as the language of instruction in American schools.* Washington, DC: Center for Applied Linguistics.

Leibowitz, A. H. (1974, August). *Language as a means of social control: The United States experience.* Paper presented at the 8th World Congress of Sociology, University of Toronto, Canada.

Leibowitz, A. H. (1982). *Federal recognition of the rights of minority language groups.* Rosslyn, VA: National Clearinghouse on Bilingual Education.

Lemoine, N. (1999). *English for your success.* Saddle Brook, NJ: Peoples Press.

Lepore, J. (2002). *A is for American: Letters and other characters in the newly United States.* New York: Alfred A. Knopf.

Levine, K. (1982). Functional literacy: Fond illusions and false economies. *Harvard Educational Review, 52*(3), 249–267.

Lévi-Strauss, C. (1966). *The savage mind.* Chicago: University of Chicago Press.

Lewin, T., & Medina, J. (2003, July 31). To cut failure rate, schools shed students [Electronic version]. *New York Times.* Retrieved July 31, 2003, from http://nytimes.com

Lewis, M. (1978). *The culture of inequality.* Amherst, MA: University of Massachusetts Press.

Lippi–Green, R. (1997). *English with an accent: Language, ideology, and discrimination in the United States.* London: Routledge.

Luebke, F. C. (1980). Legal restrictions on foreign languages in the Great Plains states, 1917–1923. In P. Schach (Ed.), *Languages in conflict: Linguistic acculturation on the Great Plains* (pp. 1–19). Lincoln: University of Nebraska Press.

Luke, A. (1998). *Literacy, textbooks, and ideology: Postwar literacy instruction and the mythology of Dick and Jane.* London: Falmer Press.

Luria, A. R. (1976). *Cognitive development: Its cultural and social foundations.* Cambridge, MA: Harvard University Press.

Lyons, J. J. (1990). The past and future directions of federal bilingual education policy. *Annals of the American Academy of Political and Social Science, 508,* 66–80.

Mace-Matluck, B. J., Alexander-Kasparik, R., & Queen, R. M. (1998). *Through the golden door: Educational approaches for immigrant adolescents with limited schooling.* Washington, DC, and McHenry, IL: Center for Applied Linguistics and Delta Systems.

Macías, R. F. (1979). Choice of language as a human right: Public policy implications. In R. V. Padilla (Ed.), *Ethnoperspectices in bilingual education research: Bilingual education and public policy in the United States* (pp. 39–57). Ypsilanti: Eastern Michigan University.

Macías, R. F. (1984). *Cauldron, boil and bubble: United States language policy towards indigenous language groups during the nineteenth century.* Unpublished manuscript, University of Southern California, Center for Multilingual, Multicultural Research.

Macías, R. F. (1988). *Latino illiteracy in the United States.* Claremont, CA: Tomás Rivera Center.

Macías, R. F. (1990). Definitions of literacy: A response. In R. L. Venezky, D. A. Wagner, & B. S. Ciliberti (Eds.), *Toward defining literacy* (pp. 17–23). Newark, DE: International Reading Association.

Macías, R. F. (1993). Language and ethnic classification of language minorities: Chicano and Latino students in the 1990s. *Hispanic Journal of Behavioral Sciences, 15*(2), 230–257.

Macías, R. F. (1994). Inheriting sins while seeking absolution: Language diversity and national data sets. In D. Spener (Ed.), *Adult biliteracy in the United States* (pp. 15–45). Washington, DC, and McHenry, IL: Center for Applied Linguistics and Delta Systems.

Macías, R. F. (1999). The flowering of America. In S. McKay & S.-L. C. Wong (Eds.), *New immigrants in the United States: Readings for second language education* (pp. 11–57). Cambridge, United Kingdom: Cambridge University Press.

Macías, R. F., & Spencer, M. (1984). *Estimating the number of language minority and limited-English proficient children in the United States: A comparative analysis of the studies.* Los Alamitos, CA: National Center for Bilingual Research.

MacSwan, J. (1999). *A minimalist response to intrasentential code-switching.* New York: Garland.

MacSwan, J. (2000). The threshold hypothesis, semilingualism, and other contributions to a deficit view of linguistic minorities. *Hispanic Journal of Behavioral Sciences, 22*(1), 3–45.

MacSwan, J., & Rolstad, K. (2003). Linguistic diversity, schooling, and social class: Rethinking our conception of language proficiency in language minority education. In C. B. Paulston & R. Tucker (Eds.), *Essential readings in sociolinguistics* (pp. 329–341). Oxford, United Kingdom: Blackwell.

MacSwan, J., Rolstad, K., & Glass, G. V. (2002). Do some school-age children have no language? Some problems of construct validity in the Pre-LAS Español. *Bilingual Research Journal, 26*(2), 213–238.

Martin Luther King Junior Elementary School Children v. Ann Arbor School District, 73 F. Supp. 1371 (E.D. Mich. 1979).

Mathews, J. (2001, July 22). Landmark illiteracy analysis is flawed statistics faulty, study director says. *The Arizona Republic,* p. A16.

Mayo, P. (1999). *Gramsci, Freire, and adult education: Possibilities for transformative action.* London: Zed Books.

McArthur, E. K. (1993, December). *Language characteristics and schooling in the United States, a changing picture: 1979 and 1989* (NCES Publication No. 93699). Washington, DC: U.S. Department of Education, National Center for Education Statistics.

McCarthy, M. (1991). *Discourse analysis for language teachers.* Cambridge, United Kingdom: Cambridge University Press.

McClymer, J. F. (1982). The Americanization movement and the education of the foreign-born adult, 1914–1925. In B. J. Weiss (Ed.), *American education and the European immigrant: 1840–1940* (pp. 96–116). Urbana: University of Illinois Press.

McDermott, R. (1987a). Achieving school failure: An anthropological approach to illiteracy and social stratification. In G. Spindler (Ed.), *Education and cultural process: Anthropological approaches* (2nd ed.). (pp. 173–209). Prospect Heights, IL: Waveland Press.

McDermott, R. (1987b). The explanation of minority school failure, again. *Anthropology and Education Review, 56*(4), 355–378.

McDonnell, L. M., & Hill, P. T. (1993). *Newcomers in American schools: Meeting the educational needs of immigrant youth.* Santa Monica, CA: Rand.

McKay, S. (1993). *Agendas for second language literacy.* Cambridge, United Kingdom: Cambridge University Press.

McKay, S. L., & Weinstein-Shr, G. (1993). English literacy in the United States: National policies, consequences. *TESOL Quarterly, 27,* 399–419.

McLaren, P. (1989). *Life in schools: An introduction to critical pedagogy in the foundations of education.* New York: Longman.

Mensh, E., & Mensh, H. (1991). *The IQ mythology: Class, race, and gender inequality.* Carbondale: Southern Illinois University Press.

Meyer v. Nebraska, 262 U.S. 390 (1923).

Mignolo, W. D. (1995). *The darker side of the Renaissance: Literacy, territoriality, and colonization.* Ann Arbor: University of Michigan Press.

Mignolo, W. D. (2000). *Local histories/global designs: Coloniality, subaltern knowledges, and border thinking*. Princeton, NJ: Princeton University Press.

Mikulecky, L. J. (1990). Literacy for what purpose? In R. L. Venezky, D. A. Wagner, & B. S. Ciliberti (Eds.), *Toward defining literacy* (pp. 24–34). Newark, DE: International Reading Association.

Miles, R. (1989). *Racism.* London: Routledge.

Miller, C. (1991). *Some contextual problems relative to the acquisition of literacy by Hmong refugees.* Unpublished master's thesis, California State University, Long Beach.

Milroy, J., & Milroy, L. (1985). *Authority in language: Investigating language prescription and standardization.* London: Routledge.

Mohan, B. A. (1986). *Language and content.* Boston: Addison-Wesley.

Mohan, B. A. (1989). Knowledge structures and academic discourse. *Word, 40,* 99–115.

Molesky, J. (1988). Understanding the American linguistic mosaic: A historical overview of language maintenance and language shift. In S. L. McKay & S. C. Wong (Eds.), *Language diversity: Problem or resource* (pp. 29–68). Cambridge, MA: Newbury House.

Morrow, L. M. (1983). Home and school correlates of early interest in literature. *Journal of Educational Research, 76,* 221–230.

Nash, A., Cason, A., Rhum, M., McGrail, L., & Gomez-Sanford, R. (1992). *Talking shop: A curriculum sourcebook for participatory adult ESL.* Washington, DC, and McHenry, IL: Center for Applied Linguistics and Delta Systems.

National Commission on Excellence in Education. (1983, April). *A nation at risk: The imperative for educational reform.* Washington, DC: U.S. Department of Education.

Norgren, J., & Nanda, S. (1988). *American cultural pluralism and the law.* New York: Praeger.

Nunan, D. (1988). *The learner-centered curriculum*. Cambridge, United Kingdom: Cambridge University Press.

Nunan, D. (1989). *Designing tasks for the communicative classroom*. Cambridge, United Kingdom: Cambridge University Press.

Nunan, D. (1991). *Language teaching methodology: A textbook for teachers*. Englewood Cliffs, NJ: Prentice Hall.

O'Connor, P. (1993). Workplace literacy in Australia: Competing agendas. In P. Freebody & A. R. Welch (Eds.), *Knowledge, culture, and power: International perspectives on literacy as policy and practice* (pp. 187–208). Pittsburgh, PA: University of Pittsburgh Press.

Ogbu, J. U. (1991). Immigrant and involuntary minorities in comparative perspective. In M. A. Gibson & J. U. Ogbu (Eds.), *Minority status and schooling: A comparative study of immigrant and involuntary minorities* (pp. 3–33). New York: Garland.

Ogbu, J. U., & Matute-Bianchi, M. E. (1986). Understanding sociocultural factors: Knowledge, identity, and school adjustment. In California State Department of Education (Ed.), *Beyond language: Social and cultural factors in schooling for language minority students*. Los Angeles: California State University, Evaluation, Dissemination, and Assessment Center.

Olson, D. R. (1977). From utterance to text: The bias of language in speech and writing. *Harvard Educational Review, 47*, 257–281.

Olson, D. R. (1984). See! Jumping! Some oral language antecedents of literacy. In A. Oberg, H. Goelman, & F. Smith (Eds.), *Awakening to literacy* (pp. 185–192). Portsmouth, NH: Heinemann.

Olson, D. R. (1988). The bias of language in speech and writing. In E. R. Kintgen, B. M. Kroll, & M. Rose (Eds.), *Perspectives on literacy* (pp. 175–189). Carbondale: Southern Illinois University Press.

Olson, D. R. (1994). *The world on paper: The conceptual and cognitive implications of reading and writing*. Cambridge, United Kingdom: Cambridge University Press.

Olson, D. R. (1999). Literacy and language development. In D. A. Wagner, R. L. Venezky, & B. V. Street (Eds.), *Literacy: An international handbook* (pp. 132–136). Boulder, CO: Westview Press.

O'Neil, W. (1973). The politics of bidialectism. In R. H. Bentley & S. D. Crawford (Eds.), *Black language reader* (pp. 184–191). Glenview, IL: Scott Foresman.

O'Neill, W. F. (1983). *Rethinking education: Selected readings in educational ideologies.* Dubuque, IA: Kendall/Hunt.

Ong, W. J. (1982). *Orality and literacy: The technologizing of the word.* London: Methuen.

Ong, W. J. (1988). Some psychodynamics of orality. In E. R. Kintgen, B. M. Kroll, & M. Rose (Eds.), *Perspectives on literacy* (pp. 28–43). Carbondale: Southern Illinois University Press.

Ovando, C. J., & Wiley, T. G. (2003). Language education in the conflicted United States. In J. Bourne & E. E. Reid (Eds.), *World yearbook of education 2003: Language education* (pp. 141–155). London: Kogan Page.

Penfield, J. (1982). Chicano English: Implications for assessment and literacy development. *Bilingual Education Paper Series, 6*(5).

Pennycook, A. (1997). Critical applied linguistics and education. In R. Wodak & D. Corson (Eds.), *Language policy and political issues in education* (pp. 33–41). Boston: Kluwer.

Pennycook, A. (2001). *Critical applied linguistics: A critical introduction.* Mahwah, NJ: Erlbaum.

Perdue, C. (Ed.). (1984). *Second language acquisition by adult immigrants: A field manual.* Rowley, MA: Newbury House.

Perry, T., & Delpit, L. (1998). *The real Ebonics debate: Power, language, and the education of African-American children.* Boston: Beacon Press.

Petrovic, J. E., & Olmstead, S. (2001, Summer) [Review of the book *Language, power, and pedagogy: Bilingual children in the crossfire*]. *Bilingual Research Journal, 25*(3), 251–258.

Peyton, J. K., Ranard, D. A., & McGinnis, S. (Eds.). (2001). *Heritage languages in America: Preserving a national resource.* Washington, DC, and McHenry, IL: Center for Applied Linguistics and Delta Systems.

Philips, S. U. (1972). Participant structures and communicative competence: Warm Springs children in community and classroom. In C. Cazden, V. John, & D. Hymes (Eds.), *Functions of language in the classroom* (pp. 370–394). Prospect Heights, IL: Waveland Press.

Philips, S. U. (1983). *The invisible culture: Communication and community on the Warm Springs Indian Reservation.* New York: Longman.

Phillips, K. (1993). *Boiling point: Republicans, Democrats, and the decline of middle-class prosperity.* New York: Random House.

Phillipson, R. (1988). Linguicism: Structures and ideologies in linguistic imperialism. In T. Skutnabb-Kangas & J. Cummins (Eds.), *Minority education: From shame to struggle* (pp. 339–358). Clevedon, England: Multilingual Matters.

Pitt, L. (1976). *We Americans: Vol. 1. Colonial Times to 1877.* Glenview, IL: Scott Foresman.

Portes, A., & Rumbaut, R. (2001). *Legacies: The story of the immigrant second generation.* Berkeley: University of California Press.

Ramírez, J. D. (1992). Executive summary. *Bilingual Research Journal, 16*(1–2), 1–62.

Ramírez, J. D., Wiley, T. G., de Klerk, G., & Lee, E. (1999). *Ebonics in the urban education debate.* Long Beach: California State University and Center for Language Minority Education and Research.

Redduck, J., & Hopkins, D. (Eds.). (1985). *Research as a basis for teaching: Readings from the work of Lawrence Stenhouse.* London: Heinemann.

Reder, S. (1999). Comparative aspects of functional literacy development: Three ethnic American communities. In D. A. Wagner (Ed.), *The future of literacy in a changing world* (Rev. ed., pp. 291–313). Cresskill, NJ: Hampton Press.

Reder, S., Harris, K., & Setzler, K. (2003). The multimedia adult ESL learner corpus. *TESOL Quarterly, 37*(3), 546–557.

Reder, S., & Wikelund, K. R. (1993). Literacy development and ethnicity: An Alaskan example. In B. Street (Ed.), *Cross-cultural approaches to literacy* (pp. 176–197). Cambridge, United Kingdom: Cambridge University Press.

Resnick, D. P., & Resnick, L. B. (1988). The nature of literacy: A historical exploration. In E. R. Kintgen, B. M. Kroll, & M. Rose (Eds.), *Perspectives on literacy* (pp. 190–203). Carbondale: Southern Illinois University Press.

Ricento, T., & Wiley, T. G. (2002). Introduction: Language, identity, and education and the challenges of monoculturalism and globalization. *Journal of Language, Identity, and Education, 1*(1), 1–5.

Richard-Amato, P. A., & Snow, M. A. (Eds.). (1992). *The multicultural classroom: Readings for content-area teachers.* Harlow, Essex, United Kingdom: Longman.

Richards, J. C., & Rodgers, T. S. (2001). *Approaches and methods in language teaching* (2nd ed.). Cambridge, United Kingdom: Cambridge University Press.

Rickford, J. R., & Rickford, R. J. (2000). *Spoken soul: The story of Black English.* New York: Wiley.

Risen, J. (1994, August 29). Fed ties decisions to natural 6% jobless rate. *Los Angeles Times,* p. A1.

Romaine, S. (1995). *Bilingualism* (2nd ed.). Oxford, United Kingdom: Blackwell.

Rosen, H. (1985). The voices of communities and language in classrooms. *Harvard Educational Review, 55,* 448–456.

Roy, J. D. (1987). The linguistic and sociolinguistic position of Black English and the issue of bidialectism in education. In P. Homel, M. Palij, & D. Aaronson (Eds.), *Childhood bilingualism: Aspects of linguistic, cognitive, and social development* (pp. 231–242). Mahwah, NJ: Erlbaum.

Ruíz, R. (1984). Orientations in language planning. *Bilingual Research Journal 8*(2), 15–32.

Ryan, W. (1972). *Blaming the victim.* New York: Random House.

Santos, R. L. (1985). *A methodological report on the sampling design of the 1979 National Chicano Survey* (Working Paper No. 11). Stanford, CA: Stanford Center for Chicano Research.

Schieffelin, B. B., & Cochran-Smith, M. (1984). Learning to read culturally: Literacy before schooling. In A. Oberg, H. Goelman, & F. Smith (Eds.), *Awakening to literacy* (pp. 3–23). Portsmouth, NH: Heinemann.

Schieffelin, B. B., & Gilmore, P. (Eds.). (1986). *The acquisition of literacy: Ethnographic perspectives.* Norwood, NJ: Ablex.

Schumann, J. (1978). *The pidginization process: A model for second language acquisition.* Rowley, MA: Newbury House.

Scollon, R., & Scollon, S. (1981). *Narrative, literacy, and face in interethnic communication.* Norwood, NJ: Ablex.

Scribner, S. (1988). Literacy in three metaphors. In E. R. Kintgen, B. M. Kroll, & M. Rose (Eds.), *Perspectives on literacy* (pp. 71–81). Carbondale: Southern Illinois University Press. (Reprinted from *American Journal of Education,* 1984, *93,* 6–21)

Scribner, S., & Cole, M. (1978). Literacy without schooling: Testing for intellectual effects. *Harvard Educational Review, 48,* 448–461.

Scribner, S., & Cole, M. (1981). *The psychology of literacy.* Cambridge, MA: Harvard University Press.

Shannon, P. (1989). *Broken promises: Reading instruction in twentieth-century America.* South Hadley, MA: Bergin & Garvey.

Shannon, P. (1990). *The struggle to continue.* Portsmouth, NH: Heinemann.

Shor, I. (1987). *Freire for the classroom: A sourcebook for liberatory teaching.* Portsmouth, NH: Boynton/Cook.

Shuman, A. (1993). Collaborative writing. In B. Street (Ed.), *Cross-cultural approaches to literacy* (pp. 247–271). Cambridge, United Kingdom: Cambridge University Press.

Shuy, R. (1980). Vernacular Black English: Setting the issues in time. In M. F. Whiteman (Ed.), *Reactions to Ann Arbor: Vernacular Black English and education* (pp. 1–9). Arlington, VA: Center for Applied Linguistics.

Simon, P. (1988). *The tongue-tied American* (2nd ed.). New York: Continuum.

Simpkins, G. C., Simpkins, G., & Holt, G. (1977). *Bridge: A cross-cultural reading program.* Boston: Houghton Mifflin.

Simpson, D. (1986). *The politics of American English, 1776–1850.* New York: Oxford University Press.

Singleton, D. (1989). *Language acquisition: The age factor.* Philadelphia: Multilingual Matters.

Skutnabb-Kangas, T. (1981). *Bilingualism or not: The education of minorities.* (L. Malmberg & D. Crane, Trans.). Clevedon, England: Multilingual Matters.

Skutnabb-Kangas, T. (2000). *Linguistic genocide in education: Or worldwide diversity and human rights?* Mahwah, NJ: Erlbaum.

Skutnabb-Kangas, T., & Phillipson, R. (1989). *Wanted! Linguistic human rights.* (Rolig-Papir No. 44). Denmark: Roskilde University Center.

Sledd, J. (1969). Bi-dialectism: The linguistics of White supremacy. *English Journal, 58,* 1307–1315, 1329.

Sledd, J. (1973). Doublespeak: Dialectology in the service of Big Brother. In R. H. Bentley & S. D. Crawford (Eds.), *Black language reader* (pp. 191–214). Glenview, IL: Scott Foresman.

Smith, E. A. (1993). The Black child in the schools: Ebonics and its implications for the transformation of American education. In A. Darder (Ed.), *Bicultural studies in education: The struggle for educational justice* (pp. 58–76). Claremont, CA: Institute for Education in Transformation.

Smoke, T. (Ed.). (1998). *Adult ESL, politics, pedagogy, in classroom and community programs.* Mahwah, NJ: Erlbaum.

Spener, D. (Ed). (1994). *Adult biliteracy in the United States.* Washington, DC, and McHenry, IL: Center for Applied Linguistics and Delta Systems.

Spolsky, B. (1984). A note on the dangers of terminological innovation. In C. Rivera (Ed.), *Language proficiency and academic achievement* (pp. 41–43). Clevedon, England: Multilingual Matters.

Spring, J. (1994). *Deculturalization and the struggle for equality: A brief history of the education of dominated cultures in the United States.* New York: McGraw-Hill.

Stewart, W. (1964). *Non-standard speech and the teaching of English.* Washington, DC: Center for Applied Linguistics.

Stewart, W. (1993). *Immigration and education: The crisis and the opportunities.* New York: Lexington Books.

Street, B. V. (1984). *Literacy in theory and practice.* Cambridge, United Kingdom: Cambridge University Press.

Street, B. V. (Ed.). (1993). *Cross-cultural approaches to literacy.* Cambridge, United Kingdom: Cambridge University Press.

Street, B. V. (1995). *Social literacies: Critical approaches to literacy in development, ethnography, and education.* London: Longman.

Street, B. V. (1999). The meanings of literacy. In D. A. Wagner, R. L. Venezky, & B. V. Street (Eds.), *Literacy: An international handbook* (pp. 34–40). Boulder, CO: Westview Press.

Street, J. C., & Street, B. V. (1991). The schooling of literacy. In D. Barton & R. Ivanic (Eds.), *Writing in the community* (pp. 143–166). London: Sage.

Strucker, J., & Davidson, R. (2003, November). *Adult Reading Components Study* (NCSALL Research Brief). Cambridge, MA: National Center for the Study of Adult Learning and Literacy.

Stubbs, M. (1980). *Language and literacy: The sociolinguistics of reading and writing*. London: Routledge.

Stuckey, J. E. (1991). *The violence of literacy*. Portsmouth, NH: Heinemann.

Szwed, J. (1981). The ethnography of literacy. In M. F. Whiteman (Ed.), *Writing: The nature, development and teaching of written communication: Vol. 1. Variation in writing* (pp. 13–23). Mahwah, NJ: Erlbaum.

Tannen, D. (1982). The myth of orality and literacy. In W. Frawley (Ed.), *Linguistics and literacy: Proceedings of the Delaware Symposium on Language Studies* (pp. 37–50). New York: Plenum.

Tannen, D. (1987). The orality of literature and literary conversation. In J. A. Langer (Ed.), *Language, literacy, and culture: Issues of society and schooling* (pp. 67–88). Norwood, NJ: Ablex.

Taylor, D. M. (1983). *Family literacy: Young children learning to read and write*. Portsmouth, NH: Heinemann.

Taylor, D. M. (1987). Social psychological barriers to effective childhood bilingualism. In P. Homel, M. Palij, & D. Aaronson (Eds.), *Child bilingualism: Aspects of linguistic, cognitive, and social development* (pp. 183–196). Mahwah, NJ: Erlbaum.

Taylor, D. M., & Dorsey-Gaines, C. (1988). *Growing up literate: Learning from inner-city families*. Portsmouth, NH: Heinemann.

Tchudi, S. N., & Huerta, M. C. (1983). *Teaching writing in the content areas*. Washington, DC: National Education Association.

Teachers of English to Speakers of Other Languages. (1997). *ESL standards for pre-K–12 students*. Alexandria, VA: Author.

Tollefson, J. (1991). *Planning language, planning inequality: Language policy in the community*. New York: Longman.

Trimble, L. (1985). *English for science and technology: A discourse approach*. Cambridge, United Kingdom: Cambridge University Press.

Troike, R. C. (1978). Research evidence for the effectiveness of bilingual education. *Bilingual Research Journal, 3*(1), 13–24.

Troike, R. C. (1984). SCALP: Social and cultural aspects of language proficiency. In C. Rivera (Ed.), *Language proficiency and academic achievement* (pp. 44–54). Clevedon, England: Multilingual Matters.

Trueba, H. T. (1984). The forms, functions, and values of literacy: Reading for survival in a barrio as a student. *Bilingual Research Journal, 9*(1), 41–51.

Trueba, H. T. (1989). *Raising silent voices: Educating the linguistic minorities for the 21st century.* Rowley, MA: Newbury House.

Trueba, H. T., Jacobs, L., & Kirton, E. (1990). *Cultural conflict and adaptation: The case of Hmong children in American society.* New York: Falmer Press.

Tse, L. (2001). *"Why don't they learn English?" Separating fact from fallacy in the U.S. language debate.* New York: Teachers College Press.

Tumposky, N. R. (1984). Behavioral objectives, the cult of efficiency, and foreign language learning: Are they compatible? *TESOL Quarterly, 18*(2), 295–307.

U.S. Department of Education, Office of Vocational and Adult Education, Division of Adult Education and Literacy. (2001, March). *Measures and methods for the National Reporting System for Adult Education: Implementation guidelines.* Washington, DC: Author. Available at www.nrsweb.org/reports/implement.pdf

U.S. General Accounting Office. (2002, January). *Foreign languages: Human capital approach needed to correct staffing and proficiency shortfalls* (GAO-02-375). Washington, DC: Author.

Valadez, C. M. (1981). Identity, power, and writing skills: The case of the Hispanic bilingual student. In M. F. Whiteman (Ed.), *Writing: The nature, development, and teaching of written communication: Vol. 1. Variations in writing: Functional and linguistic-cultural differences* (pp. 167–178). Mahwah, NJ: Erlbaum.

Valadez, C., MacSwan, J., & Martínez, C. (2002). Toward a new view of low achieving bilinguals: A study of linguistic competence in designated "semilinguals." *Bilingual Review, 25*(3), 238–248.

Valdés, G. (2001). Heritage language students: Profiles and possibilities. In J. K. Peyton, D. A. Ranard, & S. McGinnis (Eds.), *Heritage languages in America: Preserving a national resource* (pp. 37–77). Washington, DC, and McHenry, IL: Center for Applied Linguistics and Delta Systems.

Van Ek, J. (1978). *Threshold level for modern language learning in schools.* Harlow, Essex, United Kingdom: Longman.

Van Ek, J. (1987). Communicative teaching. In M. H. Long & J. C. Richards (Eds.), *Methodology in TESOL: A book of readings* (pp. 84–85). Boston: Heinle & Heinle.

van Lier, L. (2001). Language awareness. In R. Carter & D. Nunan (Eds.), *The Cambridge guide to teaching English to speakers of other languages* (pp. 160–165). Cambridge, United Kingdom: Cambridge University Press.

Vargas, A. (1986). *Illiteracy in the Hispanic community.* Washington, DC: National Council of La Raza.

Veltman, C. (1983). *Language shift in the United States.* Berlin, Germany: Mouton.

Veltman, C. (2000). The American linguistic mosaic: Understanding language shift in the United States. In S. McKay & S.-L. C. Wong (Eds.), *New immigrants in the United States: Readings for second language educators* (pp. 58–93). Cambridge, United Kingdom: Cambridge University Press.

Venezky, R. L., Kaestle, C., & Sum, A. (1987). *The subtle danger: Reflections on the literacy abilities of America's young adults* (Report No. 16-CAEP-01). Princeton, NJ: Educational Testing Service, Center for the Assessment of Educational Progress.

Venezky, R. L., Wagner, D. A., & Ciliberti, B. S. (Eds.). (1990). *Toward defining literacy.* Newark, DE: International Reading Association.

Vygotsky, L. S. (1978). *Mind in society: The development of higher psychological processes* (M. Cole, V. John-Steiner, S. Scribner, & E. Souberman, Trans.). Cambridge, MA: Harvard University Press.

Waggoner, D. (1993, September). Majority of non-English speakers speak Spanish but others have more difficulty with English. *Numbers and Needs, 3*(5), 1, 3-4.

Wagner, D. A. (Ed.). (1999). *The future of literacy in a changing word* (Rev. ed.). Cressskill, NJ: Hampton Press.

Wald, B. (1984). A sociolinguistic perspective on Cummins' current framework for relating language proficiency to academic achievement. In C. Rivera (Ed.), *Language proficiency and academic achievement* (pp. 55–70). Clevedon, England: Multilingual Matters.

Walsh, C. E. (Ed.). (1991). *Literacy as praxis: Culture, language, and pedagogy.* Norwood, NJ: Ablex.

Walters, K. (1992). Whose culture? Whose literacy? In D. E. Murray (Ed.), *Diversity as resource: Redefining cultural literacy* (pp. 3–29). Alexandria, VA: Teachers of English to Speakers of Other Languages.

Weinberg, M. (1983). *The search for quality integrated education: Policy and research on minority students in school and college.* Westport, CT: Greenwood Press.

Weinberg, M. (1990). *Racism in the United States: A comprehensive classified bibliography.* Westport, CT: Greenwood Press.

Weinberg, M. (1995). *A chance to learn: A history of race and education in the United States* (2nd ed.). Long Beach: California State University Press.

Weinberg, M. (1997). *Asian-American education: Historical background and current realities.* Mahwah, NJ: Erlbaum.

Weinstein, G. (1984). Literacy and second language acquisition: Issues and perspectives. *TESOL Quarterly, 18,* 471–484.

Weinstein-Shr, G. (1990). From problem solving to celebration: Discovering and creating meanings through literacy. *TESL Talk, 20*(1), 68–88.

Weinstein-Shr, G. (1993a). Directions in adult ESL literacy: An invitation to dialogue. *TESOL Quarterly, 27,* 517–533.

Weinstein-Shr, G. (1993b). Literacy and social process: A community in transition. In B. Street (Ed.), *Cross-cultural approaches to literacy* (pp. 272–293). Cambridge, United Kingdom: Cambridge University Press.

Weinstein-Shr, G. (1995). *Literacy and older adults in the United States.* Philadelphia: National Center for Adult Literacy.

Weinstein-Shr, G., & Quintero, E. (Eds.). (1995). *Immigrant learners and their families: Literacy to connect the generations.* Washington, DC, and McHenry, IL: Center for Applied Linguistics and Delta Systems.

Weiss, B. J. (Ed.). (1982). *Education and the European immigrant: 1840–1940.* Champaign: University of Illinois Press.

Wells, G. (1986). *The meaning makers: Children learning language and using language to learn.* Portsmouth, NH: Heinemann.

Wiley, T. G. (1986). The significance of language and cultural barriers for the Euro-American elderly. In C. Hayes, R. A. Kalish, & D. Guttman (Eds.), *The Euro-American elderly: A guide to practice* (pp. 35–50). New York: Springer.

Wiley, T. G. (1988). *Literacy, biliteracy, and educational achievement among the Mexican-origin population in the United States.* Unpublished doctoral dissertation, University of Southern California, Los Angeles.

Wiley, T. G. (1990). Literacy, biliteracy, and educational achievement among the Mexican-origin population in the United States. *Bilingual Research Journal, 14*(1, 2, 3), 109–127.

Wiley, T. G. (1990–1991). Literacy among the Mexican-origin population: What a biliteracy analysis can tell us. *Journal of the Association of Mexican American Educators,* 17–38.

Wiley, T. G. (1991a). *Measuring the nation's literacy: Important considerations* (ERIC Digest). Washington, DC: National Center for ESL Literacy Education.

Wiley, T. G. (1991b). Planning versus prespecification: The role of premeditation in instruction. *Action in Teacher Education, 12*(4), 47–51.

Wiley, T. G. (1993). *Issues of access, participation and transition in adult ESL* (Working Paper). Washington, DC: Southport Institute for Policy Analysis.

Wiley, T. G. (1996). *Literacy and language diversity in the United States.* Washington, DC, and McHenry, IL: Center for Applied Linguistics and Delta Systems.

Wiley, T. G. (1998). The imposition of World War I era English-only policies and the fate of German in North America. In T. Ricento & B. Burnaby (Eds.), *Language politics in the United States and Canada: Myths and realities* (pp. 211–241). Mahwah, NJ: Erlbaum.

Wiley, T. G. (1999). Comparative historical perspectives in the analysis of U.S. language polices. In T. Heubner & C. Davis (Eds.), *Political perspectives on language planning and language policy* (pp. 17–37). Amsterdam: John Benjamins.

Wiley, T. G. (2000a). Continuity and change in the function of language ideologies in the United States. In T. Ricento (Ed.), *Ideology, politics, and language policies: Focus on English* (pp. 67–85). Amsterdam: John Benjamins.

Wiley, T. G. (2000b). Ebonics: Background to the current policy context. In J. D. Ramírez, T. G. Wiley, G. de Klerk, & E. Lee (Eds.), *Ebonics in the urban education debate* (pp. 8–19). Long Beach, CA: Center for Language Minority Education and Research.

Wiley, T. G. (2001, November). *One workplace, two languages: Challenges, myths, and opportunities.* Paper presented at the summit of the Adult Bilingual Curriculum Institute, Johns Hopkins University and the U.S. Department of Labor, El Paso, TX.

Wiley, T. G. (2002a). Accessing language rights in education: A brief history of the U.S. context. In J. Tollefson (Ed.), *Language policies in education: Critical readings* (pp. 39–64). Mahwah, NJ: Erlbaum.

Wiley, T. G. (2002b). Biliteracy. In B. Guzzetti (Ed.), *Literacy in America: An encyclopedia of history, theory, and practice* (pp. 57–60). Santa Barbara, CA: ABC-CLIO.

Wiley, T. G. (2004). Language policy and English-only. In E. Finegan & J. R. Rickford (Eds.), *Language in the USA: Themes for the 21ˢᵗ century.* New York: Cambridge University Press.

Wiley, T. G., & Lukes, M. (1996). English-only and standard English ideologies in the United States. *TESOL Quarterly 30*(3), 511–535.

Wiley, T. G., & Wright, W. (in press). *The politics of language instruction in the United States.* London: Sage.

Wiley, T. G., Wrigley, H. S., & Burr, R. (1983). *Refugee resettlement in Long Beach: Needs, service utilization patterns, and curriculum recommendations.* Washington, DC: U.S. Department of Health and Human Services, Office of Refugee Resettlement.

Wilkins, D. A. (1976). *Notional syllabuses.* Oxford, United Kingdom: Oxford University Press.

Williams, S. W. (1990). Classroom use of African American language: Educational tool or social weapon? In C. E. Sleeter (Ed.), *Empowerment through multicultural education: From reproduction to contestation of social inequality through schooling* (pp. 199–215). New York: State University of New York Press.

Willis, D., & Willis, J. (2001). Task-based language learning. In R. Carter & D. Nunan (Eds.), *The Cambridge guide to teaching English to speakers of other languages* (pp. 173–179). Cambridge, United Kingdom: Cambridge University Press.

Wink, J. (1993). Labels often reflect educators' beliefs and practices. *Bilingual Education Office Outreach, 4*(2), 28–29.

Wolfram, W. (1994). Bidialectal literacy in the United States. In D. Spener (Ed.), *Adult biliteracy in the United States* (pp. 71–88). Washington, DC, and McHenry, IL: Center for Applied Linguistics and Delta Systems.

Wolfram, W., Adger, C. T., Christian, D. (1999). *Dialects in schools and communities.* Mahwah, NJ: Erlbaum.

Wolfram, W., & Christian, D. (1980). On the application of sociolinguistic information: Test evaluation and dialect differences in Appalachian English. In T. Shopen & J. M. Williams (Eds.), *Standards and dialects in English* (pp. 177–204). Cambridge, MA: Winthrop.

Wolfram, W., & Fasold, R. W. (1973). Toward reading materials for speakers of Black English: Three linguistically appropriate passages. In R. H. Bentley & S. D. Crawford (Eds.), *Black language reader* (pp. 172–184). Glenview, IL: Scott Foresman.

Woodson, C. G. (1990). *The mis-education of the Negro.* Trenton, NJ: Africa World Press. (Original work published 1933)

Wright, E. (1980). School English and public policy. *College English, 42,* 327–342.

Wrigley, H. S., Chisman, F. P., & Ewen, D. T. (1993). *Sparks of excellence: Program realities and promising practices in adult ESL.* Washington, DC: Southport Institute for Policy Analysis.

Wrigley, H. S., & Guth, J. A. (1992). *Bringing literacy to life: Issues and options in adult ESL.* San Mateo, CA: Aguirre International.

Wrigley, H. S., Richer, E., Martinson, K., Kubo, H., & Strawn, J. (2003). *The language of opportunity: Expanding employment prospects for adults with limited English skills.* Washington, DC: Center for Law and Social Policy.

Wyman, M. (1993). *Round-trip to America: The immigrants return to Europe, 1880–1930.* Ithaca, NY: Cornell University Press.

Yalden, J. (1983). *The communicative syllabus: Evolution and design.* Oxford, United Kingdom: Pergamon.

Index